JAPANESE MANAGEMENT
IN HISTORICAL PERSPECTIVE

JAPANESE

The International Conference on Business History 15

MANAGEMENT

Proceedings of the Fuji Conference

IN

edited by TSUNEHIKO YUI   KEIICHIRO NAKAGAWA

HISTORICAL

PERSPECTIVE

UNIVERSITY OF TOKYO PRESS

The Fuji International Conference on Business History has been held annually since 1974, with the third series beginning in 1984. We would like to express our deepest gratitude to the Taniguchi Foundation for their continuing sponsorship of the Conference.

Contents

Notes on Style and Usage

1. Japanese personal names appearing in this volume are given in the order customary in Japan: family name followed by given name. The exceptions are the names of the editors and contributors, which are given in Western order to avoid confusion for librarians and bibliographers.

2. Macrons have been used to indicate elongated vowel sounds in transliterated Japanese terms, personal names, and names of organizations. They have not been used, however, in names of places, e.g., Osaka, Kyushu.

3. Transliterated titles of Japanese language books are given with only initial words capitalized; English-language book titles have all important words capitalized.

Introduction

Tsunehiko Yui
Meiji University

I. On the Topic of "Japanese Management in Historical Perspective"

The subject of Japanese management has received considerable attention from both Japanese and Western scholars in recent years. Undoubtedly, this reflects the growing interest in the remarkable development and consistent international competitive position of Japanese enterprises. The Fifth Session of the Third Series of Fuji Business History Conference, which took place from January 5 to 8 in 1988, dealt with this very topic of "Japanese Management in Historical Perspective."[1] In particular, six Japan specialists from abroad were asked to participate in and contribute to the Conference.

The topic of Japanese management can be discussed from a great variety of viewpoints and disciplines, and so we found it necessary to restrict our focus. Perhaps most important, the Conference chose not to analyze issues involving government-business relations in Japan. This aspect of Japanese management, which was taken up at the Fourth Session of the Second Series,[2] is obviously an issue of great importance, yet to consider it here would have overly diluted the discussion of the session.

In addition, the Conference did not ask the participants to consider cultural aspects of Japanese business enterprises. Many who write about Japanese management tend to emphasize the cultural or ideological attitudes of managers and workers. In particular, a number of commentators who stress cultural attributes speak of "vertical society" (*tate shakai*), "total embrace" (*marugakae*), and "groupism" (*shūdan shugi*) as unique traits of Japanese management. Here again, though we recognize the significance of this approach,[3] for the sake of clarity, Conference participants did not directly delve into these cultural factors. Similarly, management in merchant houses of the pre-industrial (Edo) period was not addressed.[4] Instead, participants attempted to concentrate on the managerial and organizational aspects of modern Japanese industrial enterprises.

We assume that even among industrially advanced nations, there are different patterns of managerial development and industrial professionalization. It may be useful to provide an overview of the papers presented. Needless to say, each has its own approach, interest, and argument. The main purpose of this introduction is to place these contributions into a larger framework of historical analysis of industrialization in Japan.

II. Industrial Revolution and Entrepreneurship

The rise of modern industrial enterprises in Japan, which has had a great impact on the organization and management of business enterprises, is a relatively recent phenomenon. In the West, industrial institutions, such as factories, railways, and shipyards, which have based themselves on scientific technology, evolved over a long period of time, from the latter half of the 18th century. In Japan, however, such institutions did not appear for at least another century, more specifically, until after the Meiji Restoration of 1868, which released private business activities from stifling feudal controls.

As a consequence, the rise of modern enterprises in Japan occasioned a simultaneous technological and organizational revolution. With respect to technological developments, the enormous gap between Japan and the West had to be closed. This was done first by the study of Western books prior to the Restoration, the dispatch of Japanese students abroad immediately after the Restoration, and the establishment of institutions of higher learning after the 1870s. Project leader Nakagawa Keiichirō's paper, entitled, "The 'Learning Industrial Revolution' and Business Management," deals with one of the "unique" aspects observed in the initial phase of Meiji entrepreneurship and business management, referring to the fact that some technicians or engineers fulfilled managerial functions as well.

The origins of Meiji entrepreneurship have been a topic of great importance and interest in international comparative studies. Business and economic historians, who recently have described the origins and nature of entrepreneurs in Meiji Japan, have found that these entrepreneurs came from a wide variety of backgrounds.[5] In the West, industrial entrepreneurs mainly emerged from the bourgeoisie or business classes. By contrast, in Japan the promoters and leaders of modern business ventures came from a wide variety of backgrounds: merchants, landowners, ex-samurai, aristocrats, government officials, and even scholars. They were more akin to organizers or investors who did not have the business experience and technical knowledge that their Western counterparts did. Andrew Fraser's "Hachisuka Mochiaki: From Feudal Lord to Modern Businessman," which exemplifies one such type of Meiji entrepreneur, traces in detail Hachisuka's personality, unique career, and varied business activities with vicissitudes common to Meiji entrepreneurs during the early stages of Japan's industrialization.[6]

The joint-stock company also represented a revolutionary change in how business was organized and conducted. Not only was it unlike any other form of organization in Japan, but it was coupled with previously unknown technologies, of which it was more often than not the carrier. The joint-stock company, therefore, brought about a double revolution in technique as well as organization. In order to establish and manage a railroad enterprise, full-scale spinning factory, shipyard, or flour mill during the Meiji period, it was absolutely necessary to attract capital from numerous sources and to place the firm's operations in the hands of joint-stock companies. This form of organization enabled the firms to raise large amounts of capital and delegate authority to able managers.

In every industrialized nation, railroads appeared as the first modern enterprises in terms of both technology and organization. In Japan as well, railroad companies, together with textile enterprises, were organized as joint-stock companies and developed remarkably during the Meiji period. Steven Ericson's "Private Railways in the Meiji Era: Forerunners of Modern Japanese Management?" examines closely the management of railroad companies, a subject relatively neglected even by Japanese scholars. In this paper, Ericson presents a qualified view of "administrative evolution"—that is, the professionalization of management—in Meiji railroad companies.

III. Transitional Problems

The period from the end of the 19th century until World War One in Japan can be seen as a transitional phase in the development of enterprises. Even if the technological aspects of production had been mastered and the joint-stock form of business management had been successfully transplanted, these newly established enterprises could not have functioned well within the framework of traditional business organization and managerial practices. There were distinct, yet interdependent, managerial problems associated with this transitional phase. These problems involved the recruitment for and staffing of technical and clerical positions, as well as the formation of the industrial labor force. These aspects of the modernization of business administration posed special problems, since they were closely bound up with human relations, which could not be changed overnight.

Iwauchi Ryōichi observed the issue recruitment of educated white-collar employees in his "The Growth of White-Collar Employment in Relation to the Education System." With an expertise in sociology, he examines this topic from a broad perception of the formation and educational background of the middle class. After analyzing in detail the structure of Meiji governmental bureaucracy, in which educational credentials and seniority were given precedence, Iwauchi traces the recruitment and placement of college graduates in both the public and private sectors. His paper also addresses what he calls the "mismatch" between actual requirements in the private sector and governmental efforts.

Recently quite a few Japanese business historians have looked into the subject and significance of white-collar employees, particularly college graduates, including engineering and technical graduates, within these modern public- and private-sector enterprises. Uchida

Hoshimi, commentator of the Iwauchi paper, conducted extensive research on this topic. He presented statistical data on the growth of the employment of engineers and technicians who graduated from universities and technical colleges.[7] On the important role of engineers in the course of industrialization, Morikawa Hidemasa's work was a pioneering study.[8] Moreover, with regard to college graduates in modern private enterprises in prewar Japan, Daitō Eisuke's article presented at a previous conference,[9] as well as Yonekawa Shin'ichi's recent works,[10] will also prove useful to foreign students interested in this topic.

The formation of the industrial labor force from the late 19th to the early 20th century is a second issue of some consequence. Though several experts have already examined this topic,[11] its very complexity has made it difficult to interpret the process in an integrated form. W. Mark Fruin, in his paper, "Instead of Management: Internal Contracting and the Genesis of Modern Labor Relations," presented his own analytical framework, which he claims is applicable to labor relations in the transitional phase of industrialization. Pointing out the clear break from traditional work relations to a direct, and therefore, modern form of labor management, he emphasizes the fact that internal contracting practices functioned instead of management in labor relations and the labor market in Japan. This interesting interpretation and argument deserves more research, particularly on a comparative international level.[12]

IV. The Institutionalization of Japanese Management

When viewed from the vantage point of managerial evolution and industrial professionalization, World War One in Japan marks the turning point from an early to a more developed phase. In the United States, the integration of mass production and mass distribution triggered a managerial revolution in the late 19th century. These simultaneous and interrelated developments of large enterprises necessitated the creation of a sizable managerial hierarchy accompanied by systematic management. By contrast, the industrial enterprises established in the late 19th century in Japan were modern enterprises which utilized machinery in their production, but they were by no means *large* modern enterprises with integrated managerial hierarchies and advanced management. The development in Japan required a more step-by-step growth from early to large industrial enterprises.

It was during World War One and its aftermath that Japanese industrial enterprises developed a managerial complexity and size which made them comparable to Western firms, even in limited fields and products. Historically, the economic boom years from 1914 to 1918 gave Japanese industrial firms the chance to grow and even capture markets which had been previously served by Western enterprises. Not only in the field of consumer goods, but in those of capital goods, such as metal products, electrical, and non-electrical machinery, and chemical and transportation equipment as well, modern Japanese industrial enterprises developed with great rapidity. With overall industrial expansion, the number of industrial workers continued to grow. As of 1893, for example, there were only 445,000 workers employed in industrial fields, but by 1917, there were 2.24 million such workers (not including those employed by firms with less than 5 laborers).

It was also the period during and after World War One that professional, salaried managers of leading industrial companies, most of whom were college graduates, came to occupy the top executive positions as well as the director's seats on the boards. These high-ranking managers, mainly promoted from middle ranks, were not professionals in the sense of commanding a great deal of theoretical knowledge concerning management. Nevertheless, they did generally devote themselves to a single enterprise. Since they often obtained their positions through long-time service within the company, based on their technological know-how and managerial skills, they may be properly termed "career type" top executives. This type of manager, though typical in Japan, was not commonly found within the professional managerial class in comparable U.S. enterprises. The original style of Japanese modern management, including labor management, was largely molded by the professional attitudes of those managers. The process of managerial revolution, or the development of managerial enterprises in Japan, was examined in a comparative framework in the Second Session of the Conference, under the rubric "Development of Managerial Enterprises,"[13] a project led by Morikawa Hidemasa. Interested scholars may refer to the abovementioned proceedings in the current context for a full discussion of this topic.

However, it is evident that in the course of industrial development following World War One, there emerged a new type of industrial entrepreneur who was more experienced than his Meiji counterpart. This new type of entrepreneur did take advantage of opportunities mainly in the chemical and electrical industries, and the enterprises they managed grew quickly by their strategy of diversification into related fields based on incremental technological innovation.[14] Barbara Molony's paper, "Innovation and Business Strategy in the Prewar Chemical Industry," describes the career, idiosyncratic personality, and industrial activities with incremental innovation of Noguchi Jun, whom she terms a "scientist-entrepreneur."

Apart from technological challenges, one of the most difficult tasks facing the professional and rational-minded managerial leader after World War One was the management of industrial labor. In particular, the growth of heavy industry called for an adequate and stable supply of male laborers who were fully committed to their work. However, during and immediately after World War One, when the demand for qualified labor increased, labor turnover was high and labor discipline declined. In this environment, management was hard put to secure adequate numbers of workers and had to train and retain these workers in their organizations. The former internal (inside) contractors or subcontractors with their labor squads were not able to meet the complex technical tasks which these enterprises now confronted.

The original practice of so-called Japanese labor management (it is often described in terms of a "triad" of lifetime employment, seniority-based wages, and from the postwar era, company unions) was founded and institutionalized by leading industrial enterprises in the 1920s and the first half of the 1930s. This labor employment practice was originally described by Japanese academics expert in the field of industrial relations, such as Sumiya Mikio.[15] As is well known, however, James Abegglen's work on this topic, which appeared in 1958, had considerable impact on scholars, which extended even beyond the discipline.[16] Since then, Japanese labor employment (sometimes used as a synonym of Japanese management) has been a highly controversial issue among both Japanese and Western academics. This is because Abegglen emphasized the anthropological continuity and cultural legacies directly carried over from traditional society.

It would be impossible and may be unnecessary to describe all of the debates surrounding the contemporary labor-management system.[17] However, one important effect of Abegglen's work was to stimulate studies of the Japanese employment system from a specifically historical point of view. Historical studies of this issue are no less controversial than arguments over the contemporary situation. Almost all business historians accept the view that the economic and social conditions of the 1920s and the first half of the 1930s had important effects on the development of the employment system, yet students of this topic remain divided as to the roots or causes of this labor system.

Hazama Hiroshi, Ronald Dore, and others believe that management's "creative" adaption of tradition lay at the core of the institutionalization of lifetime employment, seniority-based wage and welfare programs.[18] Hazama, in particular, advocates "systematic paternalism" as the ideological base of Japanese labor management. By contrast, Okuda Kenji, Andrew Gordon, and others stress more dynamic factors, which involve conflict between management and workers, as central to the development of the practice. These latter scholars explicitly reject the role of "the warm-hearted treatment" of workers in the formation of the employment system.[19]

Andrew Gordon's paper, "Araki Tōichirō and the Shaping of Labor Management," is grounded in the latter view. He focuses on this obviously important, yet entirely neglected, individual who was influential as a pioneering business consultant and practitioner of scientific management in Japan.[20] By elucidating Araki's consulting activities, particularly his role in the 1920s and the 1930s, Gordon emphasizes the role of labor-management contention and compromise as crucial to the formation of Japanese labor management.

Students of labor-management relations in inter-war Japan inevi-

tably come across the seeming ambivalence in the relationship between managers and workers. On the one hand, there were strong
familistic ties between the two, yet on the other hand, the two sides
also engaged in severe conflict. To further examine labor-management relations in a more integrated fashion, studies of actual
practices at the factory level involving such factors as production
and training are indispensable.[21]

Sawai Minoru's "The Development of Machine Industries and
the Evolution of Production and Labor Management," based on an
impressive array of primary evidence, deals with production control
and labor management on the shop floor. In this paper, Sawai
describes the evolutionary development of production management,
which had as one of its primary goals the strict observance of
appointed dates for delivery orders. One of the Japanese managerial and organizational characteristics evident here is that of
engineers with high levels of education orchestrating these developments through their advancement into the workshop, which over-
came the disparity between theoretical knowledge and practical
experience.

The final paper, by Janet Hunter, an expert on the history of the
Japanese textile industry, is entitled "Factory Legislation and Employer Resistance: The Abolition of Night Work in the Cotton
Spinning Industry." In this article, Hunter traces, with great
precision and accuracy, the long history of the enactment and
enforcement of factory legislation, which attempted to abolish night
work for women. Not only valuable for the new evidence brought
to light on perceptions of women in the labor market, this paper
also contributes to the debate on Japanese management by examining the dilemma of employers who perceived the proclaimed virtues
of paternalism yet exploited female workers to the fullest extent as
a factor of production.

Critically affected by labor legislation and the labor movements
after World War Two, the management of labor developed into its
fully articulated postwar form by the 1960s.[22] Clearly, Japan's more
recent experience with the management of labor deserves careful
scholarly analysis, and we are confident that studies which compare

and contrast historical development with more contemporary events will produce significant insights.

V. Concluding Remarks

This introduction provides a context within which the papers can be properly placed and evaluated. As mentioned at the outset, our attempt in the Conference was to focus our discussion on the managerial and organizational aspects of the industrial enterprises.

Unlike much popular literature of this kind, the contributors to this volume present the results of their studies within a balanced historical framework grounded in careful research analysis. It has not been the intention of this Conference to offer radically new explanations on this subject which are merely based on simplistic ideas. Rather, we have tried to concentrate our efforts to promote a better understanding among the participants, and through them to the general public. The attentive reader will no doubt realize that the distinctive characteristics of Japanese management originate in the process of evolutionary development of industrial enterprises in which management practices have been closely connected with organizational structure. In other words, consistent with the fact that even the course and patterns of industrialization have differed among the industrially advanced, so-called capitalist nations, this Conference demonstrates that the course and patterns of the evolutionary development of management differ by country.

NOTES

1. One publication, by a business historian, is *Nihonteki keiei* (Japanese management), edited by Nakagawa Keiichirō, Nihonkeizai Shinbunsha, 1977. This includes articles which deal with various aspects (decisionmaking, organization, personnel, R&D, labor management, marketing, etc.), focusing on Japanese characteristics in enterprises and management.
2. Keiichirō Nakagawa ed., *Government and Business*, The International Conference on Business History, Vol. 5, University of Tokyo Press, 1980. Because both Japanese economic and business historians have accumulated a large number of works on this subject, it is not pos-

sible in this introduction to attempt an overall bibliographical commentary. For a bibliographical survey, see Kobayashi Masaaki, "Seifu to Kigyō" (Government and Business) in Japan Business History Society ed., *Keieishigaku no 20 nen* (20 years of the studies of business history in Japan), University of Tokyo Press, 1985, pp. 135–41. As a recent, significant work by a foreign scholar, Chalmers Johnson, *MITI and the Japanese Miracle: The Growth of Industrial Policy, 1925–1975* (Stanford University Press, 1982), should be noted.

3. Of the studies by business historians who discuss the ideological aspects of Japanese enterprises after the Meiji Restoration, the following works are useful. Chō Yoshio ed., *Jitsugyō no shisō* (The thought of modern business enterprises), Chikuma shobō, 1964; Morikawa Hidemasa, *Nihongata keiei no genryū* (The spiritual source of Japanese-style management: Nationalism of Japanese business), Tōyōkeizai shinpōsha, 1974; Johannes Hirschmeier and Tsunehiko Yui, *The Development of Japanese Business*, George Allen & Unwin, 1981 (section IV of each chap.); Byron K. Marshall, *Capitalism and Nationalism in Prewar Japan: The Ideology of the Business Elite, 1868–1941*, Stanford University Press, 1967.

4. In the context of the continuity of the lifetime employment system, quite a bit of research on the management of the traditional merchant houses has been conducted. For example, Yōtarō Sakudō, "Traditional Labor Management in Japan, 1710–1890," in Keiichirō Nakagawa ed., *Labor and Management*, The International Conference on Business History, Vol. 4, University of Tokyo Press, 1979, pp. 127–40; Chimoto Akiko, "Meiji kōgyōka to zairaiteki koyō kankei no henten" (Changes in the traditional employment system in Meiji industrialization), *Shakai keizai shigaku*, Vol. 50, No. 1 (1986).

5. For example, see Johannes Hirschmeier, *The Origins of Entrepreneurship in Meiji Japan*, Harvard University Press, 1964; Hirschmeier and Yui, *op. cit.*, pp. 70–110. For a bibliographical commentary, Ishikawa Kenjirō, "Kigyōka" (Entrepreneur), Japan Business History Society, *op. cit.*, pp. 94–100.

6. On the same subject, see Ishikawa Kenjirō, "Meiji zenki ni okeru kazoku no ginkō tōshi" (Investment in banking by aristocrats in Meiji Japan), *Ōsakadaigaku keizaigaku*, Vol. 22, No. 3 (1972); Ishikawa K., "Kazoku shihon to shizoku keiesha" (The capital of aristocrats and business administration of ex-samurai); Tsunehiko Yui ed., *Kōgyōka to kigyōsha katsudō* (Industrialization and entre-

preneurship), Nihonkeizai Shinbunsha, 1976, pp. 122–30.

7. For example, Uchida Hoshimi, "1920 nen no gakusotsu gijutsusha bunpu" (A statistical survey of college graduate engineers in 1920), *Tokyo-keizaidaigaku kaishi*, No. 152 (1987).

8. Morikawa Hidemasa, *Gijitsusha: Nihon kindaika no ninaite* (The engineers, the promoters of industrialization in Japan), Nihonkeizai shinbunsha, 1975.

9. Eisuke Daitō, "Recruitment and Training of Middle Managers in Japan, 1850–1939," in Kesaji Kobayashi and Hidemasa Morikawa ed., *Development of Managerial Enterprises*, The International Conference on Business History, Vol. 12, University of Tokyo Press, 1986, pp. 151–79.

10. Shinichi Yonekawa, "University Graduates in Japanese Enterprises before the Second World War," *Business History*, Vol. XXVI, No. 2 (1984).

11. For instance, Hyōdō Tsutomu, *Nihon ni okeru rōshikankei no tenkai* (The development of industrial relations in Japan), University of Tokyo Press, 1973; Sumiya Mikio, *Nihon chinrōdō no shiteki kenkyū* (A historical study of wage-workers in Japan), Ochanomizu shobō, 1976.

12. With respect to the subject of subcontract or inside contract system from a comparative historical approach, the 20th Conference of the Business History Society of Japan, held in Oct. 1984, dealt with the topic. Suzuki Yoshitaka's "Naibu ukeoisei to 19 seiki Igirisu no sangyō soshiki" (The subcontract system and workshop organization in 19th-century Britain) and Shiomi Haruhito's "Amerika ni okeru kōjōsoshiki no henshitsu to naibu ukeoisei" (American factory system and the inside contract system) were presented at the Conference. *Keiei shigaku*, Vol. 20, No. 2 (1985).

13. Kobayashi and Morikawa, *op. cit.*

14. Studies on the new types of entrepreneur, closely connected with the analysis of the development of heavy and chemical industry, have advanced remarkably. For a bibliographical survey, see Ōshio Takeshi, "Sonota zaibatsu" (The other zaibatsu), and Yamazaki Hiroaki, "Jūkagaku kōgyō (Heavy and chemical industry), Japan Business History Society, *op. cit.*, pp. 128–34, pp. 151–62.

15. See Sumiya, *op. cit.*; Sumiya M. ed., *Nihon sangyō kunren hattatsushi* (The development of industrial training), 2 vols., Nihon Rōdō Kyōkai, 1971–72; Ujihara Masajirō, *Nihon no rōshi kankei* (Industrial relations in Japan), University of Tokyo Press, 1968; Komatsu

Ryūji, *Kigyōbetsu kumiai no seisei* (The emergence of enterprise union), Ochanomizu shobō, 1971. A recent important and thorough study is Nakanishi Yō, *Nihon kindaika no kiso katei* (The foundation of modernization in Japan: Nagasaki shipyard and its industrial relations, 1855–1900), 2 vols., University of Tokyo Press, 1982–83.

16.   James G. Abeggglen, *The Japanese Factory: Aspects of Its Social Organization*, MIT Press, 1958. Generally, the scholars who attach importance to anthropological continuity point out the "group-oriented" nature of Japanese management. Their argument centers on its social origins that some stress as the logic of the "village" (*mura*) and others emphasize as the logic of the "family" (*ie*). See Iwata Ryūshi, *Nihonteki keiei no hensei genri* (The fundamental rules of Japanese management), Bunshindō, 1977.

17.   For a summation of contemporary discussion, see Haruo Shimada, "Japanese Industrial Relations, A Survey of the English-Language Literature," in Taishiro Shirai ed., *Contemporary Industrial Relations in Japan*, University of Wisconsin Press, 1983, pp. 3–27.

18.   Hazama Hiroshi, *Nihon rōmu-kanrishi kenkyū* (A historical study of Japanese labor management), Diamondsha, 1964; Hazama H., *Rōshi kyōchō no teiryū* (Underlying currents in cooperation between labor and management), Waseda Daigaku Shuppankai, 1978; H. Hazama, "Japanese Labor Relations and Uno Riemon," *Journal of Japanese Studies*, Vol. 5, No. 1 (1979).

Ronald Dore, *British Factory-Japanese Factory*, University of California Press, 1973; R. Dore, "Authority and Benevolence," *Government and Opposition*, London, Vol. 20, No. 2 (1985).

The scholars who stress the social-cultural continuity take the affirmative on this argument.

19.   Okuda Kenji, *Hito to keiei* (Men and management: A historical study of Japanese labor management), Managementsha, 1985; Andrew Gordon, *The Evolution of Labor Relations in Japan: Heavy Industry, 1853–1955*, Council on East Asian Studies, Harvard University, 1986.

For a summation of this controversial discussion and bibliographical review through 1978, Mark Fruin, "The Japanese Company Controversy," *Journal of Japanese Studies*, Vol. 4, No. 2 (1978), is useful. In this paper, Fruin discusses the moderate nature of lifetime employment in prewar Japan, based on his statistical survey in Kikkōman (Noda Shōyu) Co.

Also, for a bibliographical commentary on the Japanese employment system in prewar Japan, see Daitō Eisuke, "Nihonteki keiei" (Japanese management), in Japan Business History Society, *op. cit.*, pp. 219–25.

20. Another influential individual, as a pioneering business consultant and practitioner of scientific management, is Ueno Yōichi, who has been well known among academicians. See Saitō Takenori, *Ueno Yōichi to keieigaku no paionia* (Ueno Yōichi, as a pioneer of scientific management), Sangyō Nōritsu Kyōkai, 1986.

21. As to the recent studies on production and labor management, the following are noteworthy: Eisuke Daitō, "Industrial Training and Factory Management in Japan, 1900–1930," in K. Nakagawa and T. Yui ed., *Organization and Management 1900-1930*, Proceedings of the Japan-German Conference of Business History, Japan Business History Institute, 1983, pp. 59–71; Choki Toshio, "Nihon ni okeru kōjō soshiki no kindaika" (The modernization of factory management in Japan), *Hōseidaigaku keieishirin*, Vol. 22, No. 1 (1985); Konno Kōichirō, "Kokutetsu kōsakukōjō ni miru kagakuteki kanrihō" (Scientific management in the factories of J.N.R.), *Rōmu kenkyū*, Vol. 29, No. 10, Vol. 30, No. 1 (1976, 1977); Sasaki Satoshi, "Mitsubishi denki ni miru kagakuteki kanrihō no dōnyū katei" (The development of time-study in Mitsubishi Electronic Co. at Kobe Works), *Keiei shigaku*, Vol. 21, No. 4 (1987); Sugayama Shinji, "1920-nendai Jūdenki keiei no kakyū shokuinsō (Lower white-collar employees of heavy electric industry in the 1920s: in the case of Hitachi), *Shakai keizai shigaku*, Vol. 53, No. 5 (1987). Also, refer to footnotes in Sawai's paper in this volume.

22. On the development of labor management immediately after World War II, refer to Koji Taira, *Economic Development and the Labor Market in Japan*, Columbia University Press, 1970; Tsuda Masumi, *Nihonteki keiei no ronri* (The characteristics of Japanese management), Chūō-keizaisha, 1977. With respect to the other works which deal with the subject, see Shimada, *op. cit.*

The "Learning Industrial Revolution" and Business Management

Keiichirō Nakagawa
Aoyama Gakuin University

One of the outstanding features of the origin of Meiji entrepreneurship is that very few entrepreneurs rose from the class of craftsmen (*kō*), primarily because of the sharp discontinuity in the industrial technology of traditional Japan and modern industrial countries of the West.[1] During the earliest stage of industrialization, this enormous gap in technology had to be filled first by learning through books, mostly in Dutch and some in French and English, second by sending students mainly to the United Kingdom and some to France and the United States, and third by establishing institutions of higher learning for science and technology. In fact, almost a half century of "book learning" preceded the start of the real industrial revolution (or modern economic growth), and the long process of this "learning industrial revolution," necessitated by Japan's cultural and geographical isolation from the Western countries, contributed to the development of some industrial systems fairly different from those in Western nations. In this paper, the early development of the two representative modern industries, cotton spinning and shipbuilding, will be examined, following the sequence of the three stages of learning Western technology mentioned above, and some comments will be made on the evolution of a few characteristic industrial systems which became the basis of the so-called Japanese management system.

I. The Pioneering Cotton Spinning Mills

There was substantial development in cotton spinning and weaving as a traditional skill during the Tokugawa period in several areas of the Japanese islands. However, after the opening of the country, domestic products suffered a humiliating defeat both in quality and in price by imported British and Indian cotton goods. At the time of the crisis, the first modern cotton mill in Japan was established in Kagoshima by the Satsuma Lord on the advice of a Dutch Studies (*rangaku*) scholar, Ishikawa Seiryū, who served the lord as a secretary. The machines imported from the Platt Bros. in England, i.e., 1,848 spindle throstles, 1,800 spindle mules and 100 power looms, started production in 1867 with some 200 male and female workers under the guidance of the English mechanics who had accompanied the machines to Japan. Three years later, another cotton mill, also owned by the Satsuma Lord, began work at Sakai, near the raw cotton growing area, and this mill was constructed and operated solely on the skills of Ishikawa and several Japanese mechanics trained at Kagoshima cotton mill. The new Meiji government immediately nationalized this Sakai Mill and established Aichi Cotton Mill in 1879 as a model mill with 2,000 spindle mules, moved by a 30 h.p. waterwheel constructed at Yokosuka Naval Shipyard.[2]

This government-run Aichi Mill was also constructed and operated by Ishikawa and six or seven mechanics who had come over from Sakai Mill, and, for the several years after 1880, Aichi Mill played the role of training center for industrial skills. It admitted trainees from the so-called 2,000 spindle mills, established by ten groups of local merchants and landlords, and sent to these mills a group of engineers and skilled workers to give instructions on how to construct and operate a modern cotton mill. In this group of traveling consultants, we can find already a product of the third stage of the "learning industrial revolution," Arakawa Shin'ichirō, an engineer of the Ministry of Agriculture, Commerce, and Industry who graduated in 1879 from Kōbu Daigakkō (Institute of Technology of the Ministry of Industry) and had studied in England for four years. However, until the mid-1880s, the learning of the modern cotton industry had been introduced mostly by Ishikawa, the pioneering Dutch Studies scholar, and his disciples as well as the English mechanics who had accompanied the machines to Japan.[3]

The second stage of learning is represented by Yamanobe Takeo and the promotion of the Osaka Cotton Mill. Yamanobe, the son of a samurai who served the Tsuwano Lord, studied with Nishi Amane, a scholar of Western philosophy who studied in Holland from 1862 to 1865, and also at the Osaka branch of Fukuzawa's Keiō Gijuku. In 1877 Yamanobe left for England with a son of the Tsuwano Lord to study economics at the University of London, and in the summer of 1879 he was persuaded by Shibusawa Eiichi to move to King's College to study the technology of cotton spinning. The government-subsidized "2,000 spindle mills," all failed, primarily on account of their small scale of operation, and Shibusawa, the president of the First National Bank, noticing the enormous amount of Japan's import of cotton yarn, was determined to establish a modern cotton mill of competitive scale. He persuaded the former lords and rich merchants in Osaka and Tokyo to invest in this new venture of strategic importance, and now he was anxious to find a qualified Japanese engineer who could operate the first large-scale private cotton mill in Japan.

The engineer of such a pioneering enterprise could not simply remain as a student of engineering, and Yamanobe moved to Lancashire where he was admitted to Briggs Mill in Blackburn to watch and understand the whole process of a modern cotton mill. He ordered the machines from Platt Bros. and returned to Japan in 1880. He decided to adopt steam engine instead of waterwheel and to establish a new factory in Osaka, a traditional market center of raw cotton and cotton goods. At the same time, four young men, relatives and acquaintances of Shibusawa and Yamanobe, were sent as apprentices to Aichi Mill and other pioneering cotton mills. Thus Osaka Mill was formally established in 1883 with a capital of ¥280,000 and 95 stockholders, 38% of the total amount of capital being subscribed by 17 former lords, 30.9% by Osaka, and 28.7% by Tokyo merchants. To respond to the expectation of long-suspended dividends, Osaka Cotton Mill immediately adopted a two-shift work schedule (day and night) and, raising a high profit from its first year, proved that the modern cotton spinning mill could be successful as a private enterprise.[4]

The success of Osaka Cotton Mill and the declined interest rate after the Matsukata financial reorganization gave rise to a promotion boom of cotton spinning mills from 1886 to 1888, and graduates of Kōbu Daigakkō played vital roles in the development of major pioneering cotton mills. They were Hattori Shun'ichi of Owari, Saitō Kōzō of Mie, and Kikuchi Kyōzō of Amagasaki Mills, all graduates of the engineering department of Kōbu Daigakkō.

Hattori, the son of a Dutch Studies physician, completing six years schooling at Kōbu Daigakkō in 1881, was appointed head of the engine section of the government's Hyōgo shipyard and successfully constructed several marine engines in cooperation with two British engineers. However, Hyōgo shipyard was sold to a private entrepreneur, and Hattori became chief engineer of Owari Cotton Mill and left for England to buy spinning machines. Hattori studied at Manchester Technical School and worked at the spinning mills in Oldham and Middleton for six months to master the operation of a spinning mill. Although Owari Cotton Mill thus started its operation in 1889, chief engineer (*kōmu-shihainin*) Hattori had to handle all aspects of factory management because no engineers or skilled workers were qualified to oversee factory operations, and the members of the board of directors, all being merchants in the Nagoya area, had no idea about modern factory management.[5]

Mie Cotton Mill was established in 1882 first as a "2,000 spindle mill" by Itō Denshichi, a wealthy farmer (*gōnō*) who was responsible for the office of magistrate, to develop local raw cotton farming and to give support to the wives and daughters of distressed ex-samurai. The mill was constructed under the guidance of Ishikawa, and its 13 workers were trained at Aichi Mill. However, the mill failed in the continuous production of good quality yarn, and Itō reorganized the mill into a joint-stock company in 1886 and tried to employ an educated engineer. Saitō Kōzō, who had been working at the government's Osaka Mint, came over to Mie Mill and sailed for England to be trained in textile engineering at Oldham. Saitō adopted ring frame along with mule, and in 1889 the Yokkaichi factory of Mie Mill was successfully operating 12,800 spindle mule and 4,472 spindle ring frames. From the early 1890s, graduates of Tokyo Shokkō Gakkō (trade school) were employed by and lived with Saitō to be more effectively trained and educated.[6]

The case of Kikuchi Kyōzō was typical of the crucial role played by educated engineers in Japan's industrialization. Born in 1859 to a family of rural samurai (*gōshi*) and physicians, Kikuchi studied at the Osaka English School and graduated from the Kōbu Daigakkō in 1885. First, he was employed at Yokosuka Naval Shipyard, but in 1887 he was solicited to be the chief engineer of the newly promoted Hirano Cotton Mill. As he had majored in marine engineering, he accepted the invitation on the condition that he would be allowed to go to England for training in textile engineering. Kikuchi thus stayed in Manchester for eight months, studying at Manchester Technical School and learning the operation of cotton mills at Middleton. He negotiated with the London branch of Mitsui Bussan for the purchase, on the basis of a 2.5% commission, from Platt Bros. of 11,520 spindle ring frames to be installed at Hirano Mill. Hirano was operated successfully, expanding its scale of operation to 27,647 spindles by constructing a second factory in 1893, and Kikuchi was promoted to the general manager and chief engineer at the same time.

Meanwhile, another group of Osaka merchants was promoting Amagasaki Cotton Mill, and in 1889 they successfully arranged for Kikuchi to serve as chief engineer of Amagasaki Mill as well by partially covering Kikuchi's traveling expenses in England. In the following year, Settsu Cotton Mill, closely related to Hirano, also solicited the same services from Kikuchi, again by paying a part of the expense of Kikuchi's visit to England. At any rate, Kikuchi thus supervised the design, construction, and operation of Amagasaki Cotton Mill, which specialized in the production of *chūte* (middlegrade fineness of yarn) twist and oversaw the operation of the three cotton mills, commuting to them every day on horseback.[7]

The modern cotton spinning mills could not be promoted without expert engineers, and educated engineers were scarce. An expert engineer had to be invited at a high salary, much higher than that of the president of the company. Nevertheless, the merchants, who were the members of the board of directors, usually refused to promote such qualified engineers to the board members, saying that engineers were not the owners but simply employees of the company. However, it was not the merchant but the engineer who knew how to operate and manage the cotton mill, and the merchant capitalists of the board had to promote the engineer to the board. Many of the pioneering educated engineers were promoted as presidents of major pioneering cotton mills. Amagasaki Mill promoted Kikuchi to board member in 1893 and to president in 1901.[8]

II. Learning Modern Shipbuilding

In 1863, a wooden screw steam warship, *Chiyodagata* (158 displacement tons, 60 h.p., 5 knots), was launched at Ishikawajima, a shogunal shipyard, and it was the first bona-fide steamship built at a Japanese shipyard only by Japanese. The hull of this ship was contructed by Ono Tomogorō, Haruyama Benzō, and Sawa Tarōzaemon, and its engine was built by Hida Hamagorō and Akamatsu Daizaburō, all these five being graduates of the Nagasaki Kaigun Denshūjo (naval training school) established by the Bakufu in 1855. This school was attended by about 70 students from shogunal retainers and about 130 from vassals of local lords. Many of these students had some knowledge of Dutch sciences, especially of astronomy and gunnery.[9]

Ono Tomogorō, chief engineer of the construction of *Chiyodagata*'s hull, was born a lower-class samurai of Kasama domain, studied Japanese mathematics (*wasan*), worked as the clan's agricultural officer (*jikata-tedai*) in land surveying and civil engineering, and also served as general manager (*motojime-tedai*) of the financial affairs of the clan's office in Edo. In 1852, he was recruited to the office of astronomy of the Bakufu and had the opportunity to study Western mathematics. To reward him for his achievement in translating into Japanese a Dutch book on the art of navigation, *Handleiding voor de praktische zeefaartkunde* (1837), by Jacob Swart, he was sent to Kaigun Denshūjo in 1855.[10]

Hida Hamagorō, chief engineer for the building of the *Chiyodagata*'s engine, was born the son of a Dutch Studies physician who served as doctor to Egawa Tarōzaemon, the governor of Izu province, and studied in Edo with the leading scholars of Dutch sciences, Kawamoto Kōmin (a chemist) and Itō Genboku (founder of the first clinic for smallpox vaccination and director of Seiyō Igakusho). When a Russian warship, *Diana*, was shipwrecked off Izu peninsula, about 50 Izu shipwrights worked for some 100 days, under the direction of Governor Egawa, himself a *rangaku* scholar. Using a ship design submitted by a Russian officer, they built a schooner to carry the *Diana* crew back to Russia. This was the first attempt by Japanese artisans at Western-style shipbuilding, and two of these shipwrights were also sent to Nagasaki Kaigun Denshūjo.

At Kaigun Denshūjo, the warship donated to the Bakufu by the king of Holland and its officers and crew were mobilized to educate the students in the art of navigation, the sciences and technologies of shipbuilding, marine engine manufacturing, and gunnery, as well as mathematics and Dutch. Among the students were many who became leaders of the modernization and industrialization that was to follow, such as Katsu Rintarō and Enomoto Kamajirō, sent by the Bakufu, Sano Tsunetami, and Tanaka Giemon from Saga domain, Nomura Yakichi (later Inoue Masaru) from Chōshū, and Godai Tomoatsu from Satsuma. Ono Tomogorō studied goniometry, horology, and hydrography by means of a sextant, and Hida Hamagorō (Tameyoshi) devoted himself to the technology of engine construction. In 1860, on *Kanrin-maru*, the Bakufu's warship which sailed across the Pacific Ocean to San Francisco, navigated for the first time by the Japanese themselves, Ono was chief navigator and Hida was chief engineer.

In the following year, Ono convinced the Bakufu of the necessity of constructing gunboats for the defense of Edo Bay, and construction began on *Chiyodagata*, the first of a series of gunboats, at Mito clan's Ishikawajima shipyard. However, the construction took as long as four years because of difficulty in the water-tank experiment and lack of the machinery for engine building at Ishikawajima. The engine had to be built at the Akunoura Engine Works of the Bakufu's Nagasaki Iron Works. Akunoura was equipped with 17 machine tools imported from Holland, such as the lathe and drilling and planing machines, and greatly contributed to raising the precision level of metal fabrication. However, even this engine works was not provided with a riveting machine, indispensable for boiler manufacturing, and Hida had to be sent to Holland in 1864 to purchase this and other machine tools for Ishikawajima shipyard. While in Holland, Hida met a group of Japanese whom the Bakufu sent two years previously, such as Enomoto, Sawa, Akamatsu, and other graduates of Kaigun Denshūjo, and Nishi Amane and other students of Western philosophy, law, and medical science.[11]

Soon after Hida's departure, the Bakufu was approached by French minister Léon Roches with a proposition to help the Bakufu establish a large-scale shipbuilding yard in Edo Bay. Ono Tomogorō was in charge of surveying a suitable location for such a naval shipyard. In 1865, François Léonce Verny came to Japan to be the principal of the proposed naval shipyard, but the Bakufu decided to first establish an iron works in Yokohama to repair the Bakufu's warships and then to construct a full-scale naval shipyard in Yokosuka. Yokohama Iron Works was constructed with the help of officers and crew of a French warship at anchor in the port and was furnished with the machine tools the Saga domain had bought from Holland and had left idle. The iron works employed and allocated traditional craftsmen to the jobs most suited to their skills—for example, carpenters to the hull-building yard and blacksmiths to the iron-puddling mill—and thus could finally secure about a hundred fairly skilled workers.

The plan of Yokosuka yard was far more extensive, including two repairing docks, three building docks, and one iron mill, and employing about 40 French and 2,000 Japanese. Its construction took long, and the first dock was not completed until 1870. In the meantime, Verny was ambitious to set up a system for education in shipbuilding technology and established in the shipyard a shipbuilding school with a three-year course. However, the difficulty of mastering French in a short time and the inadequacy of basic knowledge in mathematics and physics limited the number of eligible students. In the two years before May of 1868 there were only nine, of whom six were recruited from the Bakufu's army and navy and three who had learned French at the Yokohama Language School.

Under the new Meiji regime, Verny's school was reorganized as Kōsha, also located in Yokosuka Shipyard, but French was also a prerequisite for the classes on shipbuilding and engineering, where the morning classes emphasized mathematics and physics, and in the afternoon there was workshop practice. Professional courses on ship designing and engine manufacturing were not taught until 1876. F. L. Verny and other French engineers seemed to have set their goals on developing Yokosuka shipyard into a great ship-repairing and shipbuilding center of East Asia where Western ships of increasing tonnage had started to congest. The French were not as interested as the Japanese government was, particularly the navy, in quickly improving the level of Japanese shipbuilding engineers.[12]

In 1875, Hida, who had been the head of the Shipbuilding Department of the Ministry of Navy since 1873, proposed a plan to reorganize Yokosuka shipyard and decided that the shipyard could repair and build only the ships approved by the Ministry of Navy. Furthermore, the efforts of French officers in teaching Japanese officers and workers should be evaluated and rewarded. This reorganization limited the authority of the French officers, and Verny and other engineers gradually returned to France, leaving the role of technological tutor to British engineers.

An almost identical change had been taking place at Nagasaki shipyard, first established by the Bakufu as Nagasaki Iron Works in 1857. Its Akunoura engine works constructed under the leadership of H. Hardes, an able and devoted Dutch engineer, could boast of being the largest ship-repairing works in East Asia. However, the plan to construct a large-scale repairing dock at Tategami was seriously delayed, and Hardes and other Dutch engineers were successively discharged in the 1860s. Hirano Tomiji, an assistant at the engine works, was appointed in 1870 by the Meiji government as head of Nagasaki Iron Works and devoted himself to the construction of the Tategami repairing dock. However, the control of Nagasaki Iron Works was transferred in the following year to the newly established Ministry of Industry. Hirano and his predecessor Motoki Shōzō, both products of Dutch Studies, left the iron works and started a printing business in Nagasaki and Tokyo. In 1876, the government sold Ishikawajima shipyard to Hirano, and thus started the first private shipbuilding enterprise in Japan.

Yamao Yōzō, later head of the new Ministry of Industry, left Japan for England in 1863 with Itō Shunsuke and other colleagues of Chōshū clan. Yamao studied shipbuilding technology in Glasgow as the first Japanese apprentice at Robert Napier's shipyard, also attending evening school at Anderson College. A younger samurai of Chōshū, Watanabe Kōzō, also studied shipbuilding from 1867 to 1873 in England and America, and as the head of the government's Nagasaki shipyard from 1873 to 1884 saw the construction of the large-scale Tategami repairing dock to its completion. The two young samurai of Okayama's Ikeda clan, Mizutani Rokurō and Matsuda Kinjirō, also sailed for England in 1871, and both studied shipbuilding at Hawthorne Shipyard in Newcastle. Mizutani came back to Japan to be chief engineer of Nagasaki Shipyard, and Matsuda, having participated in the construction of three Japanese capital warships in London and Hull, returned home on board the *Fusō* to become in 1883 chief engineer of the government's Hyōgo shipyard. Education abroad, mostly studying at technical night school and apprenticeship in shipyards in the daytime, was thus the second stage of the "learning industrial revolution."[13]

The third stage began in 1873 with the opening of the Kōgaku Ryō (after 1877 Kōbu Daigakkō), one of the pioneering institutes of technology in the world. Its curriculum was a six-year program, composed of preparatory, professional, and practical courses, each for two years. Its first principal was Henry Dyer, himself just graduated from Glasgow University in 1872 and obtained the first Bachelor of Science in the world. Among the 11 best merit-graduates of Kōbu Daigakkō in 1879 who were sent to Great Britain for advanced study, Miyoshi Shinrokurō specialized in shipbuilding and studied at Glasgow University, particularly in the John Elder Memorial Course of shipbuilding. After practicing at Napier shipyard, Miyoshi returned home to be the first professor of shipbuilding of Kōbu Daigakkō. In the meantime, Sadate Jirō and Ieiri Yasushi, both 1880 graduates of the mechanical engineering department, were employed by Nagasaki shipyard. C. D. West, a graduate of Trinity College in Ireland, came to Japan in 1883 after practicing as a shipbuilding engineer in Glasgow and helped Miyoshi teach the shipbuilding class.[14]

When the government sold Nagasaki shipyard to Mitsubishi in 1884, only Mizutani and two assistant engineers stayed with the shipyard, and therefore J. E. Calder and five other British engineers, who had worked since 1875 at Mitsubishi Yokohama Iron Works, had to be transferred to Nagasaki shipyard. It is no wonder that the management of the shipyard was almost in the hands of British engineers in the early days of Mitsubishi Nagasaki Shipyard. However, by 1897 Shioda Taisuke, Katō Tomomichi, Sugitani Yasuichi and seven other graduates of Kōbu Daigakkō and Kōka Daigaku (established when the Engineering Department of Tokyo University merged with Kōbu Daigakkō in 1886) and 11 graduates of Tokyo Kōgyō Gakkō (Tokyo Technical College, established in 1889 and successor of Tokyo Shokkō Gakkō, organized in 1881) were successively recruited to fortify the engineering staff of Nagasaki shipyard.[15]

In the latter half of the 19th century, shipbuilding in the world, particularly in Great Britain, was in the process of momentous technological innovations, and the growing staff of professional engineers could play a crucial role in absorbing the newest technology from the West. Nagasaki shipyard could thus launch between 1889 and 1890 three steel ships charged with triple compound engines for Osaka Shōsen Kaisha, and in 1896 the shipyard successfully constructed a 6,000-ton liner, *Hitachimaru*, one of the six passenger ships Nippon Yūsen Kaisha allocated to the newly opened European regular service. Further, between 1907 and 1911, Nagasaki shipyard pioneered the construction of the ocean-going turbine steamers by launching the *Ten'yō* and two other large-scale steamers, each 13,500 tons, 20 knots, and powered by Parsons turbines. As far as technology was concerned, Japanese shipbuilding seems to have been firmly established.[16]

III. The Japanese Industrial and Management Systems

The three stages of the "learning industrial revolution" have been reviewed in the cotton and shipbuilding industries. An almost identical process can be traced in the iron and steel industry during its early stage of development. Ōshima Takatō, the son of a physician of Nanbu clan, cooperated with Tezuka Ritsuzō of Chōshū clan in translating a Dutch book into Japanese, *Het Gietwezen in 's Rijks IJzer- Geschutgieterij te Luik* (The method of casting in the Liege National Gunnery), in 1854 and three years later successfully smelted iron with a Western-type iron furnace constructed at Kama-ishi in Nanbu. The Meiji government planned to establish a large-scale iron mill at Kamaishi with equipment wholly imported from England and operated by C. H. Godfrey and 16 other English and German engineers and skilled workers. This undertaking failed, however, after eight years of trial, and the government gave up the plan, which had expended an enormous sum of ¥2.4 million.

The residue of the government iron mill was sold to an iron merchant, Tanaka Chōbei, and his clerk, Yokoyama Kyūtarō, who constructed two small furnaces, similar to that built by Ōshima 30 years earlier. They successfully smelted some pig iron in 1886 with the help of skilled workers trained at the government mill. With the same small furnaces, each of 5- to 6-ton capacity and resuming the operation of the abandoned 25 tons of governmental furnaces, with the assistance of Komura Koroku, a graduate of Kōka Daigaku, Tanaka Iron Mill at Kamaishi produced, in 1894, 15 thousand tons of pig iron, 65% of the national output.

Thus the Japanese iron industry still remained small, and, at the end of the Sino-Japanese War in 1895, the government decided to establish once again a large-scale iron mill. Ōshima Michitarō, a son of the Dutch Studies engineer, was appointed chief engineer and, making a tour of inspection through the United States and Germany where he studied from 1877 to 1882 at Freiberg Berg-akademie, drew up the plan for the new mill; its annual output of pig iron was set at 120,000 tons in the integrated iron and steel mill. Thus the government-run Yawata Seitetsusho started to operate its 160-ton iron furnace in 1901. However, it experienced repeated problems with the iron furnace and its output turned out to be a miserable 16.7 tons a day, in spite of the efforts of Ōshima, the German engineers, and the skilled workers called in from Ta-naka Iron Mill.[17]

Noro Kageyoshi was invited to examine the reasons for the failure. Noro, son of the highest class samurai of Nagoya domain, studied metallurgy with Kurt Netto at Kaisei Gakkō (later Tokyo University), mechanical and electric engineering at London University, and metallurgy at Freiberg Bergakademie. As profes-sor of Kōka Daigaku (the Department of Engineering of the Imperial University) from 1889, Noro was once a consultant for

Tanaka Iron Mill, and based on this experience he was able to detect some structural defects in the failing furnace and the unsuitableness of coke ovens and coal at Yawata Mill. Although Ōshima's plan was too heavily dependent on German technology, the basic difficulty was in the expanded scale of operation. A second and smaller furnace was constructed and continued successful production since 1906. The operation of the steel mill had been smooth from its beginning under the supervision of Imaizumi Kaichirō, a student of Noro at Kōka Daigaku.[18]

The development of the institutions for technological higher learning at the early stage of Japan's industrialization deserves notice. For example, Henry Dyer was enthusiastic in establishing Kōbu Daigakkō as a model for systematic education of technology that had not yet been realized in his own country. However, we must not overlook the role of the Dutch Studies school as a basis for the successful "learning of industrial revolution." At the end of the 18th century, the Dutch edition of a French encyclopedia, N. Chomel's *Algemeen Huishoudelijk-, Natuur-, Zedekundig- en Konstwoordenboeck*, was translated into Japanese, and in the early 19th century some 60 samurai studied in Nagasaki with P. F. von Siebold, a Dutch physician, on various aspects of Western science and technology. Tekijuku in Osaka, taught by a Dutch Studies physician Ogata Kōan, attracted 637 students not only from the samurai class but also from farmer and merchant classes.[19]

With years of accumulation of knowledge only from books, and never being able to observe its physical reality, the curiosity of the Japanese about Western industrial civilization had been so much heightened that as early as 1855 Nagasaki Kaigun Denshūjo could immediately attract about 200 scholars and students, more or less educated in Dutch Studies. The mentality of scientific rationalism combined with the spirit of adventure had penetrated them, and further most of them had been well trained for functional responsibility in the tradition of bureaucracy of the Bakufu and domain governments. It is no wonder that many of them rose to eminence as government and business leaders in the Meiji era, seizing the opportunity of being sent to the West as students or members of diplomatic missions.[20]

On the other hand, merchants at the end of the Tokugawa period

were not educated enough to know about Western industrial civilization and could not perceive the entrepreneurial opportunities in
the new age and new world. They had the monetary resources, but
they had to organize joint-stock companies not only to finance on
an internationally competitive scale, for example, cotton mills
but also to recruit educated engineers who were very scarce at the
beginning of industrialization. And the merchant capitalists who
knew little of modern factory management had to promote, usually
with some reluctance, the educated engineers to the members of
the board of directors at the early stage of the development of their
companies. As a result, the ratio of the engineers in the total number
of top management, the *jōmu* (managing director) and above,
before World War II was as high as 40%, according to Morikawa
Hidemasa. A survey by the Ministry of Education in 1930 of 59
engineering firms also reported that of the 47 top business managers,
division managers and above, 26 were graduates of the engineering
department, whereas only 15 were graduates of the departments of
law and economics. According to the same survey, in 79 factories
in the textile industries, of the 13 top business managers, 5 were
graduates of engineering departments and 8 graduates of law and
economics.[21]

In the modern cotton mills and shipbuilding yards, the commercial side of the enterprise, such as marketing, purchasing, and
financing, also required the ability of educated *shōgyō gishi* (business engineers). Especially in the case of cotton spinning, the Japanese mills established second and third factories in areas distant
from the first ones in sharp contrast to the British "one-site mills."
The merger movement at the turn of the century accentuated multiunit enterprises. As each factory had to be staffed with educated
mechanical and "business engineers" as well as specialists on labor
management, the headquarters of the mills also had to be buttressed
with a growing number of professional managers.

In relation to the development of such management hierarchy,
the boards of directors and the stockholders meetings of industrial
firms steadily lost their authority, which had not been firmly established during the companies' formative stages. Although the pioneering industrial firms had to be organized on a joint-stock basis,

the functions and authority of the board of directors was never clearly established. According to Yui Tsunehiko, the responsibilities and authority were first concentrated on the president, and other members of the board had no obligations other than attending board meetings once a month, and they were usually not paid a salary. After the company law was established by the 1893 Commercial Code, the chief engineer (*shihainin*) was promoted to *senmu-torishimariyaku* (executive director) to help the president, and since the beginning of this century the *jōmu-torishimariyaku* (managing directors) were appointed from among the *buchō* (division heads) class to share the responsibilities of the president and *senmu*. In this way, the expanding top management functions were fullfilled by the *shachō* (president), *senmu*, and *jōmu*, mostly promoted from among the company employees, and the power of merchant capitalists, who were the ordinary members of the board, was constantly decreased.[22]

Further, a study by Yonekawa Shin'ichi on cotton mills at the turn of the century clearly shows that the system of long-term employment had apparently developed for the white-collar employee, i.e., the junior mechanical and "business engineers," and the system of payment and promotion on seniority as well as the bonus system were extensively applied even to the lowest level of engineers and other white-collar workers.[23]

Concerning the laborers in the process of the "learning industrial revolution," traditional craftsmen could build small mechanical instruments, such as *wadokei* (Japanese-style clock), but could not cast a cogwheel for the large-scale waterwheel of gunnery without the knowledge of a Dutch Studies scholar of mathematics and sciences. It was the same with traditional shipwrights who could be employed in the building of Western sailing ships only under the direction and training by Dutch Studies engineers. Without such training or guidance by engineers, traditional craftsmen were like unskilled workers and could not be organized into an effective craft union. In addition, the skilled craftsmen preferred to be promoted to the lower class of engineers by mastering modern industrial skill.

At any rate, the recruitment and management of modern skilled workers were extremely difficult. For example, Nagasaki shipyard, bought by Mitsubishi in 1887, could not maintain, on account of the unstable market, the overstaffed labor management organization of the government shipyard and therefore adopted the *oyakata* (gang boss) system for recruiting and training unskilled workers. Some other shipyards went so far as to subcontract work on hull building to several *oyakata* who recruited workers through their personal relations. This *oyakata* system induced the gang bosses to move with their own workers from shipyard to shipyard, seeking better payment, and consequently the rate of labor mobility became as high as 100%.

Toward the end of the 19th century, Nagasaki shipyard shifted its objective from the repairing business to shipbuilding and found it difficult to secure enough skilled workers under the *oyakata* system. The shipyard therefore established Mitsubishi Kōgyō Yobi Gakkō to provide a five-year course at the company's expense to train new primary school graduates as *gishi* and *gikō* (lower level of engineers and mechanics). This was a pivotal turning point in the history of Japanese labor management, marking the beginning of an "internal labor market," in terms of recent labor economics. At Nagasaki shipyard, the system of *minaraikō*, that is, unskilled workers trained not by *oyakata* but by superiors or colleagues in the same workshop, had existed since the days of the government-run shipyard, and on the founding of Kōgyō Yobi Gakkō and the expansion of the *minaraikō* system, the *oyakata* system was abolished in 1908.[24]

In the case of cotton spinning mills, the speed of mechanization of work in the factory was so fast that subcontracting by *oyakata* did not establish itself. In Kanegafuchi Cotton Mill, even recruitment and training by *oyakata* was replaced in 1902 by a young worker training system (*yōnen shokkō yōsei seido*) by which the new male graduates from primary schools were housed in the dormitory for three years and trained and educated as apprentices trained in-house (*kogai yōseikō*) at the company's expense.[25]

In short, on account of the sharp discontinuity of technology between traditional and modern industries and the fast speed of the technological change of the developing industries, traditional craftsmen could play only a small role in Japan's industrialization, and they were unable to organize any effective craft unions in modern industries. The shortage or the lack of skilled workers had to be overcome by a joint effort by educated engineers and unskilled workers, just as in the case of Eli Whitney and his workers in America. In Japan, the shortage of capital resources led to the early formation of joint-stock companies, which resulted in the early rise of managerial hierarchies. And in just the same way, the shortage of skilled workers led to the development of an employment system based on close cooperation between engineers and workers on the floors of workshops.

IV. Postscript

From the beginning of and through gradual industrialization in Western Europe, the class of workers developed their skills on the basis of traditional crafts, and it was these skilled workers and the craft unions that raised and maintained the level of their profession in major manufacturing industries. The unions themselves instituted and managed an apprentice system, and skilled workers were responsible for managing workshops, in many cases taking subcontract factory work from mill owners. In the United States also, skilled mechanics were the "masters of trade" who trained unskilled workers for particular jobs, maintaining an apprentice system themselves, and contrived to improve the work efficiency under a system of "inside contract."[26]

In Japan, however, where traditional craftsmanship had little in common with the newly introduced Western technologies, workers' skills had to be developed not on the basis of traditional crafts, but by learning from abroad; learning from and practicing with Dutch Studies scholars, foreign engineers and skilled workers, and the earliest Japanese college-educated engineers. From the early stages of industrialization, it was not the "journeymen apprentice system" (*shokunin totei seido*), but the "factory apprentice system" (*kōjō totei seido*) that played a decisive role as an essential institution for training workers and gave rise to more or less sophisticated arrangement for in-firm training and education.[27]

At the start of Osaka Cotton Spinning Mill, for example, workers employed from surrounding villages were totally inexperienced in modern mechanical spinning, and they had to be trained and educated by the chief engineer, Yamanobe, and four young machin-

ists who had studied the manual of cotton spinning, which Yamanobe translated from English, and had been trained at the government's Aichi and other spinning mills. As a result of its early switch
from mule to ring frames, the level of skills required was greatly
reduced, and the percentage of female workers at Osaka Mill
increased to 70% in 1892. These young women, recruited increasingly from distant rural areas, were housed in dormitories and
educated in reading, arithmetic writing, and sewing at the company school.

These workers were not in a position to dominate the workshops
by dint of their skill as in the case of adult male spinners in the
British cotton mills, and their need and possibility of being subcontractors or being unionized to protect their own skills were
limited. On the other hand, the administrative system for controlling the work at each factory expanded in the 1890s by appointing *gishu*, chief mechanics responsible for the operation of each
section of the factory, and *gidan* and *gijo*, male and female workers
who had served in the factory more than three years diligently and
were to help *gishu* by examining the conditions of machines and
overseeing workers. *Gidan* and *gijo* were paid monthly salaries on a
scale of six degrees, and an administrative hierarchy was established
at each factory: from the top to bottom were *kōmu kakari* (factory
superintendent), *gishu*, *gidan/gijo*, assistant *gidan/gijo*, and *shunin*, who
were responsible for allocating workers to each job.[28]

In the case of the shipbuilding industry, many of the traditional
shipwrights of Izu province, who were the first to learn Western shipbuilding in Japan, moved to Yokosuka, Ishikawajima, and other
pioneering shipyards around Tokyo. Some of them were sent to
Nagasaki Kaigun Denshūjo and even to Holland in 1862 as members
of a group of Japanese students led by Enomoto Takeaki. However,
it is not certain to what extent these Izu shipwrights contributed to
the subsequent development of skilled workers in the rising shipbuilding industry throughout the country. Particularly at the government-run and later Mitsubishi Nagasaki Shipyard, there is little
left to remind us of the participation of the Izu shipwrights. It seems
that on account of the great gap of technology between the traditional and modern Western shipbuilding and due to the lack of an

established apprentice system, Japanese shipwrights could not improve and maintain the level of their technology and were not confident or proud enough of their skills or craft to play leading roles in the development of Japanese shipbuilding technologies.[29]

The transplanting of Western shipbuilding technology had to be organized by a system of school education. A great group of teachers, 43 French engineers and skilled workers led by F. L. Verny, started in the mid-1860s to teach more than a hundred traditional carpenters and smiths the skills in keel and frame building, metal fabricating, and engineering. However, in addition to the obvious linguistic barrier, these workers, who had been partly recruited from the classes of peasants and peddlers, were not accustomed to the regularity of factory work and did not stay in the shipyard long enough to become experienced veteran shipwrights who could take on responsible jobs operating the workshops.[30]

Therefore a mechanics school, Gijutsu Denshūjo, was established in 1866 to educate farm boys in French and basic engineering, and this system was replaced in 1871 by a second division (Hensoku Gakkō) of Kōsha, where about 50 young apprentices were taught by seven French and Japanese teachers every morning or afternoon. The students of this school, many of whom were the sons of distressed ex-samurai families, were expected to qualify as foremen who would supervise and train unskilled workers on the shopfloors. However, these educated mechanics were eager to be promoted to the junior level of the engineering staff, mainly because the shogunate or daimyo government practice of employing samurai as factory officials and commoners as factory workers was still influential on the behavior of people. This sense of class distinction between factory officials and workers obstructed the growth of such real skilled workers as the British shipwrights who continued to control as subcontractors the operation of workshops through the 19th century. As a result, there were few master shipwright subcontractors at Yokosuka shipyard in 1873, and 109 *kōshu*, or low-class educated engineers, were directly responsible for supervising and training 1,314 workers on the shopfloors.[31]

In addition, the *kōshu* were responsible primarily for working conditions and attitudes of the workers, helping the communication between them and French engineers and workers, while the task of managing and developing shipbuilding processes and technologies were wholly entrusted in the hands of French engineers. The Japanese engineers did not shift their major tasks from supervising workers to managing processes and technologies until the mid-1880s when the French had mostly left and the skilled Japanese workers ultimately became competent enough to supervise unskilled workers.

The situation was almost the same with the government's Nagasaki shipyard. The Japanese officials, many of whom had participated in Nagasaki Kaigun Denshūjo, were primarily in charge of supervising the work attitude of workers, and the Dutch engineers and skilled workers, who were originally expected to be technological staff, had to play the role of foremen, being employed for on-the-job training of unskilled workers. The Japanese workers were slow in mastering the new skills and becoming qualified enough to operate workshops, and it was not until after Nagasaki shipyard was sold to Mitsubishi in 1887 that the shipyard could partially adopt the system of subcontracting to *oyakata* skilled workers.[32]

However, the "journeymen apprentice system" under which *oyakata* moved with their apprentices from shipyard to shipyard seeking better working conditions, was not suitable for the introduction of rapid technological innovations in the shipbuilding industry. Workers' skills could keep pace with the progress of technology only by constant and close contact and communication with professional engineers. It is no wonder that in the 1890s Mitsubishi Nagasaki Shipyard aggressively recruited a growing number of educated engineers, and by establishing Kōgyō Yobi Gakkō in 1899 in its own yard, decisively returned to the "factory apprentice system," an epoch-making development of "internal labor market" in Japan.

NOTES

1. Ishikawa Kenjirō, "Meijiki ni okeru kigyōsha katsudō no tōkeiteki kenkyū" (Statistical study of entrepreneurship in the Meiji period), *Osaka daigaku keizaigaku*, Vol. 23, No. 4, 1974. Of the 422 prominent businessmen born before 1869, the sons of craftsmen comprised

only 5%, while the sons of samurai reached 48% and the sons of merchants 23%.

2. Horie Yasuzō, "Kindai Nihon no senkuteki kigyōka: Ishikawa Seiryū to Ōshima Takatō" (Pioneering entrepreneurs in modern Japan), *Keizai ronsō*, Vol. 84, No. 3, 1958: Okamoto Yukio, "Wagakuni bōseki kigyō sōsetsuki ni okeru gijutsu mondai ippan" (Technological problems of the cotton spinning firms in their formative years), *Kōnan keizaigaku ronshū*, Vol. 14, No. 1, 1973. Iijima Manji, *Nihon bōseki shi* (History of cotton spinning in Japan), 1949, pp. 1–13.

3. Okamoto, *op. cit.* Of about ten traveling consultants dispatched from Aichi Mill, all except Arakawa were journeyman mechanics trained and educated by Ishikawa at Kagoshima, Sakai, and Aichi mills. They consulted each other on the building of factories, installment and operation of machines, and the choice of powers.

4. Ishikawa Yasujirō, *Kozan no hen'ei* (Biography of Yamanobe Takeo), Tokyo, 1922, pp. 98–160. Shibusawa Eiichi Denkishiryō Kankōkai, *Shibusawa Eiichi denki shiryō*, Vol. 10, talk by Okamura Katsumasa. Tōyō Bōseki KK, *Tōyō Bōseki 100 nenshi*, Vol. 1, 1986, pp. 14–34. The crucial importance of qualified engineers is revealed in their high salaries. In 1883, their salary was 50 yen a month, while the salary was 30 yen for a chairman and 20 yen for a director. The technological engineers' salaries were also much higher than those of *shōmu shihainin* (business managers). (Okamoto Yukio, "Wagakuni bōsekigaisha bokkōki no gijutsusha mondai" (Problems of engineers at the emerging stage of the Japanese cotton spinning mills), *Seinan gakuin shōgaku ronshū*, Vol. 20, No. 3, 1973.

5. Okamoto, "Gijutsusha Mondai," *Seinan ronshū*, pp. 20–23; Kinugawa Taichi, *Hompō menshi bōseki shi*, 1937, Vol. 4, pp. 311, 320–22; Tōyō Bōseki KK, *op. cit.*, pp. 178, 180, 201. Hattori's monthly salary was 100 yen while that of sub-prefectural governor was 60 yen.

6. Fujitsu Seiji, "Mie bōseki seiritsu zenshi" (Formative stage of Mie Cotton Spinning Mill), *Ikkyō ronsō*, Vol. 77, No. 6, 1977; Tōyō Bōseki KK, *op. cit.*, pp. 163–76.

7. Nitta Naozō, ed., *Kikuchi Kyōzō Ōden* (Biography of Kikuchi Kyōzō), 1948, pp. 27–176. The book *Cotton Spinning*, brought back by Kikuchi from England, was adopted as the first important textbook at the Department of Engineering of the Imperial University. (pp. 111–13). The president of the Hirano Mill, Kanazawa Nihei, was an able merchant-businessman in Osaka, but he did not come to the mill more than once a month and entrusted Kikuchi with the

management of the mill as well (pp. 106–8).

8. Nitta, *ibid.*, pp. 163–76, 195–200. The emphasis of the role of engineer does not mean that merchant skills were not important. Kikuchi was ably supported by Tashiro Jūemon, who had been brought up in cotton trade and was appointed the business manager of Amagasaki Mill in 1893.

9. Zōsen Kyōkai, ed., *Nihon kinsei zōsenshi* (History of shipbuilding in modern Japan), 1911, pp. 96–98; Tsuchiya Shigeaki, *Kindai Nihon zōsen kotohajime* (History of early shipbuilding in modern Japan), 1975, pp. 136–44; Shinohara Hiroshi, *Kaigan sōsetsu shi* (Founding the Japanese Navy), 1986, pp. 31–64.

10. Fujii Tetsuhiro, *Ono Tomogorō no shōgai* (Life of Ono Tomogorō: Technocrats in Bakumatsu and Meiji), 1985, pp. 17–57. Ono became an official of the Ministries of Interior and Industry and helped Edmund Morrel in surveying for the Nippon Railway (Tokyō to Aomori) and other railways.

11. Tsuchiya, *op. cit.*, pp. 31–47, 60–92, 136–58; Fujii, *op. cit.*, pp. 47–65; Shinohara, *op. cit.*, pp. 31–44.

12. Zōsen Kyōkai, *op. cit.*, pp. 103–5, 276–79, 919–23; Kamiki Tetsuo, "Kindai ikōki ni okeru ishokukōgyō no teichaku katei" (Process of establishment of Western industries in early modern Japan), *Kokumin keizai zasshi*, Vol. 154, No. 1, 1985; Kamiki Tetsuo, "Kindai ikōki ni okeru zōsen gijutsu denshū" (Learning shipbuilding technology in early modern Japan), in *Kinsei ikōki ni okeru keizai hatten* (Economic development in early modern Japan), edited by Kamiki Tetsuo and Matsuura Akira, 1987, Ch. 5; Tomita Hitoshi and Nishibori Akira, *Yokosuka Seitetsusho no hitobito* (People at Yokosuka Iron Works), 1983, pp. 136–62. The emphasis on French and basic science education seems to have delayed and obstructed the development of professional shipbuilding education at Kōsha, but it made possible the rise of many pioneers in introducing French culture and technology—language education, laws, accounting, and chemistry. Tatsumi Hajime, Wakayama Tsurukichi, and several other graduates of Kōsha who studied at Ecole des Constructions Navales at Cherbourg became leading engineers in the naval construction in Japan.

13. Nakanishi Hiroshi, *Nihon kindaika no kisokatei: Nagasaki Zōsensho to sono rōshi kankei, 1855–1900* (Basic process of Japan's modernization: Nagasaki Shipyard and its labor relations), University of Tokyo Press, 2 vols., 1982–83. For Watanabe Kōzō, Mizutani Rokurō, and

Matsuda Kinjirō, see Nakanishi, *ibid.*, Vol. 2, pp. 400–29; Kita Masami, *Kokusai Nihon o hiraita hitobito* (People who opened Japan to the world), 1984, Ch. 2, "Yamao Yōzō to Henry Dyer."

14. Nakanishi, *op. cit.*, Vol. 2, pp. 530–36. The Kōbu Daigakkō was one of the earliest institutes of technology in the world, although there had already been many institutes that specialized in mining, civil engineering, or shipbuilding technology. As an institute of general technology, only a few, such as the Massachusetts Institute of Technology and Rensselaer Polytechnic Institute, preceded the Kōbu Daigakkō. (Uchida Hoshimi, "Shoki ryūgaku gijutsusha to Ōbei no kōgaku kyōiku kikan" (The engineers who studied abroad at the early stage and European and American institutions for technological education), *Tokyo keizai daigaku jinbun shizen kagaku ronshū*, No. 71, 1985.

15. Mitsubishi Zōsen KK, Nagasaki Zōsensho, Shokkōka, *Mitsubishi Nagasaki Zōsensho shi* (History of Mitsubishi Nagasaki Shipyard), Vol. 1, 1928, pp. 33–42.

16. *Ibid.*, pp. 53–57, 73–76; Iwasakike Denki Kankōkai, ed., *Iwasaki Yanosuke den* (Biography of Iwasaki Yanosuke), Vol. 2, pp. 273–323; Inoue Yōichirō, "Nihon kindai zōsengyō kakuritsuki ni okeru Mitsubishi Nagasaki Zōsensho" (Nagasaki shipyard in the process of establishing modern shipbuilding in Japan), *Keiei shigaku*, Vol. 3, No. 1, 1968. At Nagasaki Shipyard in 1904, except the president who was also a director of the Mitsubishi Head Office in Tokyo, all of the vice-presidents, assistant vice president, and the heads of shipbuilding yard, engine and boiler works and electric manufacturing works were engineers, and among them three were the graduates of Kōka Daigaku, one studied abroad, one was a graduate of Tokyo Shokkō Gakkō (later Tokyo Engineering College), and one was from the Navy.

17. Saegusa Hiroto and Iida Ken'ichi, *Nihon kindai seitetsu gijutsu hattatsu shi* (History of the development of modern ironwork techniques in Japan), 1957, pp. 201–14, 224–26, 234–46.

18. Imazu Kenji, "Imaizumi Kaichirō, wagakuni seikō jigyō no paionia" (Imaizumi Kaichirō, a pioneer of steel-making in Japan), *Kinzoku*, No. 15, 1965.

19. Imazu Kenji, "Edo jidai no chiteki suijun" (Intellectual level of the Edo period), in Miyamoto Mataji, ed., *Edojidai no kigyōsha katsudō* (Entrepreneurship in the Edo period), 1977.

20. Among the trainees from the Bakufu were Katsu Yasuyoshi (Min-

ister of the Navy), Enomoto Kamajirō (ministers of Communication, of Agriculture and Commerce, of Education, and of Foreign Affairs), Akamatsu Daizaburō (Vice-President of the Yokosuka Naval Shipyard and Commander-in-Chief of the Saseho and Yokosuka Naval Yards), a trainee from Satsuma, Godai Saisuke (Vice-Minister of Foreign Affairs and President of the Osaka Chamber of Commerce), and among the trainees from Saga, Sano Tsunetami (ministers of Finance and of Agriculture and Commerce, founder of the Red Cross Society in Japan), and Nakamuta Kuranosuke (President of Yokosuka Naval Shipyard). Shinohara, *op. cit.*, pp. 34–46.

21. Morikawa Hidemasa, *Gijutsusha: Nihon kindaika no ninaite* (Engineers: The leaders of Japan's modernization), 1975, pp. 123–42. Monbushō Jitsugyō-Gakumukyoku Chōsashitsu, *Kaisha kōjō jūgyōin gakureki chōsa hōkoku* (Report on the school careers of the employees in business offices and factories), edited by Hazama Hiroshi as Vol. 9 of *Nihon rōmukanri shiryōshu* (Materials on Japanese labor management), Gozandō, 1987, pp. 205–13, 635.

22. Yui Tsunehiko, "Meiji jidai ni okeru jūyaku soshiki no keisei" (Formation of the board of directors organization in the Meiji period), *Keiei shigaku*, Vol. 14, No. 1, 1979. Yui Tsunehiko, "The Development of the Organizational Structure of Top Management in Meiji Japan," *Japanese Yearbook on Business History*, 1984, Japan Business History Institute.

23. Yonekawa Shin'ichi, "Meijiki daibōseki kigyō no shokuinsō" (White-collar employees of the large-scale cotton mills in the Meiji period), *Shakai keizaishigaku*, Vol. 51, No. 4, 1986.

24. Hazama Hiroshi, *Nihon rōmukanri shi kenkyū: Keiei kazokushugi no keisei to tenkai* (Study on the history of Japanese labor management: Formation and development of managerial familism), 1964, pp. 393–482; *Mitsubishi Nagasaki Zōsensho shi*, pp. 70–72. During the days of governmental shipyards, all the workers were directly employed by the shipyard authority. Unskilled workers were trained by French engineers and skilled workers under the *minaraikō* system. On account of the early departure of French engineers and workers, the system of payment according to the nature of crafts or jobs was not established, and instead a system of paying on status and seniority emerged. Thus, due to the shortage of skilled workers, an in-factory training system already had started to supersede the development of inter-firm labor market.

25. Hazama, *op. cit.*, pp. 307–18.

26. Nakagawa Keiichirō, *Igirisu keieishi* (British business history), 1986, pp. 273–76; Nakagawa Keiichirō, "New England sangyō kakumei to tairyō seisan taisei no hatten" (New England industrial revolution and the development of mass production), *Keizaigaku ronshū*, Vol. 29, No. 4, Vol. 30, No. 1, 1964.

27. Horie Yasuzō, "Meiji 30 nendai no shokkō kōyō no jōkyō" (Workers' employment in the Meiji 30s), *Keizai keiei ronshū*, 1974; Horie Yasuzō, "Nihonteki keiei no shūdanshugi no rūtsu" (Roots of Groupism in Japanese Management), *Keizai keiei ronshū*, Vol. 18, No. 1, 1983.

28. Sumiya Mikio, ed., *Nihon shokugyō kunren hatten shi* (Development of Japanese workers' training), 1970, Vol. 1, pp. 64–69. Tōyō Bōseki KK, *op. cit.*, pp. 130–46. Hazama, *op. cit.*, pp. 245–316.

29. Nakanishi, *op. cit.*, Vol. 1, pp. 208–10.

30. Sumiya, *op. cit.*, pp. 11–14.

31. Sumiya, *ibid.*, pp. 17–20, 22–25.

32. Hazama, *op. cit.*, pp. 399–415. Nakanishi, *op. cit.*, Vol. 1, pp. 166–68. At Nagasaki Shipyard, just before the Meiji Restoration there had emerged some skilled workers, giving rise to a *de facto oyakata* system. However, due to the absence of a craft guild system and craftsmen ethics, these skilled workers could not be responsible for training workers and for the operation of workshops. Instead, according to Nakanishi, the upper levels of unskilled workers became responsible as *kashira* and *kogashira* for maintaining the workshop in operation. (Nakanishi, pp. 166–70).

Comment

W. Mark Fruin
California State University, Hayward

Professor Nakagawa Keiichirō's paper on the "Learning Industrial Revolution" and business management in Japan is an illuminating description of the early process by which Western industrial technology was transferred to Japan. He argues that this process occurred in three phases, beginning with the dissemination of book learning during the declining days of the Tokugawa Bakufu, moving to the overseas studies by scores of young Japanese in the United Kingdom, the United States, and France during the 1860s and 1870s, and culminating in the establishment of a number of institutions for the study of science and technology during the 1870s and 1880s. The most important of these, the Kōbu Daigakkō, which would become the nucleus of the Engineering School of Tokyo University, was founded in 1873 as the Kōgaku Ryō.

By detailing the early development of two modern industries, cotton spinning and shipbuilding, Nakagawa shows how closely related the second and third phases of the "learning industrial revolution" were. Many of the young Japanese who were sent abroad for study returned to establish and promote in-company training programs and institutions of higher learning.

Nakagawa further describes the difficulties that the "learning industrial revolution" caused for the commercially minded founders of many early joint-stock companies. The owners of the first joint-stock companies were typically merchants or ex-warriors, and they were, as a consequence, unfamiliar with Western technology and factory management methods. They clashed repeatedly with the overseas-trained engineers and managers who were hired to oversee the actual transfer and implementation of Western technology.

As a result of the friction and conflict between traditionally minded owners and technologically trained managers, the joint-stock company at the turn of the 20th century quickly moved to a stage where ownership and management were increasingly separated. By 1900, many owners had retired from active, day-to-day management, while engineers and others with a social or natural science education were serving as the chief officers and board members of the more successful joint-stock companies in most industries.

The last phase of the process of industrial technology transfer was not discussed by Nakagawa. This is the stage when the process of technology transfer is taken out of the hands of a limited number of enterprising engineers and managers, and it is incorporated as an ongoing institutional process. It is unfortunate that Nakagawa did not discuss this phase because it clearly constitutes another stage—Stage Four—in his model of the "learning industrial revolution."

From the 1890s, the leading industrial enterprises in Japan were learning how to learn. I call this process organizational learning, that is, the process by which organizations (more precisely, the people in them) learn, develop a collective memory, and pass down values, methods, and routines to those who follow in the organization. As a consequence, organizations, or industrial enterprises in this case, develop patterns of imitation (technology transfer), learning, and action that differentiate them from all other organizations.

As early enterprises became more successful, they mobilized people both within and without their own institutional boundaries to build support for additional industrial and enterprise development. The process of many industrial enterprises' internalizing knowledge and acting upon this information, I believe, was the end result of Nakagawa's "learning industrial revolution."

If we accept Nakagawa's provocative hypothesis, and I think we should, we can more easily understand not only the speed of Japanese industrial development, beginning with its antecedents in what is generally called Dutch Studies, but also the special emphasis placed on technology transfer and organizational learning in leading industrial firms in Japan. The "learning industrial revolution" is a key feature of the development of business management in Japan.

Hachisuka Mochiaki (1846–1918): From Feudal Lord to Modern Businessman

Andrew Fraser
Australian National University

As Yui Tsunehiko points out, Japan's business leaders in the crucial years between 1868 and 1911 were very different from those of Europe and North America, who were often sustained by several generations of family inheritance, corporate organization, and professional expertise.[1] While grappling with the problems of unequal treaties, modern technology, and new market strategies, their Japanese counterparts were drawn from a wide medley of bureaucrats, scholars, traditional traders, successful speculators, and former feudal lords, all of them virtual amateurs in modern business management.

Most of the 250 or so former feudal lords had quite modest financial assets, but in aggregate they were a significant force in the economy, as symbolized by the formation of the 15th National (Peers) Bank in 1877 with a capital of ¥18 million.[2] This was by far the largest bank in Japan at the time, easily exceeding the financial assets of budding combines such as Mitsui and Mitsubishi, now so eminent in the business world.[3] Headed by Princes Shimazu and Mōri, after 1871 the top 20 former feudal lords played important roles as fund raisers and investors in a wide range of commercial and industrial enterprises, often employing exofficials and designated merchants from their previous domains as financial managers and company officials. They are now beginning to attract detailed research as important case studies of business management in Japan's early modern era.[4]

This paper singles out the activities of one such new-style businessman, Marquis Hachisuka Mochiaki. Until 1871, he was feudal lord of the Tokushima domain, centered on Awa province. With an assessed income of 250,000 *koku* (worth about ¥700,000 in Meiji currency at the time), this domain was the seventeenth largest in Japan. When all domains were taken over by the central government in 1871, Hachisuka was pensioned off with a yearly stipend of 19,317 *koku* (worth about ¥60,000). Just before this, he paid off all the debts of his domain, amounting to ¥340,000, to a grateful central government.[5] He is reputed to have done this by a massive sale of forest land; as a result, in striking contrast to most other prefectures, after 1871, 90% of Tokushima forest land was privately owned.[6] In addition, Hachisuka was allowed after 1871 to keep one of his former domain residences in Tokyo, and he owned two or three smaller villas and property in Tokushima city. One can only estimate his total capital assets at this time, but they must have amounted to about ¥1 million, a figure supported by later evidence such as his proposal to invest this amount in railways in 1872 and his general account (*sōkanjō*) for 1887. He was certainly one of Japan's richest men.

Rather than tracing Hachisuka's business activities in chronological order, this paper groups them under specific headings. While primarily concerned with capital accumulation and investment strategies, the paper also seeks to explore Hachisuka's distinctive attitudes to business and the level of professional expertise displayed by him and his financial managers.

I. Government Bonds

In 1876, along with all other members of the former feudal class, Hachisuka's yearly stipend in rice was capitalized to government stipend-bonds (*kinroku kōsai*) repayable over 30 years. His holding amounted to ¥500,000. While their 5% annual interest was well below half the average rate at the time, these bonds carried important privileges. If deposited in national banks, they could be used as collateral for nonconvertible note issue of up to 80% of their face value, and as prime securities for loans. Thus it is no surprise to see in his general account of 1887 that he still held ¥300,000 in 5% government bonds at the time.[7] One can surmise that Hachisuka continued to hold a major part of his assets in government stipend-bonds until 1900, when they had all been redeemed.

II. Banking

Almost all former feudal lords deposited their government stipend-bonds in the 15th National (Peers) Bank in 1877. Only Nabeshima, former lord of the Hizen domain, and Hachisuka refused to do so. Having studied politics and economics at Balliol College, Oxford, Hachisuka was a firm believer in the values of English economic liberalism. The reason he gave for not joining the Peers Bank was his disapproval of its special privileges and government protection, a very unique attitude to adopt at the time.[8] On the surface, therefore, Hachisuka had no significant holding of bank shares.

However, his former retainers banded together in 1878 to pool their stipend-bonds in the 89th National Bank of Tokushima. With a capital of ¥260,000, this was one of the largest banks in the province. Looking at the shareholder's list for 1890-91, we see that the largest investor was Ikeda Noboru, a trusted chief retainer (*karō*) of the former domain, who held nearly 300 of the 2,600 shares (1 share: ¥100).[9] Next, nine members of the Hachisuka family held around 300 shares in total; eight prominent local merchants held another 300. The remaining 1,700 shares were held in small amounts by some 300 former samurai and local merchants. While not formally shareholders in the bank, Hachisuka and his business managers often borrowed from it, and Ikeda's large investment probably included shares held on Hachisuka's behalf.

National banks at first were a profitable investment, with their rights to note issue and their role as repositories for government funds. But after the formation of the Bank of Japan in 1882, they were required to redeem their note issue progressively over the next 15 years and lost their role as fundholders for the government. Like many others of its kind, the 89th National Bank was basically a "family" business advancing loans to such privileged customers as Hachisuka himself. After the bank lost ¥70,000 in the financial panic of 1890, Hachisuka asked his friend and business associate Shibusawa Eiichi to recommend a professional manager, and

thereafter under merchant leadership the 89th National Bank made
a successful switch to become a private bank in 1897, with branches
in Osaka and Tokyo.[10] Even so, in 1904 the 89th Bank was forced
to close with debts of around ¥1 million when involved in the failure
of the Senju Paper Company (see below), and was only able to re-
open after receiving a loan from Hachisuka, which he raised by
mortgaging his Tokyo residence and selling bonds and shares on
its behalf.[11] Thereafter, the bank failed to repay this loan, and
went into voluntary dissolution in 1909.

Hachisuka was more fortunate in his investment in the Tokushima
Bank set up in 1882 with a capital of ¥50,000. This was a savings
bank with unlimited liability established at a time when national
banks were specifically forbidden to handle such business. Hachisuka
himself held ¥5,000 of the shares; a former chief retainer (*karō*),
Kashima Masanori, also held ¥5,000 (roughly equivalent to his
holding of government stipend-bonds). Two or three local merchants directing the bank held similar amounts; the rest were held
by 170 others, many of them former samurai.[12] Unlike the 89th
Bank, the Tokushima Bank under able merchant management
proved a most successful enterprise. By 1900 its capital had increased
to ¥250,000, and it now ranked as one of the leading banks of the
province.[13] Whether Hachisuka increased his shareholding after
1887 is not known, but he must have found this bank a profitable
investment.

III. Residential Property

Hachisuka changed the location of his Tokyo residence several
times after 1871; then in 1882 he settled at No. 1, Hamachō, Shiba-
ku. In area, its land was 13,256 *tsubo* (44,000 square meters),
worth at least ¥1 per *tsubo* in 1907.[14] He invested large sums in
building an impressive three-story mansion on it, and sometimes
held garden parties in its grounds attended by several hundred
people.[15] Other comparable mansions were worth up to ¥500,000
at the time, and when forced to mortgage it to pay off the debts of
the 89th Bank in 1904, Hachisuka might have been able to raise
several ¥100,000.[16] He also owned two or three smaller villas and
vacant ground in Tokushima worth ¥55,000, which he sold to the

city in 1904 for use as a park.[17] While one can only guess at values, residential and urban property was certainly among Hachisuka's major assets.

IV. Landed Estates

After 1871, Hachisuka bought two or three landed estates in Tokushima as mulberry plantations to promote the local silk industry, both as a scheme for samurai relief and as attempts at landlord "direct" management. He sold one such estate of 100 *chōbu* (100 hectares) to local entrepreneurs in 1881 for around ¥10,000; another of 40 *chōbu* was sold the same year. The failure of these ventures was due partly to the supremacy of indigo as a cash crop, but also to the refusal of tenant farmers to work as wage laborers.[18]

In the 1880s leading officials and government-connected businessmen began to acquire large landed estates in north Japan and Hokkaidō, when railway development made them an attractive investment. Former feudal lords like Hachisuka were also encouraged to acquire such estates, both as rich capitalists able to raise the necessary funds and as noblemen who needed to be shielded from the declining value of government bonds and losses in commercial and industrial ventures.[19] Hachisuka at first planned a joint estate with two other noblemen in 1889, but then went ahead on his own in 1893, investing ¥152,000 in an estate of 6,164 *chō* (6,000 hectares). Although he hired foreign experts and imported modern machinery, for the first few years the estate made a steady loss of ¥7,000 a year. In 1896 he was forced to drop plans for "direct" management and began to recruit tenant farmers, mainly from Tokushima Prefecture. But the difficult terrain, labor insecurity, defaulted tenant fees, and low prices for commercial products at long distances from city markets continued to make the estate unprofitable.[20]

However, after 1900 Hachisuka was able to extend his landholdings on favorable terms, when the threat of war with Russia and the undesirable prospect of foreigners acquiring estates after treaty revision made Hokkaidō development an urgent government priority. At the same time, with loans from the Hokkaidō Development and Hypothec Banks, and the application of new engineering skills, he switched from such low-priced crops as beans and flax to wet-field rice cultivation. By 1904 he had recovered all his previous losses, and his clear profit for the next decade averaged ¥24,000 a year.[21] The estate was now centered on 2,756 *chō* (2,500 hectares) of arable land, cultivated by 753 tenant households. The steep rise in the price of rice after 1900 coupled with the high rate of tenant fees made Hachisuka's Hokkaidō estate easily the most profitable of all his investments.[22] Even so, one may note that once again his plans for "direct" management had failed; only the Koiwai estate in Iwate Prefecture owned by the Iwasaki family, founders of the Mitsubishi combine, has survived to the present day as a successful modern enterprise devoted to dairy products.[23]

V. Railways

Hachisuka went to England in 1871 for an extended period of overseas study and was immediately convinced of the urgent need for railway development in Japan. When Council of State Vice-President Iwakura Tomomi came to London in 1872, Hachisuka proposed to invest ¥1 million in railways, a measure of his assets at the time.[24] His business manager Komuro Shinobu returned to Japan in 1874 and as Hachisuka's agent (*dairi*) was instrumental in setting up a Tokyo Railway Company in 1875.[25] At the head of 20 other former feudal lords, Hachisuka proposed to invest ¥825,900 (28% of total capital) in the company, which would have made him by far its largest shareholder. But the reduction in the incomes of former feudal lords consequent on the capitalization of stipends in 1876 and the government's decision not to sell off existing railways to the new company led to its dissolution in 1878.[26] When a new Japan Railway Company was formed in 1881 to construct a trunk line from Tokyo to Aomori in North Japan, Hachisuka invested the rather modest sum of ¥70,000.[27] As in the case of his refusal to join the 15th National Bank, Hachisuka's small investment in the Japan Railway Company reflects his distaste for government control of railways; he shared Shibusawa's conviction that they should be private enterprises run by businessmen. In addition to large government subsidies and future options to purchase, shareholders were guaranteed a dividend of 8% per annum. In 1890, these and other leading company shares were singled out by the Bank of Japan as prime securities (*tanpohin*), negotiable at face value on the same terms as government bonds. The Japan Railway Company paid a regular dividend of around 12% per annum, and Hachisuka probably retained his shares until 1907, when the company was nationalized on generous terms, enabling him to recover his capital. After 1890, he also invested in the Nishinari (¥15,000), Hokuetsu (¥50,000), and Kyoto (¥50,000) railway companies.[28] These lines proved unprofitable, especially in their first years of operation, but were nationalized in 1907, again saving Hachisuka from capital loss.

VI. Insurance

Hachisuka's next major venture was the Tokio Marine Insurance Company, the first of its kind in Japan. In 1878 he invested ¥82,000 (out of a total capital of ¥600,000) and became the first company president (*tōdori*). The government guaranteed the company against the loss of up to two-thirds of paid-up capital, and it progressively increased its resources from ¥1 million in 1883 to ¥3 million in 1906. Dividends throughout these years averaged 12%.[29] Hachisuka certainly continued to hold his original investment in 1887; his business manager Fujimoto Bunsaku was chief director of the company in 1894, and a successor was a director of the company in 1903. These shares were also singled out by the Bank of Japan in 1890 as prime securities. Despite rather amateurish management in the 1880s, leading to a crisis in 1892–93 when the company expanded its activities overseas, increased professionalism and government support enabled the company to recover from the loss of over half its paid-up capital in 1895.[30]

VII. Shipping

Significant advancements took place in shipping in the early 1880s. Hachisuka's business adviser, Komuro Shinobu, became a director and branch manager of the Kyōdō Un'yu Kaisha, set up in 1882 with assets of ¥5 million. When this company was amalgamated with Mitsubishi shipping interests in 1885 to form the Nippon Yusen Kaisha, Komuro lost his job. But it is very interesting

to see that Kondō Rempei, another former samurai of the Tokushima domain, swiftly rose to be head of the new company.[31]
There is no record that Hachisuka held shares in shipping companies, but his ex-retainers were prominent in this field.

VIII. Trading Companies

Even before the abolition of his domain in 1871, Hachisuka and
his business managers planned with leaders from other domains and
Osaka businessmen to set up the Hōraisha, a company to engage in
exports, shipping, currency trading, commodity markets, and industry.[32] In 1874, when the Hōraisha fell into difficulties, seven
former retainers of Hachisuka set up a similar company, Yūrinsha,
with a capital of ¥220,000. They each received sums of between
¥50,000 and ¥20,000 divided into 220 shares; this capital was
provided by Hachisuka as a loan repayable in ten years, on which
5% interest per annum was to be paid to him regardless of profit
or loss.[33] Thereafter, the seven shareholders engaged in a wide range
of trading activities, but by 1881 the company had dissolved, amidst
rumors of heavy losses due to unwise speculation, adverse trading
circumstances, and general mismanagement.[34] Related to this con-
sortium was the purchase by a Tokushima former designated-
merchant of the *Boshin Maru* (316 tons), a steamship which after
1871 became the private property of Hachisuka, who sold it to him
for ¥30,000 repayable over ten years. After a decade of activity in
overseas shipping and tea-trading from Yokohama, this merchant
was bankrupted in 1881 when the ship was wrecked in a storm.[35]
Hachisuka probably lost much of the ¥250,000 he loaned to these
ventures.

Even so, in 1882 he invested a further ¥200,000 in a new trading
company, Narutogumi. This again took the form of a loan repayable over five years from his three business managers to specialist
traders, one of whom, Kanda Yukiyasu, had Tokushima connections.[36] The company operated from Yokohama, dealing in foreign
currency and raw silk exports. Results were good at first in the
export boom of the early 1880s, when the government encouraged
such trading companies by generous loans from the Yokohama
Specie Bank. Nevertheless, Japan's export trade remained largely in

foreign hands, and in a sudden switch the government decided in 1885 to allow foreigners to raise loans from the Yokohama Specie Bank, ordering it to recall those made to Japanese trading companies. By 1886, many "direct export" companies such as Naruto-gumi had sharply turned unprofitable.[37] Once again, it seems, investment in a trading company had proved a failure.

Trading companies were highly risky and speculative ventures in the 1870s and 1880s. Even powerful combines such as Mitsui, anxious to protect themselves against losses, were unable to persuade the government to allow them to trade as limited liability companies.[38] Hachisuka's trading ventures were conducted under the current law of "unlimited responsibility" (*mugen sekinin*), and he probably lost much of his capital investment in them. As with large losses when saving the 89th Bank in 1904, his obligation as a former feudal lord to protect his ex-retainers had worked to his financial disadvantage. Only trading companies enjoying special government support, such as Mitsui Bussan, managed to flourish in this demanding business.

IX. Industry

Hachisuka's first major industrial investment was in the Osaka Cotton Spinning Company, set up in 1882 with a capital of ¥280,000. This company received no government subsidies or guarantees; but by able management, the use of modern machinery, switching from water to steam power, and the import of cheap Chinese and Indian cotton, it quickly became a profitable enterprise, paying dividends of 20%.[39] In 1886, Hachisuka doubled his original investment from ¥16,200 to ¥30,000, but in 1889, he no longer held shares in the company, perhaps because he was collecting capital at this time for his Hokkaidō estate. He might have profited from the stock market boom of 1887 to sell his shares at a good profit.[40] Even so, in 1893 Hachisuka again held ¥22,400 worth of shares in the Osaka Cotton Spinning Co., and his hilding remained at about this level until 1905, when he had sold out, probably as a result of the crisis in his finances at this time.[41]

In the 1880s and 1890s, Hachisuka invested in a wide range of pioneering industrial enterprises, usually in association with Shibusawa Eiichi, now one of the leading businessmen of the new age. These investments are often hard to trace in detail because of the current system of share subscription by installments. In 1882, he was a promoter of the Tokyo Electric Company, with a paid-up investment of ¥6,000 after initially contracting to put up ¥100,000. His business manager, Fujimoto Bunsaku, played a prominent role in its management. Over the years, this company progressively increased its capital, though suffering a severe reverse in 1890–92 when new electric fittings in the Diet building broke down, causing severe fire damage. Nevertheless, the company recovered to pay dividends of around 15% for the next decades.[42] Hachisuka next invested ¥50,000 in the Tokyo Gas Company, launched in 1885; Fujimoto Bunsaku was also a promoter of the company, holding shares worth ¥10,000. Despite several setbacks, this company consistently paid dividends of around 15%.[43] Less successful was the Japan Brickmaking Company of 1887, in which Hachisuka invested ¥30,000 and Fujimoto ¥12,500. The first such enterprise in Japan, with a factory in Saitama Prefecture equipped with machinery imported from Germany, the company ran into serious technological problems, requiring Hachisuka and Shibusawa as its leading promoters each to pay ¥10,000 in 1894 to cover its debts. It was not until 1897 that the company paid its first dividend.[44] Some of Hachisuka's other ventures, such as the Japan Hatmaking Company and Chemical (Shamitsu) Manufacturing Company, proved dismal failures and had to be written off as total losses.[45]

Other industrial investments closely related to Hachisuka's landed estate were more profitable. For example, the Hokkaidō Flax Company, set up in 1887 at Sapporo with a capital of ¥800,000. Hachisuka was a promoter of this company, holding ¥10,000 in shares, while his business adviser Komuro Shinobu held a further ¥20,000. Shareholders were guaranteed a yearly dividend of 6%, and the company received over ¥200,000 in government subsidies between 1889 and 1895, by which time it had developed into a profitable enterprise.[46] He was also a promoter of the Tokyo Artificial Fertilizer Company set up in 1887 with a capital of ¥250,000. Engaged in the manufacture and import/export of superphosphate, and the first of its kind in Japan, the company lost half its capital when a fire gutted the factory in 1893, but then recovered to make a profit of ¥120,000 in 1898 on its increased capital of ¥500,000.[47] How much Hachisuka invested in the company is not known, but as one of its promoters his shareholding would have been substantial, perhaps as much as in the flax company. He grew flax on his estate, and superphosphate fertilizer was widely used both by his own farmers and those of Tokushima Prefecture, so these investments were not only profitable but a valuable contribution to his other business interests.

Meanwhile, in 1889, with assistance from Hachisuka, his three chief business managers and leading Tokushima merchants set up the Senju Paper Company with a capital of ¥250,000, and with Komuro Shinobu as its head. The company then built a factory in North Kyushu, equipped with imported machinery. The factory's production of Western-style paper increased steadily throughout the 1890s, until the failure of a new electrical process for producing caustic soda and bleaching liquids, and severe competition in the industry, precipitated a sudden crisis. In 1904, the debts of the company amounted to over ¥1.3 million; as third mortgage-holder on the Kokura factory, the 89th Bank of Tokushima was forced to close as a result, and reopened only after Hachisuka mortgaged his Tokyo residence, bonds, and shares to support it.[48]

Thereafter, the Senju Paper Company continued to flounder. In 1908, Hachisuka went in person to attend the bankruptcy auction in Kokura and bought the derelict factory for ¥400,000. For the next few years, he ran the company from the office of a Tokyo printing works owned by one of his former retainers until it had recovered profitability. With support from leading Tokyo business-men, he was then able to float a new company in 1912 with a capital of ¥1 million. Hachisuka held 8,000 first-preference shares out of the total of 20,000 shares; their capital value would have been around ¥350,000.[49] Even so, he must have made an overall capital loss in the paper business, though dividends on the new shares soon rose to over 10%.

X. Conclusion

As we have seen, Hachisuka's yearly stipend in 1871 was worth ¥60,000. When income tax was first introduced to Japan in 1887, he reported a taxable income of ¥36,340, almost exactly the sum he received that year in interest on bonds and dividends from company shares (¥35,867). His total assets listed in his general account of 1887 amounted to ¥1,107,600; subtracting ¥483,199 in expenditures, this left him with a credit balance of ¥634,400. In 1899, his reported income was ¥54,011. His rate of income appreciation from bonds and company shares was therefore very modest, though about average for other former feudal lords.[50] In 1910, his reported income had dropped to ¥4,949, an indication that he now held very little of his assets in bonds or company shares, though his Hokkaidō estate and paper company were profitable enterprises. Even so, he had made large capital losses in the 40 years since the abolition of his domain, especially in commercial and industrial ventures, a reminder of the handicaps businessmen suffered in this era of unequal treaties and technological inexperience.

Harsh criticisms have been made of the poor quality of entrepreneurship in Meiji Japan and the scarcity of managerial ability, resulting in a premature concentration of economic power in a few zaibatsu combines, with the complicity and collaboration of the government.[51] It is a fact that Hachisuka's business managers were not versed in modern technology, with the possible exception of Komuro Shinobu, who had studied railways in England from 1872 to 1874. His chief business manager after 1882 was Fujimoto Bunsaku, educated as a medical doctor and then employed as a Tokushima district head. Others were ex-officials of the Tokushima domain or local merchants.

By 1900, Hachisuka had already shifted his priorities from industry to landlordism and tenant farming; after 1910, he no longer appears in the lists of large shareholders in commercial companies. Yet this does not detract from Hachisuka's contribution as a patron, fund raiser, risk taker, and innovator in the first desperate decades of Japan's drive to economic self-sufficiency and industrial development. His business strategy was to keep most of his assets in government bonds and real estate, while investing in fairly safe commercial, communications, and industrial enterprises backed by guaranteed dividends of at least 6% and protected by government subsidies. But at times as much as one-third of his capital was invested in risky commercial and industrial ventures, perhaps a high proportion compared with smaller and more cautious businessmen.

Hachisuka was renowned for his calm indifference to financial losses, refusal to be panicked into selling shares, and absolute trust in his business managers.[52] This was perhaps an offshoot of his status as a former feudal lord, but in some ways he resembles the English landed aristocrats of the 19th century, who showed considerable skill in adjusting to the political and economic trends of the new industrial age.[53]

After 1871, Hachisuka's manager Komuro Shinobu formed close ties with the Chōshū business network centered on Inoue Kaoru, Shibusawa Eiichi, and the Mitsui combine. These ties show up in Hachisuka's official career, too, as he rose to high office in a series of posts such as ambassador to France, governor of Tokyo, chairman of the House of Peers, minister of education, and privy councillor—always under Chōshū patronage. Meanwhile, other former retainers such as Kondō Rempei established parallel ties with the Satsuma business network centered on Matsukata Masayoshi and the Mitsubishi combine.[54] Hachisuka's business career, while revealing the importance of government connections in Meiji Japan when so much depended on the power of the ruling Satsuma-Chōshū clique, also attests to his skill in casting his influence over the twin pillars of the financial world at the time.

As for the management structure of Hachisuka's business enterprises, one sees a change after 1882 to a more corporate organization. Yūrinsha of 1874 had seven members, who were supposed to take decisions by a two-thirds majority vote. But, in fact, they all went their own way within a common obligation to pay 5% per annum on their respective loan capital from Hachisuka. For example, in 1878 Komuro Shinobu and Inoue Takanori each invested ¥30,000 in the 130th National Bank, though none of the others did so.[55] The loan documents of Narutogumi of 1882, on the other hand, are stamped with the seal of "Hachikai" and jointly signed by Hachisuka's household steward and his two new business managers.[56] Even so, the management of Hachisuka's finances remained very loose; he still relied heavily on his adviser Komuro Shinobu, who after 1881 often acted as a business executive in his own right.

The top management of commercial companies in Meiji shows almost no differentiation between shareholding directors and actual managing executives. This, Yui Tsunehiko observes, is a distinctive feature of Japanese top management and continues to the present day, in sharp contrast with most Western industrial nations.[57] In many of Hachisuka's company investments, one sees his business advisers and managers holding blocks of shares, often on his behalf, as a qualification to hold managerial posts.

Yūrinsha, Narutogumi, and Senju Paper Company were dominated by Tokushima business leaders, who provided much of the capital and most of the top management. On the surface, such companies seem less "modern" than the big joint-stock enterprises with shareholders drawn widely across business circles. But many big enterprises in which Hachisuka invested, such as the Tokyo Electric and Hokkaidō Flax Companies, were rent by internal feuds and disorders, so in the conditions of the time, companies based on personal and local loyalties were not necessarily less efficient than the big joint-stock enterprises.[58] In some ways, even such powerful combines as Mitsui and Mitsubishi remained "family" organizations, as appears in their reliance on internally generated capital for development rather than on funds raised in stock exchanges, another distinctive feature of Japanese business in the modern era.[59]

XI. Postscript

Hachisuka's son Masaaki inherited the title of marquis in 1918 and remained in prosperous circumstances, though without his father's distinguished official career. The Hokkaidō estate made huge profits between 1914 and 1918, but tenancy disputes erupted in 1920 and continued until 1929, when 80% of the land was relinquished to tenants on contracts to pay current fees for the next 20 years. Land reform in 1948 completed this transfer, and the Hachisuka estate closed down.[60] Comparing the Hachisuka family's troubles in these turbulent years with those of other former feudal lords, one might note that even Shimazu, the greatest of them, fought a hard battle to survive.[61] In 1949, Hachisuka's grandson Masauji sold his Tokyo residence to the Australian government for $1 million, but died a few years later in Atami, leaving no heirs or financial assets. The former Hachisuka residence is now the Australian Embassy, and its land is rumored to be worth ¥1,000 million, tempting the government to sell it off at the present time of financial stringency. So perhaps a final lesson in the Hachisuka business story is how fragile personal fortunes can be in Japan, as elsewhere.

NOTES

1. T. Yui, "Development and Organization of Large Industrial Enterprises in Japan," *Meiji daigaku shakai kagaku kenkyūjo kiyō*, Vol. 25, No. 1 (1986), pp. 57–58.

2. For this bank and its significance, see Ishikawa Kenjirō, "Meiji zenki ni okeru kazoku no ginkō tōshi. Daijūgo kokuritsu ginkō no baai" (Investment in banking by peers in early Meiji), *Ōsaka daigaku keizaigaku*, Vol. 22, No. 3 (Dec. 1972), pp. 27–82. Ishikawa Kenjirō, "Kazoku shihon to shizoku keieisha" (Peer capital and "shizoku" managers) in Miyamoto M., Nakagawa K., Yui T., *Kōgyōka to kigyōsha no katsudō* (Industrialization and entrepreneurship), *Nihon keieishi kōza*, Vol. 2, Tokyo, 1976, pp. 122–30. For the role of former feudal lords in general, see Senda Minoru, "Kazoku shihon no seiritsu, tenkai: Ippanteki kōsatsu" (Emergence and development of peer capital), *Shakai keizai shigaku*, Vol. 52, No. 1 (April 1986), pp. 1–37.

3. In the mid-1880s the total assets of Mitsubishi were estimated at ¥6 million (see *Chōya shimbun*, 17 Sept. 1885). Mitsui's were about the same.

4. See Imuta Toshimitsu, "Kazoku shisan to tōshi kōdō; kyūdaimyō no kabushiki tōshi o chūshin ni" (Peer assets and investment patterns), *Chihō kin'yū kenk'yū*, No. 18 (March 1987), pp. 1–49. Also, Takeda Haruhito, "Meiji zenki no Fujitagumi to Mōri ke yūshi" (Fujitagumi and the Mōri family in early Meiji), *Keizaigaku ronshū*, Vol. 48, No. 3 (Oct. 1982), pp. 2–22.

5. *Kōbunroku 1873 Ōkurashō*, 2A 9 kō 581, item 2. Kokuritsu Kōbunshokan, Tokyo.

6. Tokushima Kenshi Hensan Iinkai, comp., *Tokushima kenshi* (History of Tokushima prefecture), 6 vols., Tokushima, 1964–67, 5: 299. This policy was masterminded by a high official of the domain, Inoue Takanori, who later became Hachisuka's household steward and one of his business managers.

7. *Awa Hachisuka ke monjo mokuroku* (Catalog of the archives of the Hachisuka family), item 1487. Kokuritsu Shiryōkan, Tokyo.
8. Kasumi Kaikan, *Kazoku kaikan shi* (History of Kazoku Kaikan), Tokyo, 1966, p. 624.
9. *Awa Hachisuka ke monjo mokuroku*, item 1477.
10. *Tokushima kenshi*, 5: 440.
11. Tsuyuki Kametarō, *Hachisuka Mochiaki kō kakuretaru kōseki* (The hidden achievements of Marquis Hachisuka Mochiaki), Tokyo, 1937, pp. 29–30.
12. Hachisuka's holding appears in *Awa Hachisuka ke monjo mokuroku*, item 1487; Kashima Masanori's in Kokuritsu Kokkai Toshokan, *Sanjō ke monjo mokuroku* (Catalog of the archives of the Sanjō family), Tokyo, 1973, Vol. 1, Shorui no bu, item 30 (16).
13. *Tokushima kenshi*, 5: 446–47. Tokushima Shishi Hensanshitsu, *Tokushima shishi* (History of Tokushima city), 3 vols., Tokushima, 1973–83, 3: 410.
14. Tsuyuki, *Hachisuka Mochiaki*, p. 1. Mizumoto K., Ōtaki T., "Meiji sanjūnendaimatsu Tōkyō shi jūtaku shoyū jōkyō" (Housing conditions in Tokyo in the Meiji 30s), *Shōkeihō ronshū*, Vol. 13, No. 2 (Sept. 1962), pp. 185, 194.
15. See, for example, *Chōya shimbun*, 1 May 1888.
16. Takekoshi Yosaburō, *Prince Saionji*, Kyoto, 1933, p. 65. See also *Tōkyō keizai zasshi*, No. 904, 29 November 1897, for a report on the purchase of Gotō Shōjirō's residence by the government.
17. Kawano Yukio, *Tokushima jō no rekishi* (History of Tokushima castle), Tokushima, 1980, p. 63.
18. *Ono son shi* (History of Ono Village), 5 vols. ms, Tokushima Kenritsu Toshokan, Tokushima, Vol. 4, Ch. 11, Kangyō. Also, *Abe Okito nikki* (Diary of Abe Okito), Hokkaidōritsu Toshokan, Ebetsu. Entry for 14 Aug. 1881.
19. Hatate Isao, *Nihon ni okeru dainōjō no seisei to tenkai* (Emergence and development of large farms in Japan), Tokyo, 1963, pp. 38, 83–84. Inoue Kaoru Kō Denki Hensankai, comp., *Segai Inoue kō den* (Biography of Marquis Inoue Kaoru), 5 vols., Tokyo, 1933–34, 4: 18ff.
20. Hatate, *op. cit.*, pp. 147–53, 164–66.
21. *Ibid.*, pp. 160–64, 170–77, 185.
22. *Ibid.*, p. 168. For the rise in tenancy fees, see Takahashi Kamekichi, *Nihon kindai keizai keiseishi* (Economic history of modern Japan), Tokyo, 1977, Vol. 2, p. 120.
23. Hatate, *op. cit.*, p. 10.

24. Iwakura Kō Kyūseki Hozonkai, comp., *Iwakura kō jikki* (Biography of Marquis Iwakura), Tokyo, 1927, Vol. 2, pp. 1015–17.

25. For Komuro Shinobu (1839–98), see Yamada Tatsuo, *Komuro jinan ō fushi shōden* (A short biography of Komuro), 1924.

26. Hatate, *op. cit.*, pp. 21–23.

27. Shibusawa Seien Kinen Zaidan Ryūmonsha, comp., *Shibusawa Eiichi denki shiryō* (Biographical materials of Shibusawa Eiichi), Tokyo, 1956, Vol. 8, p. 572.

28. *Shibusawa Eiichi denki shiryō*, vol. 9, p. 20, records that Hachisuka held ¥50,000 and his business manager ¥2,500 in the Hokuetsu Railway Company. See also Tsuyuki, *op. cit.*, p. 25. For Hachisuka's holding in the Kyoto Railway Company, see *Tōkyō nichi nichi shimbun*, 3 Feb. 1895.

29. *Shibusawa Eiichi denki shiryō*, Vol. 7, pp. 604, 615, 646, 653–59. *Nihon kaisha shi sōran* (Directory of Japanese company histories), Tokyo, 1954, p. 284. Ryūmonsha, *Seien sensei 60 nenshi* (Biography of Shibusawa Eiichi), Tokyo, 1900, Vol. 2, pp. 5–21.

30. Yui Tsunehiko, "Kaijō hokengyō no sōgyō to kakuritsu. Tōkyō kaijō hoken kaisha no baai" (Establishment and development of marine insurance), *Keiei shigaku*, Vol. 3, No. 1 (1968), pp. 62–66. *Nihon kaisha shi sōran*, p. 781.

31. For a most detailed analysis of these events, see William D. Wray, *Mitsubishi and the NYK 1870–1914*, Cambridge, Mass., 1984.

32. Ōmachi Keigetsu, *Hakushaku Gotō Shōjirō* (Count Gotō Shōjirō), Tokyo, 1914, pp. 469–70. Yasuoka Shigeaki, *Zaibatsu keiseishi no kenkyū* (Study on the formation of zaibatsu), Kyoto, 1970, pp. 167–72.

33. Among the private papers of the Hibino family, Tokushima.

34. Of the original seven partners, only Komuro Shinobu was still prominent in business after 1882. One of them, Nishikawa Hajime, was well known in Osaka business, political, and newspaper circles in the 1870s. He was bankrupted by speculation on the Osaka rice exchange. For similar failures at this time, see Senda, *op. cit.*, pp. 6, 9, 12–13.

35. Izumi Yasuhiro, "Meiji ishin to ai shōnin" (The Meiji Restoration and indigo merchants), *Kōkō chireki* (Tokushima kōkō gakkō), No. 8 (March 1972), pp. 23–25.

36. *Awa Hachisuka ke monjo mokuroku*, item 1454.

37. Umino Fukuhisa, "Bōeki shijō ni okeru 1880 nendai" (The trade market in the 1880s), *Rekishigaku kenkyū*, No. 253 (May 1961), pp. 22–25. Tsuyuki Kametarō, *Keison Fujimoto Bunsaku sensei* (Biog-

raphy of Fujimoto Bunsaku), Tokyo, 1937, p. 22. *Tōkyō nichi nichi shimbun*, 7 Sept. 1888, records the difficulties of a similar company, Dōshinsha.

38. Yasuoka Shigeaki, "Zaibatsu keiseishi ni okeru yūgen sekinin sei" (Limited liability in the formation of zaibatsu), *Shakai keizai shigaku*, Vol. 35, No. 2 (1969), pp. 76–77.

39. Niwa Kunio, "The Reform of the Land Tax," *The Developing Economies*, Vol. 4, No. 4 (Dec. 1966), p. 470. *Shibusawa Eiichi denki shiryō*, Vol. 10, pp. 11–12, 58. Yamaguchi Kazuo, *Nihon sangyō kin'yūshi kenkyū, bōseki kin'yū hen* (A study of industrial finance, cotton spinning), Tokyo, 1970, pp. 330–31, 338–39. Ryūmonsha, *Seien sensei 60 nenshi*, Vol. 1, Tokyo, 1900, pp. 1068–75.

40. Terabe Tetsuji, *Ginkō hattatsushi* (Development of banking business), Osaka, 1953, p. 156. Ryūmonsha, *Seien sensei 60 nenshi*, Vol. 2, pp. 702–3.

41. Yamaguchi, *op. cit.*, pp. 345, 377.

42. *Shibusawa Eiichi denki shiryō*, Vol. 13, p. 5ff. Nitta Muneo, *Tōkyō dentō kabushiki kaisha kaigyō 50 nenshi* (50-year history of Tokyo Electrical Company), Tokyo, 1936, pp. 5–59. Noyori Hideichi, *Tōden chūroku* (A critial review of the Tokyo Electric Company), Tokyo, 1915, pp. 10–11, 42–46.

43. *Shibusawa Eiichi denki shiryō*, Vol. 12, p. 614ff.

44. *Ibid.*, Vol. 11, p. 542ff.

45. *Ibid.*, Vol. 12, p. 272. Tsuyuki, *Keison Fujimoto*, pp. 22–25. Tsuyuki, *Hachisuka Mochiaki*, pp. 15–16.

46. *Shibusawa Eiichi denki shiryō*, Vol. 10, p. 669–83.

47. *Seien sensei 60 nenshi*, Vol. 2, pp. 264–73. Tsuyuki, *Hachisuka Mochiaki*, pp. 13–14.

48. Murata Tatsuzō, *Kokura seishi kōba enkaku gaiyō* (Outline of Kokura Paper Factory), Tokyo, 1924, pp. 1–4.

49. *Ibid.*, pp. 6–8. Tsuyuki, *Hachisuka Mochiaki*, p. 20.

50. Furushima Toshio, Wakamori Tarō, Kimura Motoi, *Meiji zenki kyōdō shi kenkyūhō* (Methodology of local history in early Meiji), Tokyo, 1970, pp. 142–43.

51. Mikio Sumiya and Koji Taira, ed., *An Outline of Japanese Economic History 1603–1940*, Tokyo, 1979, pp. 256–57.

52. Tsuyuki, *Hachisuka Mochiaki*, pp. 3–4, 28.

53. Philip Magnus, *King Edward the Seventh*, London, 1964, pp. 64, 69.

54. I have explored these connections in a series of articles on Hachisuka Mochiaki, Komuro Shinobu, Abe Okito, and Nakajima Masutane

published in *Papers on Far Eastern History* (Department of Far Eastern History, Australian National University), 1970–73.

55. "Kokuritsu ginkō seiritsu negai" (Proposal for the establishment of a national bank), 29 March 1878, ms, archives section, Fuji Bank Head Office, Tokyo.

56. *Awa Hachisuka ke monjo mokuroku*, item 1454.

57. T. Yui, "The Development of the Organizational Structure of Top Management in Meiji Japan," *Japanese Yearbook on Business History 1984*, Japan Business History Institute, Tokyo, 1984, pp. 1–2.

58. See, for example, Noyori, *op. cit.*, pp. 45–46; *Shibusawa Eiichi denki shiryō*, Vol. 10, pp. 683–84.

59. Yasuoka Shigeaki, *Nihon no zaibatsu* (Zaibatsu of Japan), *Nihon keieishi kōza*, Vol. 3, Tokyo, 1976, pp. 13, 27.

60. Hatate, *op. cit.*, p. 109.

61. Senda, *op. cit.*, pp. 30–31.

Comment

Kensuke Hiroyama
Nagasaki University

This paper is a brief sketch of Hachisuka Mochiaki and his business activities. Professor Andrew Fraser is an outstanding Australian Japanologist whose major interest is the early stages of political modernization and human relations, especially in Awa province, now Tokushima Prefecture. Mochiaki was the last feudal lord (*daimyō*) of this area.

The writer singles out the activities of a new-style businessman who had been educated to become a respectable feudal lord and who faced new political and economic environments. In order to do so, he groups Mochiaki's business activities under nine headings: government bonds, banking, residential property, landed estates, railways, insurance, shipping, trading companies, and industry.

Fraser's major interest is not in the economic aspects of history, but in the political aspects, especially political parties. This is why the paper has a limitation from the viewpoint of business history. It does not give us new findings or fresh interpretations of Mochiaki's activities. But it successfully shows us that Mochiaki had been a respectable person both in business and in society.

Strictly speaking, Mochiaki was not a businessman in any sense, but he was one of the enlightened former feudal lords and a kind of patron of modern business. Two special features in his background were the fact that he was the last feudal lord of Awa and that he studied abroad, especially in England. Mochiaki was born as a grandson of Tokugawa Ienari, the eleventh shogun, in 1846, and became the last Tokushima *daimyō* in January 1868, at the same time as the beginning of the Meiji Restoration.

In treating a person from the viewpoint of business history, we must explain basic characteristics of his personality in relation to business circumstances. In the case of Mochiaki, education was one of the most fundamental elements. His attitude toward business and political administration was formed through the education he received in his youth. His experience as the last feudal lord of Awa required him to be respectable, and his experience as a student abroad developed in him a flexibility in his thinking and attitude toward new social and economic conditions and institutions.

Mochiaki studied in England from 1872 to 1879 before he was appointed envoy extraordinary and minister plenipotentiary to France, Spain, Portugal, and Switzerland in December 1882. After returning to Japan, his major interest was not in business but in political administration. In May 1890, he was the governor of Tokyo metropolis; in July 1891, a member of the House of Lords (Kizokuin) and its chairman; in September 1896, the Minister of Education; in 1916, an auditor and the president of the disciplinary court.

Fraser does not refer to Mochiaki's career and positions in the political world. But at the time of the beginning of industrialization, government-business relations were one of the most important fields in Japanese business history. I hope that Fraser will in the future expand on the relationship between Mochiaki's political life and business or between education and industrialization in Meiji; was Mochiaki's position in the modern business world that of a coordinator like Godai Tomoatsu or Shibusawa Eiichi?

Private Railroads in the Meiji Era:
Forerunners of Modern Japanese Management?

Steven J. Ericson
Brown University

The managements of major Japanese corporations today emphasize long-term growth over short-run profits and enjoy almost total
freedom from interference in their programs by stockholders. Judg-
ing from Western experience, one might expect to find the origins
of these tendencies in the private railway companies of the Meiji
period. For in the West, railway concerns, as the first examples of
large-scale business enterprise, were "pioneers in modern corporate
management." Such railroads as the Pennsylvania in the United
States and the London & North Western in England spearheaded
the separation of management from ownership, the appointment of
full-time salaried managers to top decision-making posts, and the
creation of elaborate managerial hierarchies in private corporations.[1]

In Meiji Japan as well, railway firms clearly represented big business. In 1896, for example, seven of the ten largest joint-stock companies in terms of total assets were railroad enterprises.[2] Private
railways accounted for over one fourth of the total paid-up capital
of joint-stock ventures in the 1890s and early 1900s, and in 1905,
after a decade of consolidation, the top five railroads held 75% of
the paid-up capital and 68% of the operating mileage of all Japanese
railway companies.[3] To be sure, Japan's "big five" barely approached the size of the largest railroads in the West. Whereas the
London & North Western Railway had more than 1,800 miles of
track and over 55,000 employees in 1890, and the Pennsylvania
Railroad over 11,000 miles of track and 103,000 workers in 1906,
the comparable figures in 1906 for the Nippon Railway, Japan's

TABLE 1   The Five Largest Japanese Railroad Companies, March 1906.

Railway	Paid-up Capital (¥1,000)	Length of Line open (miles)	No. of Employees
Nippon	50,400	860	13,089
Kyushu	48,739	446	7,972
San'yō	30,850	406	7,064
Kansai	24,182	280	3,816
Hokkaido Colliery	12,500	208	3,709

Source: *Tetsudō kyoku nenpō*, 1905, Teishinshō Tetsudō Kyoku, 1906.

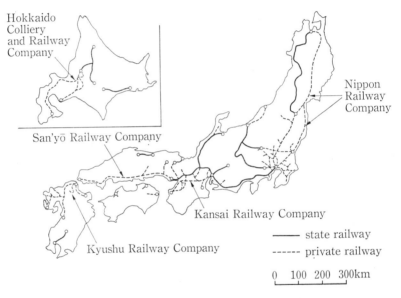

FIG. 1   Japan's Railway Network in 1906.

private rail giant, were 860 miles and about 13,000 employees (see Table 1).[4] The U.S. case suggests, however, that once railroad firms come to operate 100–200 miles of track, they begin to face problems of coordination that require the adoption of advanced administrative methods and structures.[5] The operations of the five biggest railway concerns of Meiji Japan all exceeded the 200-mile mark. Did they, then, exhibit a pattern of managerial evolution approximating that of major Western railroads and lead the way in the introduction of modern business management in Japan?

I. The Professionalization of Top Management in the San'yō and Kyushu Railways

The example of the San'yō Railway Company under Ushiba Takuzō suggests that the principal Meiji railroads did indeed resemble their Western counterparts in this regard. A Keiō graduate, Ushiba had served in the Finance Ministry and on the boards of several business enterprises before coming to the San'yō Railway in 1894 to take on the newly created post of general superintendent (*sō-shihainin*).[6] The San'yō, founded in 1888, was the first Japanese company to establish such a position. In reporting this milestone, the *Jiji shinpō* noted that the office of superintendent (*shihainin*) had already become a commonplace among business firms, but that in any given company the holder of that office managed the enterprise under orders from the president and directors. On the other hand, the need for a *general* superintendent, implying an executive with a greater say in top management decisions, had only recently arisen, especially in railroads that were just completing their lines or beginning to work them on a large scale. The need was particularly acute, the journal asserted, when, "as at present, the directors of the various companies are all connected with several firms and, pressed with work, are unable to devote themselves entirely to one company."[7] Ushiba therefore was a harbinger of the full-time career managers who from the late 1890s came to play an increasingly important role in the top-level decision making of the larger railroads. Ushiba himself became managing director of the San'yō in 1898 and chairman of its board in 1904.

The man he succeeded as San'yō chairman was Matsumoto Jūtarō, an Osaka entrepreneur who personified traditional railroad management. In drawing up plans for the Hankai Railway Company in the mid-1880s, for example, Matsumoto had stood by the old Sakai highway and estimated the traffic volume by counting beans in the sleeve pocket of his kimono.[8] As president of the 130th National Bank and a major stockholder in several of the private railroads, he exemplified Meiji railway owner-executives who served part-time on railroad company boards while simultaneously engaging in other business enterprises. Matsumoto was unusual, however, in the number of railway firms over which he concurrently presided—five, to be exact, in the early 1900s![9] Needless to say, he was unable to supervise the day-to-day operation of those roads: that task he left to full-time superintendents or managing directors like Ushiba.

Under Ushiba's direction the San'yō Railway achieved high standards of both construction and service. From the mid-1890s on, the company invested extensively in upgrading its plant and equipment and led the industry in introducing a variety of customer services and amenities. The innovations came in rapid succession. In 1895, the San'yō began operating express trains pulled by the latest American locomotives; instead of the earlier compartmentalized carriages, these trains all featured American-style bogie cars with corridors running their length. The company installed "red caps" at principal stations in 1896 and porters on through-trains in 1898. In the latter year, the railroad initiated an express package delivery service, and in 1899 it adopted electric lighting for all classes of passenger carriages. The firm also pioneered the use of dining cars in 1899 and sleeping cars in 1900. Finally, in 1903 it inaugurated Japan's first limited express train.[10] These and other innovations made the San'yō far and away the country's most modern and progressive railroad; as a Western observer noted in 1898, "its cars [are] incomparably the best appointed in Japan, as its service is the best organized."[11]

Ushiba also displayed considerable public relations skill vis-à-vis San'yō stockholders, coming out with a sophisticated rationale for the expanded investment required to finance his program of improvements. Beginning in the late 1890s he sought to rally the owners behind the company's strategy of plant renovation by urging them to extend their time horizons and appealing to their sense of civic duty. Stockholders ought not to begrudge the huge outlay of capital needed to upgrade the railway, he argued in 1899, since such investment would "open a permanent source of profits and at the same time fulfill [the company's] grave responsibility towards society."[12] By January 1906, Ushiba had refined his position considerably. In a series of articles he published that month, he insisted that private railroads must restrict their dividends and use the resulting surplus to carry out needed improvements. Ushiba went on to criticize the general tendency whereby railroad companies "compete for the highest dividend rate" and "the more their profits increase, the more they have to pay them out to shareholders." If the firms fail to restrain their dividend rates, he warned, they "will block the source of progress and improvement and thus lose their permanent interests."[13] Ushiba's appeals evidently were effective, for the San'yō Railway had little trouble implementing a policy of dividend limitation in the mid-1900s.[14]

The case of the Kyushu Railway Company under Sengoku Mitsugu lends further support to the notion of Meiji railroads as pioneers of modern Japanese management. Born into a samurai family of the Tosa domain, Sengoku had graduated from the Engineering College in Tokyo in 1878, eventually becoming an engineer in the state railways. In the latter half of the 1880s, the Railway Bureau had lent him to the Nippon and Kōbu railroads to supervise line construction work for those private firms and had then dispatched him overseas for a year and a half to investigate the latest methods of railway building in the West. In 1896 Sengoku resigned from the state railways to launch a career in private railroad management. Bursting onto the Kyushu railway scene, he developed in no time into a professional manager par excellence. As chief officer of the Chikuhō Industrial Railway and then of the Kyushu, he relentlessly pursued a program of business expansion, ignoring the protestations of conservative stockholders and prompting his peers to describe him as being "cold and stubborn as a rock."[15] When the Chikuhō Industrial merged with the Kyushu in 1897, Sengoku became vice president and managing director of the latter and the following year rose to the presidency. As top executive of the Kyushu, Sengoku "changed the previous conservative policy and firmly adopted a positive strategy."[16] On the one hand, he vigorously expanded the company's network by buying up the construction licenses of other railways and, on the other hand, invested heavily in upgrading existing lines.[17]

Sengoku's program was a far cry from that of the preceding

administration. Representative of the latter was Imamura Seinosuke, a Tokyo businessman who, like Matsumoto Jūtarō, was also
a bank president as well as an owner-executive of several railroad
companies. A director of the Kyushu Railway from the time of its
founding in 1888, Imamura had played a key part in that company's adoption of a retrenchment program in the early 1890s.
According to the railroad's first president, Takahashi Shinkichi,
Imamura had from the outset urged him "to try to curtail expenditures and raise the dividend."[18] Once the financial panic of 1890
had struck, Imamura had stepped up his pressure and, "as a
temporary expedient, advised President Takahashi to reduce the
company's operations, to take a very conservative policy, and to
endeavor to maintain the status quo."[19] With owner-capitalists like
Imamura initially controlling its board, it is no wonder that the
Kyushu Railway, in the words of contemporary observers, should
have been "dominated from the start by the vulgar view that it
had to economize on building outlays" and have proceeded "as if
it were carrying out temporary construction work."[20]

    Stockholders who shared Imamura's conservative proclivities were
naturally aghast at Sengoku's massive investment program. Perhaps
partly because he lacked Ushiba's tact in dealing with stockholders,
Sengoku's aggressive pursuit of his program provoked a sharp
reaction among the owners. Compounding the problem was the fact
that the Kyushu Railway, like other Meiji railroad companies, had
no system of depreciation accounting and therefore financed improvements out of operating revenues. As a result, Sengoku's huge
expenditure on renovations, together with his expansion of the
maintenance and other staff, put pressure on the company's profits,
causing the dividend rate to plunge after 1897. Dismayed by this
outcome, a group of stockholders began vehemently criticizing
management's expansionary policy and in mid-1899 launched a
campaign to oust Sengoku from the presidency.[21] The upshot was
a classic confrontation between ownership and management with
"the stockholders desiring an increase in dividends even to the point
of reducing the business, and the directors insisting on expanding
the business even if it means cutting dividends."[22] The critics, led
by bankers, stockbrokers, and other railroad capitalists, were

opposed by the nascent Mitsubishi zaibatsu and local mine owners, who since the Chikuhō merger had gained control of the Kyushu board.[23] Through the mediation of oligarch Inoue Kaoru, the conflict was eventually settled in management's favor, it being determined that Sengoku's program had simply been making up for the serious neglect of essential capital expenditures by the previous administration.[24] Thus, Sengoku went on pursuing his positive policies, thrusting aside a second attempt by disgruntled stockholders to interfere with his program in 1902.[25]

Ushiba and Sengoku were prominent examples of the full-time salaried managers, many of them recruited from the government bureaucracy, who in at least some of the private railroads were beginning to take over strategic decision making from traditional owner-executives like Matsumoto and Imamura. As administrative experts with little share in their companies' ownership, Ushiba and Sengoku lent a high degree of professionalism to the top managements of the San'yō and Kyushu railways.

II. The Development of Managerial Hierarchies

Not only did the San'yō and Kyushu make substantial progress in separating management from ownership and in appointing educated career managers to the high command, but they also developed sophisticated and extensive administrative structures. In 1905, for instance, the San'yō staff was organized under its top management into five departments in charge, respectively, of transportation (*un'yu*), motive power (*kisha*), construction and maintenance (*kenchiku*), accounting (*kaikei*), and general affairs (*shomu*), the latter being concerned with record keeping and statistical analysis.[26] At the time, out of a total work force of about 6,700, the San'yō apparently had more than 1,200 salaried or white-collar employees (*shokuin*), for an administrative intensity, that is, the ratio of salaried employees to manual laborers, of over 22%.[27]

To staff their administrative organizations, the private railways tapped a variety of sources. As in the case of senior executives, the companies initially drew on the government bureaucracy for many of their middle- and lower-level managers. Often, state railroad engineers, engaged to assist in line construction, would stay on to supervise various operational departments. However, as Japan's system of higher education grew, the railroad firms were more and more able to recruit talent directly from universities and higher schools, particularly the Engineering College of Tokyo Imperial University and the predecessors of Keiō and Hitotsubashi universities. Out of a sample of 36 railway company middle managers ranging from branch office head to department chief, 17 entered the firms immediately upon graduation from university or higher school, 13 were ex-government engineers or administrators, 4 came from the private sector (the most unusual being a former Christian minister who switched careers in 1891), and 2 were prefectural assembly members.[28] Of the 14 who joined private railways prior to 1890, 8 hailed from the state bureaucracy, and the remainder were new university or higher school graduates. After 1890, the ratio of ex-bureaucrats to new school leavers was reversed as the railroads turned increasingly to institutions of higher learning.

Meiji railroad companies appointed a number of their middle as well as top managers from the outside. In fact, there was considerable lateral movement among the firms and between them and the state railways, as the lengthy resumés of many railroad administrators indicate. But more and more the private railways drew managerial talent from within, as evidenced by the increase in university graduate hiring and the advancement of engineers to administrative positions. By the mid-1890s, the government railways were forced to develop their own technical experts—partly owing to the plundering of their staffs by the private roads—by resorting "to the extraordinary measure of selecting coolies that show intelligence and giving them special training."[29] The private railways were able to take similar steps at the managerial level because of changes on the supply side. In particular, the Railroad School (Tetsudō Gakkō), established in Ueno in 1897, began producing a train of clerical and technical functionaries for the railroads, freeing up the more promising among such operatives for promotion to the lower managerial ranks and creating a ripple effect on up through the administrative hierarchy.

Engineer-administrators with their advanced technical training brought a good measure of professionalism to the lower and middle managements of railway companies. Indeed, by mid-Meiji, Japanese engineers had achieved a high level of expertise, as evidenced by the hiring in 1892 of a Kyushu Railway engineer "to work on the Indo-Siamese Railway, which was planned and surveyed by Englishmen."[30] Besides receiving formal education and training in Japan, many private railroad engineers traveled overseas for study or observation, including at least 7 of the 22 with engineering backgrounds in the above sample of middle managers. One even graduated from Rensselaer Polytechnic Institute in 1878, then served two years in the U.S. Army Corps of Engineers building embankments along the Mississippi before coming home to join the state railways and a series of private railroad firms.[31] Another became chief of motive power in the Nippon Railway after earning a physics degree from Tokyo Imperial University in 1882 and spending the next 15 years in Germany studying acoustics and mechanical engineering.[32] These were rather exceptional cases, it being more common for railroad companies to send their engineer-administrators on brief inspection tours to observe first-hand the latest developments in Western railway technology and management. For example, the compilers of a list of the Kyushu Railway staff in mid-1905 noted that the heads of the Construction and Motive Power departments and of the Passenger Office in the Transportation Department were all "traveling abroad (*yōkōchū*)."[33]

Another source of technical information on contemporary Western railroads was the translation of recent publications by Western experts. These included an 1876 survey of British railway construction and operation, which appeared in Japanese translation six years later, and an 1886 study of American railroads in comparative perspective, which made its Japanese debut in 1894.[34] Also in the latter year, the San'yō Railway Company published a translation by one of its senior staff members of the 1891 edition of *The Working and Management of an English Railway*.[35] Authored by George Findlay, general manager of the London & North Western Railway Company, this book was intended to serve as "a practical guide or hand-book for those, who, whether in this country or in our numerous colonies, may find it necessary, for whatever reasons, to acquire a knowledge of the principles upon which a great English railway is constructed and managed, and the methods and appliances by means of which its business is carried on."[36] Undoubtedly, the San'yō and most other Japanese railway companies patterned their administrative structures on the British model of centralized "departmental" organization, which was better suited to the relatively short distances of the Japanese railroads than was the decentralized "line-and-staff" structure typical of the mammoth American roads.[37]

III. The Administrative Backwardness of Most Meiji Railroads

The evidence presented thus far suggests that there was a fairly close fit between the patterns of managerial development of major Japanese and Western railway firms. As predicted by the Western model, scale of operation was certainly a factor in the growing sophistication of the San'yō and Kyushu managements; after all, those two companies alternated as the second and third largest private railroads in Meiji Japan. Yet certain conditions peculiar to the San'yō and Kyushu railways point to the conclusion that ultimately their administrative experiences were exceptional among Meiji railroad concerns. In the case of the San'yō Railway, one such factor was competition. The San'yō was in the rather unusual position of facing intense competition from steamship companies whose vessels plied the Inland Sea routes adjacent to the course of the railway. Such rivalry put constant pressure on the San'yō to cut rates and improve services and therefore partly explains the progressiveness of its management. Another factor setting apart both railroads was the involvement of Mitsubishi. The second largest stockholder in Meiji railroad companies after the 15th National Bank, Mitsubishi differed from most railway owners in its primary concern for the indirect benefits of railway investment. And by far the principal targets of such investment by this emergent zaibatsu were the San'yō and Kyushu railways. Control and extension of these roads formed a key part of Mitsubishi's overall business strategy in western Japan, as the combine sought to integrate them with its other operations, especially coal mining. Mitsubishi thus became the top stockholder in both firms, supporting the rise in the San'yō, as in the Kyushu, of full-time salaried managers devoted to expansion of the enterprise.

Almost all of the other Meiji railroad companies, including the largest railway, the Nippon, failed to follow in the tracks of the San'yō and Kyushu. In fact, the vast majority showed hardly any progress at all on the managerial front. This administrative retardation was manifested in the fact that through much of the Meiji period, by contemporary Western standards, Japanese trains were generally slow; the railroads poorly equipped and maintained; and managements laggard in making necessary improvements.

Admittedly, for the Japanese of early Meiji, whose only means of overland transport had been by foot, palanquin, or packhorse, the railroad revolutionized travel time. In 1872, for instance, a newspaper writer marveled at being able to cover the eighteen miles from Shinbashi to Yokohama by rail in just 54 minutes, exclaiming that this was something that previously would have been "impossible to do without wings."[38] And the following year another newspaper broke the incredible story of a woman whose child slept the whole time she made the 30-mile round trip from Yokohama to Shinagawa on business; the journey "barely took two hours, and the child had yet to wake up!"[39] Even as late as 1900, the composer of the famous "Railway Song" voiced a common refrain when he exulted: "It's like a dream! Having raced past the 53 post stations [of the old Tōkaidō highway], we rest in a Kobe inn, thanks to the fact that trains give people wings."[40]

In early Meiji, the speeds attained by Japanese trains were not far behind those in the West. Around 1860, for example, American railroads had averaged 10 to 15 miles an hour, and speeds of more than 30 miles an hour had been "virtually unknown."[41] But by the turn of the century, Japanese trains had clearly fallen behind their Western counterparts in this regard. As the *Jiji shinpō* complained in December 1898, the railways "have never advanced one step since the time of their construction, with the exception of the San'yō road. . . . The trains creep along at the same slow pace as of old."[42] A British tourist that year seemed to confirm this observation, reporting that the fast train from Tokyo to Kobe, the 376-mile Tōkaidō run celebrated in the "Railway Song," took almost 20 hours to complete its journey, for an inclusive speed of 19 miles per hour.[43] As for actual train speed, a 1903 study of the three principal trunk lines on the main island showed the average speed of trains on the Tōkaidō to be 25 miles an hour compared to only 20 for those on the Nippon Railway and nearly 30 for those on the San'yō.[44] When limited express service was finally inaugurated on the Tōkaidō in 1912, the trains still averaged only 30 miles per hour compared to 55 for the fastest trains in Germany.[45]

The Tōkaidō was the pride of the government railways, which accounted for about a fourth of Japan's overall network around the turn of the century. The British traveler of 1898 was speaking on the basis of his experience with the national rail system when he remarked that "all notion of speed, haste, or flurry are [sic] utterly foreign to [the Japanese] nature" and that the Japanese railway terminal presents "an air of rest and quiet, which is in singular contrast to the bustle and noise of an European railway station."[46] This relaxed air was even more pronounced on state lines that were off the beaten track; in Shimazaki Tōson's 1906 novel *The Broken Commandment*, the Tokyo-bound train for which the protagonist waits at a provincial stop on the government's Naoetsu line is "20 minutes late."[47] Repeated complaints in the press about "the long delays and the unpunctuality"[48] of railways in general suggest that the state lines were not exceptional in this regard.

Granted, financial and technical factors—the relative shortage of investment capital in Meiji Japan and the choice of the narrow gauge—placed constraints on both the speed and reliability of Japanese railways, but slack management played a part, and not just on the government lines. Sei Keitarō, who eventually became Ueno stationmaster, began his career in 1893 as an assistant at one of the Nippon Railway Company's local stops. In those days, Sei recalled:

> Things were easy-going, and occasionally on fair-weather days in early spring, while waiting for the next train . . . , the staff would leave one member at the station as a caretaker (*rusuban*), and the stationmaster and everyone else would head for the nearby hills to view the cherry blossoms. No one at that time had anything like a pocket watch. So when it came time for the train to arrive, the caretaker would raise a flag attached to a long pole, which was clearly visible from the hills. Seeing the flag, the staff would break off their flower-viewing and return to the station, each member taking up his post.[49]

As late as 1903, newspapers were still grumbling about "the lax and perfunctory methods" of the Nippon Railway.[50] Insofar as such methods prevailed among Meiji railroads, it is small wonder that for the most part Japanese trains of that era were undistinguished in either speed or precision.

Meiji railway firms were also laggard in providing amenities for travelers, in spite of the fact that passenger income accounted for 60–70% of their total revenue in the 1890s and early 1900s. The early trains were a far cry from the well-appointed Shinkansen of today. Well into the Meiji era, the railroads employed British-style "matchbox" carriages divided into compartments by long wooden benches. Once inside, passengers were literally confined to their compartments, for there was no way to pass through the car, and shortly before departure a railroad employee would lock all the doors from the outside "in the approved paternal government style," as an American tourist put it in 1891.[51] The latter practice obtained on the Nippon and other private lines as well. To top it off, the third-class carriages were "absolutely destitute of upholstery" as well as heat.[52] And none of the cars had lavatories, which made for a mad scramble for platform facilities at train stops and forced the government, ever eager to present a civilized front to the West, to impose stiff fines of up to ¥10 for passengers caught urinating from the window en route and a prorated ¥5 for those caught breaking wind therefrom.[53] Travelers began to find relief only in 1889 when the state lines, which thereafter would generally follow the San'yō's lead in service improvements, had the distinction of introducing onboard toilets. Still, it was some years before such facilities became widespread, as the novelist Shiga Naoya suggested in a short story published in 1908: while riding in a toiletless carriage on the main line of the Nippon Railway, the narrator endures the flustered pleas of a mother to her distressed boy—"Can't you hold it just a little longer?"—only to discover that the next station has no restrooms.[54]

Meiji trains also had poor interior lighting at night. As evening approached, railroad employees would clamber onto the tops of the carriages at a station stop and suspend oil lamps through holes in the roof. The feeble light thus generated was barely enough for one to make out the figures of fellow passengers. The railroads began to install electric lighting in the late 1890s, but this innovation, too, was slow to disseminate; for example, while traveling on the Tōkaidō line after the Russo-Japanese War, the title character of Natsume Sōseki's 1908 novel *Sanshirō* observes at one train stop: "The sun was down. . . . Station workers were tramping along the roof of the train, inserting lighted oil lamps into holders from above."[55] In short, the following complaint by a Westerner in 1898 was not entirely off the mark a decade later: "The miserable oil lamps of ancient days still defy the traveler to read by their light, and the carriages present an unaltered aspect of conservative comfortlessness."[56]

Not surprisingly, the railroads were late in developing a sense of service toward the traveling public. On the national railways, it was only after the San'yō had begun pioneering consumer services in the late 1890s and the Kansai Railway had engaged the parallel state line in a fierce rate war in 1902 that the authorities "descended from their eminence of official magnificence and consented to address their customers in polite phraseology."[57] Earlier, railroad employees had sold tickets "as though they were doing the passenger a great favor," but for their part passengers had "often stood up for their rights, some even going so far as to haggle over the fare."[58] The same condescending attitude (*noseteyaru shugi*) pervaded the Nippon Railway, whose staff "smelled like bureaucrats."[59] As late as 1903, a newspaper assailed "the *de-haut-en-bas* temper in which the Company's business is conducted. . . . In the parlance of the railway officials, its clients in the northern regions are known generically as *dobiyakusho* (rustics), the petty officials of the Company regarding themselves as people quite above such an agricultural herd."[60]

In fairness to Meiji railroads, it should be noted that they lagged just slightly behind their Western counterparts in introducing passenger amenities. In the United States, "sleeping cars did not come into general use until after the Civil War,"[61] and trains on the Pennsylvania Railroad began to feature sanitary facilities only in 1878, diners in 1882, steam heating in 1885, and electric lighting in 1902.[62] On the British railroads, these amenities had all made their appearance by the early 1890s, but they did not become widespread until a decade later. And in class-conscious Britain, where cheaper fares had originally ridden in open freight cars, railway company attitudes toward customer service resembled those on the more conservative of the Japanese roads. In 1892, the Great Western put into service the first British train with a corridor running its entire length; this gave third-class passengers access to lavatories, "a startling innovation on the Great Western, which never forgot that they were the 'lower orders.' " When this firm added dining cars in 1896, it restricted their use to first-class passengers, "a rule that was only gradually relaxed from 1900 onwards."[63]

Yet, in addition to speed, there was one related area in which late Meiji railroads were decisively behind their contemporaries in the West, namely, the condition of lines and rolling stock. Most railroad companies in Meiji Japan sought to minimize capital expenditures by avoiding tunneling and double tracking as well as by neglecting or delaying needed repairs and improvements. As a British railroad executive observed in 1904, "Japan must be congratulated on the cheap construction of her railway system, but it is impossible to have a thoroughly efficient system without paying for it. . . . Nothing strikes one more forcibly in Japan than the impermanence of things."[64] In this regard, Meiji railway firms resembled U.S. railroads of a generation or two earlier. On antebellum American lines, durability was also "sacrificed for lower capital costs,"[65] with the result that roadbeds and rails "were almost toylike. Most lines were poorly built, sometimes not with rails at all but iron straps that could pop up, pierce the car floor, and impale the passengers."[66]

In Japan, such economizing reached a peak during the recession brought on by the financial panic of 1890. In 1893, for instance, an army officer criticized "the over-economical methods of construction adopted by private companies, whose lines follow winding routes and ascend steep gradients simply because the engineers were required to cut everything as low as possible." The officer cited as examples a branch of the Nippon Railway "where gradients as steep as 1 in 40 exist" and a section of the Kyushu "where the sinuosity of the road is quite remarkable. It would have been possible to make the former comparatively level and the latter much less tortuous had not paramount importance been given to the question of outlay."[67]

As we have seen, the Kyushu Railway reversed its "cheap construction" policy once Mitsubishi gained control of the company and backed Sengoku's elevation to its presidency, but to the bitter end—the government eventually nationalized the major private railroads in 1906 and 1907—the Nippon Railway did little to renovate its shoddy lines and equipment. Indeed, the conservatism of the Nippon presents a sharp contrast to the progressive management of the San'yō and Kyushu railways. The Nippon, like most other Meiji railroad concerns, was pressured by its stockholders to pay profits out almost entirely as dividends rather than to plow them back into the enterprise. To meet such investor demands, the company simply had to ignore or postpone essential improvements. Dominating the top management of the Nippon was the firm's leading stockholder, the 15th National Bank, founded in 1877 as an investment organ for the nobility. Reflecting the bank's risk-avoiding and dividend-maximizing tendencies, the senior executives of the Nippon lacked the vision and enterprise displayed by Ushiba and Sengoku. In 1900, for example, the railroad's president admitted that private roads, including his own, were poorly equipped as compared to those of the state, then added lamely that "since the funding needed to [upgrade facilities] is lacking, circumstances do not permit it."[68]

The demand for renewal expenditures could not be ignored indefinitely, however, and in fact the Nippon's average fixed investment per mile of line did rise from about ¥47,000 in 1897, the year in which the company completed its network, to ¥62,000 in 1905. Yet even this substantial increase represented far less than what was accomplished at the San'yō and Kyushu railways, which saw their average fixed investment per mile of line soar during that same period from ¥58,000 to ¥88,000 and from ¥61,000 to a staggering ¥114,000, respectively.[69] Mitsubishi virtually guaranteed the supply of capital required by the latter two firms, whether in the form of bond and stock purchases or loans, but evidently the 15th National Bank was not as forthcoming with financial support for the Nippon.

The failure to carry out necessary renovations meant that the Nippon and most other Meiji railway companies remained well behind their Western counterparts in the solidity and repair of their plant and equipment. In 1902, the former railway commissioner of India, Sir William Bisset, came to Japan to investigate the suitability of railways as security for loans by British capitalists. Bisset concluded that although Japan's railroads on the whole were "at least equal to the railways of India,"[70] the San'yō and the state's Tōkaidō line were in fact the only railways in Japan "worthy of the name."[71]

The managerial backwardness of the Nippon Railway found expression not only in its conservative investment behavior, but also in its relatively unsophisticated management structure. In 1905, despite operating more than twice the mileage of the San'yō Railway, the Nippon featured a much simpler bureaucracy, consisting of the board of directors and departments for general affairs (*shomu*), finance (*keiri*), and operation (*eigyō*).[72] It also carried a proportionately smaller administrative staff. With under 1,500 salaried employees at the time, the Nippon had an administrative intensity of about 14%, compared to the 22% recorded by the San'yō.[73]

Several factors contributed to the managerial retardation of private railway concerns in Meiji Japan. One factor was the relative scarcity of venture capital, which limited the ability of railroad managements to pursue expansionary programs. Another was the overwhelming passenger orientation of most railroads, for in the West it was largely problems of coordination associated with the pricing and transshipment of freight that led to advances in administrative practice and organization. In this regard, Meiji railway companies generally made little progress in developing through-traffic, both reflecting and perpetuating the comparative unsophistication of their managements. In this area, too, the San'yō Railway took the lead, arranging for connecting service with the government's Tōkaidō line and the Kyushu Railway in 1898, but only as part of its fierce rate war with the Osaka Commercial Shipping Company that year.[74] Yet, despite the conclusion of individual agreements between the railways for through-traffic, direct passenger service from Tokyo to Shimonoseki was not inaugurated until August 1905, and direct long-haul freight service did not really begin until after the nationalization.[75]

Perhaps the primary reason for the administrative backwardness of most Meiji railroads was that their top managements were dominated by cautious, dividend-seeking investors. During the Meiji period, private railways on the average raised about 80% of their capital through stock issues.[76] To be sure, ownership was somewhat dispersed, with the Nippon, Kyushu, and San'yō having respectively about 4,700, 5,500, and 3,700 stockholders in 1902.[77] This level of dispersion, however, was not on the order of that of the major British railway firms, each of which had "at least 20,000 individual investors,"[78] nor of the Pennsylvania Railroad, whose stockholders numbered around 41,000 in 1906.[79] Moreover, stockholding in the leading Japanese railroads was actually fairly concentrated; in 1902, for instance, the top ten investors in the Nippon, Kyushu, and San'yō held respectively 33, 18, and 21% of the total stock.[80] The high ratio of share capital and the relatively high concentration of stockholding together gave investors a sure basis for influencing, if not determining, the business strategies of Meiji railway concerns.

The railroads' principal stockholders included institutional investors, such as banks, insurance companies, and the Imperial Household Ministry, as well as individual investors, such as nobles, landlords, and big-city capitalists, ranging from stockbrokers to textile merchants.[81] The major private railways drew most of their capital not from the immediate localities they served but from distant urban centers, especially Tokyo and Osaka. Consequently, the leading stockholders in these firms tended to be concerned more with the direct return on their investment than with the external economies of railroad development, in which they were unlikely to share. Another important characteristic of Meiji railroad investments was the marked rise of financial institutions as railway owners from the late 1890s on. By 1905, banks and insurance companies had emerged as railroad investors to such an extent that those appearing on major stockholders' lists alone that year held a sixth of all the shares of the five largest railroads combined.[82] These various investors, individual and institutional alike, were for the most part risk-avoiding and profit-maximizing; interested mainly in obtaining stable but high dividends, "they naturally sought security over growth in the enterprise."[83]

Stockholder influence over private railway decision-making was reflected in the considerable overlap between the principal owners and top executives of the railroads. In a sample of 12 railway firms from 1896, for instance, 42 of the 75 presidents and directors appear on their companies' major stockholders' lists.[84] The situation had changed little, if at all, by the early 1900s. Whereas 39% of the officers in the 1896 sample numbered among the top ten shareholders in their firms, 37% of all private railway presidents and directors in 1902 did so as well.[85] This overlap helps to explain why investors were able to affect railway company policy to the point of dominating it, as revealed in corporate decisions on capital expenditures, dividend payouts, and the like. In short, even in late Meiji railroads, the separation of management from ownership and the emergence of a professional managerial class were still in their early stages.

IV. The Railway Nationalization and Managerial Spinoff

Meiji railroad concerns as a whole may not have pioneered modern business administration in Japan, but might not the San'yō and Kyushu railways at least be said to have done so? According to some scholars, the railway nationalization of 1906–1907 provided the occasion for a wholesale transfer of administrative expertise from the advanced railway companies to other private enterprises by prompting a major exodus of career managers from the nationalized railroads. There were indeed some notable instances of managerial spinoff from the latter to other sectors of the economy. For example, Nishino Keinosuke, head of the San'yō Railway's transportation department, left the field in 1906, becoming managing director of the Imperial Theater, where he helped to revolutionize management practices in the entertainment industry. Then, in 1912, he transferred his considerable administrative skills to the insurance business as the newly appointed superintendent of the Tokio Marine Insurance Company.[86] Similarly, Ida Seizō, chief of the accounting and purchasing departments of the San'yō, moved on to the Kirin Beer Company in 1907, eventually rising to the managing directorship of that Mitsubishi subsidiary.[87]

I would argue, however, that such cases were exceptional and that contrary to the above interpretation, the railway nationalization in effect blunted the direct impact of railway companies on other private businesses by *minimizing* the extent of managerial spinoff. The state railways promised continued employment to all of the staff, save top managers and temporary workers, of the 17 railroad firms slated for nationalization. Government employment meant greater prestige, as the president of one railroad company, on the day of its conveyance to the state, suggested in exhorting his staff: "From now on you are going to be government officials and render further service to the railway world!"[88] The employees of the railroad concerns were also assured that for the most part their pay would remain the same, and no doubt many were heartened by the fact that as a whole state railway employees received a higher average wage than did their counterparts in any of the five major private railways.[89] As a result, the vast majority of the former officers of the nationalized firms joined the government railways.

After 1907, the state rail system experienced a noticeable improvement in efficiency and service, thanks in large measure to the infusion of managerial talent from the purchased railroads. Out of the 48,409 employees transferred from the latter to the state railways, 340 were in a middle to top management category. A number of these executives became prominent officials in the new Imperial Railway Department; for example, the former superintendent of the Kyushu Railway took charge of the Kyushu branch office and two middle managers from the San'yō headed the Department's transportation and engineering divisions, respectively.[90] Such men accounted in large part for the vitality of the national railway system in the early decades of this century.

By the same token, the nationalization in a sense deprived private business of the full impact of the rise of salaried career managers in the San'yō and Kyushu railways. In light of this fact and the administrative backwardness of most other Meiji railroad companies, the roots of contemporary Japanese management are ultimately to be found elsewhere, most likely in the nascent zaibatsu, whose diversified operations achieved a scale and complexity necessitating the early adoption of sophisticated administrative methods and structures. Meanwhile, the managerial legacy of private railroad enterprise in the Meiji era went largely to the state railways. The latter proved to be the major beneficiary of the administrative advances recorded by the San'yō and Kyushu. On the other hand, the national railways faced the burden of unfinished renovation work inherited from the Nippon Railway and other delinquent companies that had been dominated by conservative investors. This work only compounded the huge debt incurred by the state system in buying out the private railways, a debt that foreshadowed the eventual bankruptcy of that system. As the *Jiji shinpō* noted prophetically in 1906, in view of the massive improvements required, the nationalized railways "may well become a perfect white elephant which the Government may be glad to put up to auction in years to come."[91] With the privatization of the state rail network in 1987, Japan's railroads have indeed come full circle, and the former national railways are now experiencing a new infusion of private managerial talent.

NOTES

1. Alfred D. Chandler, Jr., "The Railroads: Pioneers in Modern Corporate Management," *Business History Review*, Vol. 39 (Spring 1965), pp. 16–40; T. R. Gourvish, "The Railways and the Development of Managerial Enterprise in Britain, 1850–1939," in Kesaji Kobayashi and Hidemasa Morikawa, eds., *Development of Managerial Enterprise*, The International Conference on Business History, Tokyo, University of Tokyo Press, 1986.

2. Nakagawa Keiichirō, Morikawa Hidemasa, and Yui Tsunehiko, eds., *Kindai Nihon keieishi no kiso chishiki* (Guide to modern Japanese business history), Tokyo, Yūhikaku, 1974, pp. 450–51.

3. Nakanishi Ken'ichi, *Nihon shiyū tetsudōshi kenkyū: toshi kōtsū no hatten to sono kōzō* (A study of Japanese railways), 2nd ed., Kyoto, Minerva shobō, 1979, p. 53; *Tetsudō kyoku nenpō* (Annual report of the Department of Railways), 1907, ed., Teishin Shō Tetsudō Kyoku (Tetsudō-in, 1909), appendix, pp. 22–46 passim.

4. George Findlay, *The Working and Management of an English Railway*, 3rd ed., London, Whittaker & Co., George Bell & Sons, 1890, p. 11; Kishichi Watanabe, "Comment," in Kobayashi and Morikawa,

eds., *Development of Managerial Enterprise*, p. 208; *Tetsudō kyoku nenpō*, 1905 (Teishin Shō Tetsudō Kyoku, 1906), pp. 260–61, appendix, pp. 23, 39.

5. Alfred D. Chandler, Jr., "The United States: Seedbed of Managerial Capitalism," in Alfred D. Chandler, Jr., and Herman Daems, eds., *Managerial Hierarchies: Comparative Perspectives on the Rise of the Modern Industrial Enterprise*, Cambridge, Mass., Harvard University Press, 1980, p. 16; Alfred D. Chandler, Jr., *The Visible Hand: The Managerial Revolution in American Business*, Cambridge, Mass., Belknap Press of Harvard University Press, 1977, p. 96.

6. Sugiyama Kazuo, "Kigyō no zaimu-tōshi katsudō to bunkateki haikei: Meiji ki no tetsudō gyō, men-bōseki gyō o jirei to shite" (Financial investment of modern enterprises and its cultural background), *Keiei shigaku*, Vol. 10 (Aug. 1975), p. 77n43.

7. "Nihon no kaisha ni mo . . . korekara wa sō-shihainin o oku hitsuyō ari: San'yō tetsudō kaisha sossen shite kettei" (The necessity of general superintendents in Japanese enterprises), reprinted in *Shinbun shūsei Meiji hennenshi*, ed. Dō hensankai, 15 vols., 1936, Vol. 9, p. 33.

8. Kamemura Masanao and Makimura Shiyō, eds., *Ōsaka ben* (Osaka dialect), Osaka, Seibundō Shoten, 1951, Vol. 3, p. 116.

9. Sugiyama, *op. cit.*, p. 77n42.

10. *Nihon kokuyū tetsudō 100 nenshi: tsūshi* (100-year history of the Japanese National Railways), ed. Nihon Kokuyū Tetsudō, 1974, pp. 127–28; *Nihon kokuyū tetsudō 100 nenshi*, ed., Nihon Kokuyū Tetsudō, 14 vols., 1969–74, Vol. 4, pp. 425–27; Aoki Kaizō, *Jinbutsu kokutetsu 100 nen* (Personalities in 100 years of the National Railways), Chūō Senkyō Kabushiki Kaisha Shuppan Kyoku, 1969, p. 66.

11. "Railway and Steamship Competition," *Japan Weekly Mail*, 3 Sept. 1898, p. 239.

12. Ushiba Takuzō, "Tetsudō eigyō no hōshin" (Policies in railway management), *Tetsudō jihō*, No. 14 (May 1899), reprinted in *10 nen kinen Nihon no tetsudō ron*, ed. Kinoshita Ritsuan, Tetsudō Jihō Kyoku, 1909, pp. 274–86.

13. Ushiba Takuzō, "Shisetsu tetsudō rieki haitō seigen ron" (On the limitation of dividends in private railway companies), *Tetsudō jihō*, Nos. 329–34 (Jan. 1906), reprinted in *10-nen kinen Nihon no tetsudō ron*, pp. 185–219.

14. Sakurai Tōru, "San'yō tetsudō kabushiki kaisha no shihon chikuseki jōken to kokuyūka mondai: kokka dokusen seisei ni kansuru kisoteki kōan" (Accumulation of capital and the problem of nationalization

in the San'yō Railway), *Shōgaku shūshi*, Vol. 49 (Feb. 1980), p. 70.

15. Murakami Teiichi, *Minami Kiyoshi den* (Biography of Minami Kiyoshi), Hayami Tarō, 1909, p. 77.

16. Adachi Ritsuen, *Imamura Seinosuke-kun jireki* (Biography of Imamura Seinosuke), Otani Matsujirō, 1906, p. 198.

17. *Nihon kokuyū tetsudō 100 nenshi*, Vol. 4, pp. 546–49, 551–54.

18. Adachi, *op. cit.*, p. 177.

19. *Ibid.*, p. 179.

20. Kikuchi Takenori, *Nakamigawa Hikojirō-kun* (Nakamigawa Hikojirō), Jinmin Shinbunsha Shuppanbu, 1903, p. 57; "Kyūshū tetsudō kabushiki kaisha chōsa hōkokusho" (Report of investigation into the Kyushu Railway Company), Feb. 1900, in *Shibusawa Eiichi denki shiryō* (Biographical materials on Shibusawa Eiichi), ed. Shibusawa Seien Kinen Zaidan Ryūmonsha, 68 vols., Dō Shiryō Kankōkai, 1955–71, Vol. 9, p. 278.

21. *Kyū-tetsu 20 nenshi* (20-year history of Kyushu Railway), ed., Kyūshū Tetsudō Kabushiki Kaisha Sōmu-ka, 1907, pp. 17–18. See also *Shibusawa Eiichi denki shiryō*, Vol. 9, pp. 237–302.

22. "Kyū-tetsu jiken no saitei" (Arbitration of the Kyushu Railway case), *Tōyō keizai zasshi*, 17 Feb. 1900, p. 276.

23. Tōjō Tadashi, "Meiji ki tetsudō kaisha no keiei funsō to kabunushi no dōkō: 'Kyūshū tetsudō kaikaku undō' o megutte" (Railway management disputes and stockholders during Meiji), *Keiei shigaku*, Vol. 19, No. 4 (Jan. 1985), pp. 21–25.

24. "Kyūshū tetsudō kabushiki kaisha chōsa hōkokusho," p. 278.

25. *Kyū-tetsu 20 nenshi*, p. 18.

26. *Teikoku tetsudō yōkan* (Imperial railway directory), 3rd ed., Tetsudō Jihō Kyoku, 1906, pp. 163–81.

27. *Ibid.*

28. *Tetsudō senjin roku* (Pioneers in railways), ed. Nihon Kōtsū Kyōkai, Nihon Teishajō Kabushiki Kaisha, 1972, passim.

29. "Railway Construction," *Japan Weekly Mail*, 20 June 1896, p. 694.

30. "A Japanese Railway Engineer Abroad," *Japan Weekly Mail*, 7 May 1892, p. 617.

31. "Hirai Seijirō," *Tetsudō senjin roku*, pp. 305–6.

32. "Tanaka Shōhei," *Tetsudō senjin roku*, p. 209.

33. *Teikoku tetsudō yōkan*, pp. 134, 140, 142.

34. Daniel Kinnear Clark, "Railways," in G. P. Bevan, ed., *British Manufacturing Industries*, London, 1876, Vol. 9, pp. 168–214, translated as *Eikoku tetsudō kiryaku*, tr. Taguchi Toranosuke, Hagiwara

Yōsuke, 1882; Arthur T. Hadley, *Railroad Transportation: Its History and Its Laws*, New York and London, G. P. Putnam's Sons, 1886, translated as *Tetsudō un'yu ron*, Tokyo, Yūhikaku, 1894.

35. 4th ed., London, 1891, translated as *Eikoku tetsudō ron*, tr. Hayami Tarō, Kobe, San'yō Tetsudō Kabushiki Kaisha, 1894.

36. Findlay, *op. cit.*, p. 2.

37. For more on the "departmental" and "line-and-staff" structures, see Chandler, 1977, *op. cit.*, pp. 106–7.

38. Cited in Watanabe Kōhei et al., eds., *Kiteki issei: tetsudō 100 nen bungaku to zuihitsu senshū* (Essays and novels in 100 years of railways), Tokyo, Jitsugyō no Nihonsha, 1972, p. 527.

39. "Kisha no hayasa: kodomo no neta aida ni Yokohama-Shinagawa kan ōfuku" (Speed of trains), *Shinbun zasshi*, No. 104 (June 1873), reprinted in *Shinbun shūsei Meiji hennenshi*, Vol. 2, p. 52.

40. Watanabe et al., *op. cit.*, p. 498.

41. Alfred D. Chandler, Jr., and Richard S. Tedlow, *The Coming of Managerial Capitalism: A Casebook on the History of American Economic Institutions*, Homewood, Ill., Richard D. Irwin, Inc., 1985, p. 183.

42. Cited in "State Purchase of Private Railways," *Japan Weekly Mail*, 14 Dec. 1898, p. 632.

43. D. T. Timins, "By Rail in Japan," *The Railway Magazine*, 2 (March 1898), p. 236.

44. "Sandai tetsudō no sokuryoku chinsen hikaku" (Comparison of the speed and fares of the three major railways), *Tokyo keizai zasshi*, 28 Feb. 1903, p. 31.

45. Sawa Kazuya, *Nihon no tetsudō: 100 nen no hanashi* (Japanese railways), Tsukiji Shokan, 1972, p. 125.

46. Timins, *op. cit.*, pp. 232–33.

47. Shimazaki Tōson, *The Broken Commandment*, tr. Kenneth Strong, Tokyo, University of Tokyo Press, 1974, p. 119.

48. "Behaviour of Travellers by Railway in Japan," *Japan Weekly Mail*, 4 May 1901, p. 468.

49. Nagata Hiroshi, ed., *Meiji no kisha: tetsudō sōsetsu 100 nen no kobore banashi kara* (Meiji trains), Kōtsū Nihonsha, 1964, p. 57.

50. "The Japan Railway Company," *Japan Weekly Mail*, 14 Feb. 1903, p. 162.

51. Percival Lowell, *Noto: An Unexplored Corner of Japan*, Boston, Houghton, Mifflin and Company, 1891, p. 36.

52. Timins, *op. cit.*, p. 234.

53. "Kisha untenchū ni shōben: bakkin jū en nari" (Urinating in the

train), *Tokyo nichinichi shinbun*, 15 April 1873, and "Kisha chū de hōhi shite, bakkin go en" (Passing wind in the train), *Tokyo nichinichi shinbun*, 19 Nov. 1881, reprinted in *Shinbun shūsei Meiji hennenshi*, Vol. 2, p. 31, and Vol. 4, p. 491; Sawa, *op. cit.*, pp. 34–35.

54. Shiga Naoya, "Abashiri made," in Watanabe et al., *op. cit.*, pp. 11–17.

55. Natsume Sōseki, *Sanshirō: A Novel*, tr. Jay Rubin, Seattle, University of Washington Press, 1977, pp. 4–5.

56. "State Purchase of Private Railways," *Japan Weekly Mail*, 14 Dec. 1898, p. 632.

57. "Japanese Railways," *Japan Weekly Mail*, 9 Aug. 1902, p. 138, citing an article in the *Tokyo nichinichi shinbun*.

58. Shibusawa Keizō, comp. and ed., *Japanese Life and Culture in the Meiji Era*, tr. Charles S. Terry, Centenary Cultural Council Series, Tokyo, Ōbunsha, 1958, pp. 223–24.

59. Mainichi Shinbun Maebashi Shikyoku, ed., *Gunma no Meiji 100 nen* (Meiji centennial in Gumma), Maebashi, 1968, pp. 242–43.

60. "The Japan Railway Company," *Japan Weekly Mail*, 14 Feb. 1903, p. 162, citing *Jiji shinpō*.

61. Chandler and Tedlow, *op. cit.*, p. 183.

62. George H. Burgess and Miles C. Kennedy, *Centennial History of the Pennsylvania Railroad Company, 1846–1946*, Philadelphia, The Pennsylvania Railroad Company, 1949, pp. 757–60.

63. Jack Simmons, *The Railways of Britain: An Historical Introduction*, London, Routledge & Kegan Paul, 1961, p. 147.

64. Alfred W. Arthurton, "The Railways of Japan," *The Railway Magazine* 15 (Dec. 1904), p. 503.

65. Albert Fishlow, *American Railroads and the Transformation of the Antebellum Economy*, Harvard Economic Studies, Cambridge, Mass., Harvard University Press, 1965, p. 308.

66. Chandler and Tedlow, *op. cit.*, p. 183.

67. "Japanese Railways from a Military Point of View," *Japan Weekly Mail*, 21 Oct. 1893, p. 466.

68. *Tōyō keizai shinpō*, 1900, p. 463, cited in Sakurai Tōru, "Nippon tetsudō kabushiki kaisha no shihon chikuseki jōken to kokuyūka mondai (1): kokka dokusen seisei ni kansuru junbiteki kōsatsu" (Capital accumulation and the problem of nationalization in the Nippon Railway Company), *Osaka shidai ronshū*, No. 25 (1976), p. 73.

69. *Tetsudō kyoku nenpō*, 1907, appendix, pp. 22, 24, 41.

70. "Sir William Bisset," *Japan Weekly Mail*, 24 May 1902, p. 560.

71.   "Bisset-shi no honpō tetsudō hyō" (Mr. Bisset views Japanese rail-
      ways), *Tōyō keizai shinpō*, 5 June 1902, pp. 29–30.
72.   *Teikoku tetsudō yōkan*, pp. 85–108. The Nippon had actually followed
      the seemingly perverse course of simplifying its structure as it ex-
      panded, reducing the number of its departments from seven in
      1899 to four in 1903 and finally to three in 1904. Yamada Eitarō,
      "Nippon tetsudō kabushiki kaisha enkakushi" (History of the Nip-
      pon Railway Company), pt. 2, pp. 255, 331, 363, Hitotsubashi Uni-
      versity Library, Tokyo.
73.   *Teikoku tetsudō yōkan*, pp. 85–108.
74.   Sakurai, 1980, *op. cit.*, p. 59.
75.   Shibusawa, *op. cit.*, p. 223.
76.   For example, in fiscal 1900, when the Railway Bureau began to
      report complete data on the capital structure of the private railways
      in operation, the aggregate paid-up capital of those firms accounted
      for 79% of their total capital. *Tetsudō kyoku nenpō*, 1900, Teishin
      Shō Tetsudō Kyoku, 1901, pp. 55, 203.
77.   Hoshino Takao, "Nippon tetsudō kaisha to Dai 15 kokuritsu ginkō
      (2)," (Nippon Railway Company and the 15th National Bank),
      Musashi daigaku ronshū, Vol. 19 (Aug. 1971), p. 19; *Nihon teikoku
      tōkei nenkan* (Annual Statistics of Imperial Japan), 1902, ed. Naikaku
      Tōkei Kyoku, 1903, p. 704.
78.   Gourvish, *op. cit.*, p. 188.
79.   Burgess and Kennedy, *op. cit.*, p. 802.
80.   Sugiyama Kazuo, "Meiji 30 nendai ni okeru tetsudō kaisha no dai
      kabunushi to keieisha" (Large stockholders and managers of railway
      companies in the Meiji 30s), *Seikei daigaku keizai gakubu ronshū*, Vol. 7
      (1977), p. 160.
81.   Takechi Kyōzō, "Nisshin senso go tetsudō kaisha no kabunushi to
      sono keifu" (Stockholders of railway companies after the Sino-
      Japanese War), *Seitō joshi tanki daigaku kiyō*, No. 6 (Sept. 1976),
      pp. 1–61; Sugiyama, 1977, *op. cit.*; Steven J. Ericson, "Railroads in
      Crisis: The Financing and Management of Japanese Railway Com-
      panies during the Panic of 1890," in William D. Wray, ed., *Manag-
      ing Industrial Enterprise: Cases from Japan's Prewar Experience*, Cam-
      bridge, Mass., Council on East Asian Studies, Harvard University,
      forthcoming.
82.   *Teikoku tetsudō yōkan*, passim.
83.   Sugiyama, 1975, *op. cit.*, p. 57.
84.   "Dai kabunushi ichiranhyō" (List of major stockholders of railways),

Tetsudō zasshi (retitled *Tetsudō* from No. 19), No. 5 (June 1896), pp. 21–23, No. 7 (July 1896), pp. 23–24, No. 8 (July 1896), pp. 22–24, No. 26 (Nov. 1896), pp. 30–32; "Jūyaku kachō ichiranhyō," (List of directors and presidents), *Tetsudō zasshi*, No. 9 (July 1896), pp. 29–31, No. 10 (July 1986), pp. 23–26. The definition of "major stockholders" ranges from owners of 100 or more shares in the case of the smaller companies to owners of 1,000 or more in that of the largest firm.

85. *Ibid.*; Sugiyama, 1977, *op. cit.*, p. 157.
86. *Tetsudō senjin roku*, p. 268.
87. *Ibid.*, p. 18.
88. Ōe Soten, "Watashi no onjin Tanaka-san" (My benefactor Mr. Tanaka), in *Tanaka Gentarō ōden*, cited in *Nihon kokuyū tetsudō 100 nenshi*, Vol. 4, p. 450.
89. Hoshino Takao, "Nippon tetsudō kaisha to Dai Jūgo kokuritsu ginkō (3)," *Musashi daigaku ronshū*, Vol. 19 (March 1972), p. 138.
90. Miyano Takeo, "Tetsudō kokuyū hō ni yoru shisetsu tetsudō no baishū to sonogo (Taishō zenhanki goro made) no sochi" (Railway nationalization law and the acquisition of private railways), *Kōeki jigyō kenkyū*, Vol. 24 (Feb. 1973), pp. 107, 109.
91. Cited in "Nationalization of the Railways," *Japan Weekly Mail*, 17 March 1906, p. 279.

Comment

Hiroshi Itagaki
Saitama University

Professor Ericson's paper seems to me to present a well-balanced survey of the issues concerning the rudimentary professionalization of railroad management in Meiji Japan. I shall limit my comments to posing questions or pointing out problems which I think need further inquiry. My questions are related to: (1) the separation of management from ownership and the emergence of professional managers; (2) skill formation within enterprises; and (3) the impact of the state railways on other private businesses.

Ericson ascribes conservative investment strategies and the backwardness of Meiji private railroads as a whole mainly to the fact that "the separation of management from ownership and the emergence of a professional managerial class were still in their early stages." He states that the top managements of the railroads overlapped and was dominated by risk-avoiding and short-run, profit-seeking investors, individuals and institutions alike. The exceptions were the San'yō Railway and the Kyushu Railway, which employed full-time career managers, developed relatively advanced managerial hierarchies, and adopted positive investment strategies under Mitsubishi's auspices.

I agree with Ericson that the existence of professional and sophisticated management is in general a prerequisite for rational corporate decision-making based on a long-range view. However, the separation of management from ownership itself or even sophisticated administration does not necessarily result in progressiveness and longer time horizons on the part of business operations. Many U.S. companies are allegedly seeking short-run earnings, sacrificing investment that reinforces long-term positions, in spite of the separation of management from ownership and the most sophisticated and best-organized managements in the world. In U.S. companies, stockholders urge managers to improve current earnings and increase dividend payments as a token of successful management.

On the contrary, many Japanese corporations today are freed from domination by stockholders; nevertheless, these firms have close relationships with the financial institutions which hold the former's equity and have provided funds for business expansion. A common view is that it is the financial assistance from the "group" banks that enables corporations to pursue aggressive policies and long-term growth, even at the sacrifice of short-term earnings.

Another prominent example as evidence against the separation of management from ownership assumption is provided by the Korean zaibatsu. Under the leadership of owner-capitalists, whether they be founders or second-generation owners, large Korean conglomerates have developed aggressive strategies of business expansion.

These examples show that granted efficient and developed managerial organization, it is the character of stockholders or of the relationship between investors and managers which dominates or influences corporate decision-making. The sharp contrast between the San'yō and Kyushu railways and the Nippon Railway appears to result from the difference in strategy between the leading stockholders, that is, Mitsubishi for the former two railways and the 15th National Bank for the latter company.

Ericson indicates that Meiji railroad companies, in recruiting top as well as middle managers, gradually shifted from outside sources, including the government bureaucracy and the state railways, to new graduates from universities and higher schools. My second question is the reason why the railroad companies preferred to draw managerial talent from within rather than from without. Of course, as noted by Ericson, the supply-side factor, that is, the development of the higher educational system in Meiji Japan, was important. I suppose, however, that the demand-side factor also played a considerable part. Did the method of skill formation of

Japanese railways not lead to their preference to recruit talent directly from higher schools and universities rather than to hire staff from other firms and the state railways?

Finally, the author evaluates the influence of relatively advanced managerial practices in such firms as the San'yō and Kyushu on the administration of less sophisticated enterprises in other sectors of the economy. Ericson concludes that the direct impact of railroad companies on other private businesses was muted by the railway nationalization of 1906 and 1907 and that the state railway was the major beneficiary through the absorption of managerial talent. Ericson confines his evaluation too much to the direct impact or managerial spinoff from the railways to other enterprises. It seems necessary to take account of the indirect impact, namely, the demonstration effect of the state railways for the operation of nationwide and multidivisional enterprises. In connection with the managerial impact, we should also consider that the state railways played a key role in technological transfer to the suppliers, which consisted of the various machine and material industries.

Response

Steven J. Ericson

Professor Itagaki raises some important points. First of all, I agree with his qualifier that ultimately what determined whether a given railroad company pursued progressive, growth-oriented policies was not so much the nature of the management structure as it was the character of the principal owner. The adoption of positive investment strategies depended on the owner's promotion of enterprising career administrators rather than on the separation of management from ownership per se.

Secondly, Itagaki points out the need to consider demand-side factors in explaining the changing patterns of managerial recruitment in the private railroads. As he suggests, the growing complexity and specialization of railway administration may well have necessitated the development of managers with firm-specific skills. Also, the direct recruitment and in-house training of college or higher school graduates may have been a way of combating high management turnover by fostering identification with the firm. But these are issues that bear further investigation.

Finally, Itagaki correctly states that in order to grasp the full impact of Meiji railroads on other enterprises, one ought to consider not only managerial spinoff, but also the indirect influence of the railways on other industries. In addition to the kinds of effects he mentions, one might point to the paternalistic labor management system instituted by the government railways after the nationalization, which served as a model for many private businesses. How much of this post-nationalization impact represented a legacy of the purchased railroad companies, however, remains to be seen.

The Growth of White-Collar Employment in Relation to the Educational System

Ryōichi Iwauchi
Meiji University

White-collar workers—employees who do not own capital or the means of production—are the earliest manifestation of the new middle class and first appear during industrialization. The course of industrialization varies among societies, as does the extent to which the old middle class of entrepreneurs who own small amounts of capital and employ small numbers of workers continues as a distinct social stratum.

After the Meiji Restoration, we can observe two characteristics in the rise of white-collar workers in modern Japan. First, the public sector established its hiring practices before the private sector, even before the manufacturing industry, because in order to catch up quickly with modern nations, the Meiji government promoted industrialization, importing Western technologies and institutions. The Ministry of Industry (Kōbushō, from 1870 to 1885) was established for this purpose. The ministry employed Western engineers and scholars as well as supervisors and foremen, and Western instructors to train Japanese engineers, managers, and translators. Second, most early manufacturing facilities, especially those in the private sector, began with a smaller number of executives and managers, compared to manual workers, in contrast to their Western counterparts. Often, there was no clear distinction between middle-level managers and executives, on the one hand, and general managers and capitalists on the other. In the early stage of Japan's industrialization, the division of labor in industrial organizations was not fully formed. Consequently, the functions of middle management were not clearly distinguished, and white-collar workers as a distinct stratum had not yet developed.

This paper describes the growth of white-collar workers in modern Japan by focusing on (1) the development of engineers and engineering-related occupations; and (2) the increase of non-technical white-collar workers and the subsequent formation of a hierarchical status system among them. It will refer, in particular, to the role of the educational system in the development of industrial organization and the formation of the so-called Japanese management system.

I. The Planning of Technical Manpower Policy

While technology was being imported, the employment of Western scientists and engineers in educational and manufacturing facilities was inevitable, and their contributions were highly valued. But at the same time, as emphasized in the prospectus of the Institute of Technology (Kōbu Daigakkō), an educational institution affiliated with the Ministry of Industry, Japan "should not rely indefinitely on foreign engineers and Japanese people must acquire their own technology."[1]

During the Meiji era, foreign scholars at higher educational institutions in Japan lectured in their own languages. Students, after studying at these institutions, went abroad for further study, and many of them eventually replaced foreign professors and engineers on their return to Japan. A large number of Western scientists and engineers were employed by the central government during the 1870s, their numbers reaching 527 in 1875 (205 were in engineering and 322 in teaching and other fields).[2]

The government tried to replace these foreigners with Japanese by providing training at higher technological institutions and by sending them for study abroad. The Institute of Technology, founded by the Ministry of Industry in 1877, was incorporated into the Imperial University (Tokyo) as the College of Technology, and 435 professional engineers graduated by 1877 with degrees in civil, mechanical, and electrical engineering, shipbuilding, architecture, applied chemistry, mining, and metallurgy. The Tokyo Craftsman's School (Tokyo Shokkō Gakkō), founded in 1881, changed its name in 1890 to the Tokyo Technical School (Tokyo Kōgyō Gakkō) and

TABLE 1   Graduates from Higher Technological Institutions.

Institution	Number of graduates			Total
	Up to 1880	1881–89	1890–1900	
Tokyo Imperial University[1]	103	332	650	1,085
Kyoto Imperial University[2]	—	—	39	39
Tokyo College of Technology[3]	—	140	615	755
Others	—	—	162	162
Total	103	472	1,466	2,041

[1] Before 1885, called the College of Technology (Kōbu Daigakkō).

[2] From its College of Science and Technology.

[3] Includes graduates from the Tokyo Craftsman's School and the Tokyo Technical School.

was upgraded in 1901 to an institution of higher education, the Tokyo College of Technology (Tokyo Kōtō Kōgyō Gakkō). The second imperial university, established in Kyoto in 1897, included a college of science and technology. By 1900, over 2,000 engineers had graduated from these institutions (see Table 1).

Before and after the establishment of these institutions, both government-sponsored and privately funded students studied at Western institutions of higher education. Of the 439 students who went abroad between 1875 and 1908, about 60% specialized in natural or applied science or technology, far exceeding those in the humanities and social sciences.[3] However, another group had previously studied abroad, with the intention of introducing Western technology; they had left during the 1860s and 1870s, without having attended Japanese post-secondary schools.[4] The Tokugawa shogunate and local clans sent gifted youth to Western countries in the 1860s as did the Meiji government in the decade after the Restoration. Some of the latter went abroad after attending Japanese institutions of higher education. After 1890, the Meiji government provided opportunities to learn Western technology by increasing enrollment in technical institutions and, gradually, by establishing technical colleges in smaller cities, especially in the late Meiji era. We can infer that the government was acting on a plan to produce technical manpower in a short period of time. In fact, in establishing the Tokyo Craftsman's School, it was explicitly stated that it planned to produce this type of manpower in order to "set up [a manufacturing] industry" in preparation for a period of accelerated industrial growth.[5]

Graduate engineers from domestic as well as foreign institutions played a role in promoting "productive industry" (*shokusan kōgyō*) in the Meiji era and, having knowledge of Western technology during the first stage of Japanese industrialization, they formed something of an elite group. It was decades before white-collar workers constituted a substantial part of the occupational structure in industrial organizations, because factories with small numbers of the technical elite and large numbers of manual workers continued to be common.

II. The Dominance of Graduate Officials in the Hierarchical Systems

Industrial organizations in the public sector had a detailed ranking system with a hierarchical range of statuses, especially in the period of *Dajōkan-sei*, a quasi-monarchy or government by Council of State. In early Meiji times, the ranks comprised 15 classes, the highest of which was called number one rank (*ittō*). Below the fifteenth rank was another, that of out-of-rank employee (*tōgairi*), itself divided into classes. Out-of-rank employees were outside the rigid hierarchical status system prescribed by government code. Their status was ambiguous (neither permanent nor temporary), though they might aspire to enter the hierarchical system after years of good service. The rank of *ittō* corresponded to the highest status in public administration. Some employees in lower ranks were junior managers and clerical staff and were paid monthly salaries. Even out-of-rank employees in relatively high statuses could receive monthly salaries because their responsibilities focused on supervision and control of the labor force.

Ranks were distinguished by salary, and sometimes also by title. For example, in 1877, one of the ranks among senior public officials comprised three status titles. In other cases, a job title comprised a wider range of ranks. For example, technical staff and workers in government manufacturing facilities were divided into three ranks—

senior engineer (*gishi*), junior engineer or technician (*gishu*), and technical worker (*gisei*), each of which was itself divided into upper, middle, and lower levels. Moreover, each level was divided into several sublevels, reflecting salary differentials. The salary of an upper technician with number one rank was higher than the salary of another with the same title, but with number two rank.

After the transformation of the public administration system from that of *Dajōkan-sei* to a cabinet system in 1885, public officials were reorganized into a multi-layered stratification, and new personnel were to be hired from institutions of higher education. Before 1885, the highest positions in public administration were occupied by the former warrior class (samurai), especially those from powerful clans (*han*). This illustrates the transformation from old values to the new ideology of meritocracy, in which educational achievement became a criterion in awarding occupational status. Accordingly, professional careers became more important than the ideology of the early Meiji leaders, which derived from the samurai ethos. One of the social bases for the older ethos had thus eroded by 1885, as shown in Table 2. While in the 1870s, descendants of the former samurai class accounted for about three-quarters of students at Tokyo University, this proportion declined after 1881 as higher education was gradually opened to other classes.[6]

Under the cabinet system, the appointment of three major posi-

TABLE 2   Students at Tokyo University in the Early Meiji Era: percentage by social status.

Year	Nobles	Ex-samurai	Commoners
1878	0.6	73.9	25.5
1879	0.5	77.7	21.8
1880	0.9	73.6	25.5
1881	0.0	51.8	48.2
1882	0.1	49.1	50.8
1883	0.1	52.9	47.0
1884	0.2	50.2	49.6
1885	0.2	51.7	48.1

Source: Unesco, *Technological Development in Japan*, Unesco: Paris, 1971, p. 105.
Notes: Figures from 1878 to 1880 are for the Colleges of Law, Science, and Literature; those from 1881 to 1885 include the College of Medicine.

tions—two senior ones (*chokunin-kan* and *sōnin-kan*) and a junior one (*hannin-kan*)—more clearly defined a career ladder system for public officials. *Chokunin-kan*, comprising the prime minister and ministers, were appointed directly by the emperor. Graduates of the Imperial University were appointed *hannin-kan* upon entry into a ministry and promoted to *sōnin-kan* after several years of service. Until 1897, the Imperial University in Tokyo was the only accredited state university, and graduates of other institutions were not regarded as qualified for public service. One of the earliest graduates of the Tokyo Craftsman's School, in 1886, recalled an episode during his career in public service:

> I was employed at the Ministry of Agriculture and Commerce (*Nō-shōmu-shō*). Though I was paid 25 yen (a month) as a starting salary, I was not given a raise for a long time. In those days, due to the omnipotence of the law school (*hōka bannō*), engineers were not taken seriously .... My salary was ¥25 for ten years. Later, looking over my diploma, I noticed it had been signed by the President of the Imperial University, because in 1885 the Craftsman's School was like an attached school. Armed with this diploma, I pleaded vigorously with my superior [for a salary increase], and eventually I was promoted to engineer (*gishi*) in 1895.[7]

This episode might be enough to explain the following system of organization:

1.   Graduates of educational institutions other than the Imperial University were paid according to the salary level of *hannin-kan* or its lower ranks. According to the Decree of Salaries of Junior Government officials (*Hannin-kan Kantō Hōkyū-rei*), a number nine *hannin-kan* technician was paid ¥25 a month. They had to remain below rank number six for at least three years, and above rank number five for four years.[8] Promotion from these ranks in as few as nine years was exceptional.

2.   Completion of courses at the College of Law of the Imperial University conferred on graduates privileged status as well as a degree. It was widely accepted that graduation from this college was the road to high government officialdom (*kōtō-kan*), as *chokunin-kan* and *sōnin-kan*.

Revisions of the Decree of Public Officials resulted, after the

1890s, in strengthening the dominance of graduates of the Colleges of Law of the imperial universities. They were exempted from certain promotion examinations, while those from other colleges with equivalent degrees were not. The most prestigious positions were gradually occupied by graduates from the College of Law of the Tokyo Imperial University, who monopolized the administrative machinery of Japanese society. The numbers of employees in central government rapidly increased early in the 20th century, but those in the uppermost statuses were very few: a steady 0.3% for *chokunin-kan* in some years and less than 0.5% for *sōnin-kan* after 1906 (see Table 3). The proportion of *hannin-kan* varied, depending on the number of short-term or temporary employees (*koin*) and manual workers (*yōin*). The number of *hannin-kan* exceeded 105,000 in 1921, increasing to more than 145,000 in 1923. It was about 134,000 in 1926, decreasing to a low of 112,000 until 1930.

The numerical change of *hannin-kan* reflected the growth of white-collar workers. A comparatively small number, for example, those recruited from universities and assigned to the upper ranks of *hannin-kan*, could be promoted to *sōnin-kan*, a *kōtō-kan* position. Though most spent their careers in this status, some came from *koin* and *yōin* who, after long service, could be promoted to *hannin-kan*. Thus, the status of *hannin-kan* was comprised, in its upper ranks, of candidates for *sōnin-kan* and in its lower ranks of those for whom this level of service was their terminal status.

Accordingly, this status included a wide range of employees with

TABLE 3   Employees in Central Government by Status.

Year	Status (percentage)				Total
	Chokunin-kan	Sōnin-kan	Hannin-kan	Others	
1901	0.3	5.4	46.0	48.3	97,616
1906	0.3	4.4	34.8	60.5	137,806
1911	0.3	3.2	31.7	64.8	196,251
1916	0.3	3.8	23.4	72.5	224,883
1921	0.3	3.6	32.0	64.1	328,760
1926	0.3	3.6	37.8	58.3	354,777

Source: Compiled from Shōwa Dōjin Kai, *Wagakuni Chingin Kōzō no Shiteki Kōsatsu*, Shiseidō, 1960, pp. 368–69.

more than ten ranks, or strata, of salaries. This was the prototype and source of the new middle class of Japanese society. Indeed, private sector organizations developed a dual system of personnel management for white-collar workers and a labor management system for blue-collar workers. This system segregated the two groups—*shokuin* as white-collar workers, *shokkō*, or *kōin*, as blue-collar workers—after the model of the system in public administration, especially in government-run factories.

The diversification of functions in industrial organizations required increasing the proportions of managers as well as of white-collar workers. In public administration, functions were facilitated by the expansion and development of the division of labor. From the earliest periods, administrative functions in government developed in detail with the diversification of hierarchical levels, such as departments, sections, and sub-sections (*kyoku, bu, ka,* and *kakari*).

In the private sector, the management of companies, especially of manufacturing facilities, did not expand until the 1880s, when government-run factories and mines were sold to private companies by a code for the disposal of government enterprises. The private companies, after acquiring these enterprises which had attained high productivity, changed their characteristics from *seishō* to *zaibatsu*.

Some of them tried to procure human resources by hiring graduates from institutions of higher education. As the organizations of these companies became more consolidated both in quantity and in quality, they started to employ clerical workers, superintendents, and professionals who subsequently formed a certain kind of bureaucratic organization. The typology of such industrial organizations differed from one company to another. One typology developed originally from the basis of an indigenous system of premodern enterprises, another was partially influenced by the system of the public sector.

III. Mismatch in the Labor Market

It is quite difficult to maintain balanced relationships between the supply and demand of white-collar employees in the modern Japanese labor market. In the earliest stage of the establishment of the modern educational system, after 1872, one of the Meiji leaders,

Itō Hirobumi, later a prime minister, emphasized the importance of practical learning during the critical discussion on the prevailing situation and the policies required to build a new nation. He argued that studying industrial technology for practical use was more constructive than participation in public affairs in any kind of social movement.[9]

During the revision and amendment of the Code of Education promulgated in 1872, ideas on professional and occupational education were proposed, with some implemented as early as 1873, with the Additional Two Chapters to the Code of Education (Gakusei Nihen Tsuika). Though its provisions confounded the concept of professional and occupational schools, a few institutions for technology and commerce were established around 1880. These can be considered early experiments, preceding industrialization, in anticipation of and an investment in a strategic manpower policy. Production of industrial manpower was, of course, required in preparation for rapid social change in the early Meiji period.

However, the concerns of educational institutions and of industrial demand were based on different dimensions. While in the 1890s secondary and tertiary industrial sectors remained immature, the establishment of technical and commercial schools resulted in an oversupply of manpower. However, rapid growth in these sectors of industry caused a manpower shortage. From the late 19th to the 20th century, a complex balance between education and industry prevailed in this way, especially involving the supply of white-collar workers in the private sector. The following are some of the changing relationships between school and industry in this respect.

1. Low output of educated manpower

By the 1890s, most private companies had a smaller number of white-collar employees than government-owned companies, even in the companies that had been transferred from government to private management. For example, Mitsubishi Nagasaki shipyard started private operation in 1884 with 40 non-manual workers, including 26 hourly workers, and 766 manual workers.[10] When Kawasaki Shōzaemon purchased and took over the Hyōgo Shipyard, formerly managed by the government, he discharged 19 non-manual workers and over 150 manual workers. Private factories taken over from government strictly pursued profits and rationalization of productivity by decreasing the number of employees and providing for overtime work and the renewal of equipment.[11]

Consequently, these companies did not accept many graduates from higher educational institutions, except for a few from the Tokyo Craftsman's School. Some foreign engineers, whose contracts with government-owned organizations expired, were hired by private companies. In this way, industry managed by procuring only a small number of technical personnel.

As for management, some companies originated in the Tokugawa period; others started in early Meiji. The former had to induce their managers to adapt to new systems. These individuals had been educated in the Chinese classics, hardly relevant to modern management, but they acquired modern or Western management skills by practical experience. With authority over the subordinates they directly supervised, they succeeded in establishing new management techniques without actually organizing a system of middle management.

This is why the establishment of formal education for management and business was delayed. The idea of commercial education at higher levels as well as technical education was officially announced in the Additional Two Chapters to the Code of Education in 1873. However, the code did not inspire the creation of any commercial education institution, and the three that were established were private schools. Mori Arinori, later minister of education, founded the Institute of Commercial Law (Shōhō Kōshū-jo) in 1875. He tried to develop it into a professional commerce school as in the United States and invited an American scholar from there. But its administration was transferred to Tokyo city in 1876. Hyōgo Prefecture established the Kobe Institute of Commerce (Kobe Shōgyō Kōshūjo) in 1878; and in the same year, the Mitsubishi Commerce School (Mitsubishi Shōgyō Gakkō) opened (but closed just four years later). Although the Revised Education Ordinance (Kaisei Kyōiku-rei, 1879) provided for a school of commerce as an authorized institution, the Ministry of Education did not assist in its establishment. Three additional institutions were started with private funds: Osaka Institute of Commerce (Osaka Shōgyō Kōshūjo) (1880), Yokohama School of Commercial Law (Yokohama Shōhō Gakkō, 1882), and Niigata Commercial School (Niigata Shōgyō Gakkō, 1883). However, because they were dependent on donations, these schools were maintained with some difficulty.[12] Finally, they were transferred to the control of local governments, which were better able to finance them.

In 1890, the number of graduates from commercial schools as well as the Imperial University was still small. Graduates focused their aspirations on obtaining positions in government, especially in the central government. To become a government official (*kan'in*) implied success in obtaining social status, privileged power, and a high salary. Positions in private industry were less attractive, and many companies did not seek to employ these graduates. This situation of low supply and demand for educated manpower in private employment continued for decades.

2. The Employment of Graduates in the Private Sector

Nakamigawa Hikojirō employed a large number of graduates from Keiō Gijuku University, an institution not officially defined as a university in the educational code but which nonetheless used the name. This was the beginning of the employment of large numbers of graduates in the private sector. Nakamigawa did not ask his uncle, Fukuzawa Yukichi, the rector of Keiō Gijuku University, to send students, but relied on personal contacts. In this way, he sought capable youth for staff positions. Before joining Mitsui, Nakamigawa had studied in England for four years, worked at English schools, the Ministry of Foreign Affairs, a newspaper (*Jiji Shimpō*) founded by Fukuzawa, and San'yō Railways Company as president. In this varied career, he trained himself as a professional manager, and he was an intellectual, well informed on Western affairs.

As an executive of three Mitsui companies—Mitsui Bank, Mitsui Mining Company, and Mitsui Trading Corporation—Nakamigawa carried out decisive reforms in their management, as well as in other firms. Implementing a grand strategy to expand Mitsui from a commercial to a manufacturing company, he bought, and sometimes absorbed, many cotton spinning enterprises, electric companies, paper mills, and mines. Among them were such famous firms as Kanegafuchi Bōseki (Kanebō), Ōji Seishi, Shibaura Seisakujo, Hokkaido Tankō Kisen, and Miike Tankō. He employed educated staff for these as well as Mitsui's companies. Though some were immediately promoted to executive positions, most worked as clerks or junior managers upon employment in these firms. Table 4 shows graduates of Keiō Gijuku University employed by Nakamigawa, mostly in Mitsui Bank between 1891 and 1896, by years of employment between graduation and entry into Mitsui. Those who later became outstanding executives included such figures as Wada Toyoharu, Fujiyama Raita, Mutō Sanji, Ikeda Nariaki, Fujiwara Ginjirō, and Asabuki Eiji, all of whom began as junior executives (except for Asabuki at Kanegafuchi Bōseki and two others who began as director and vice-director at Mitsui Bank).[13]

This pattern of employment of graduates from higher education had two aspects. First, employment began after a period of work elsewhere; in cases influenced by Nakamigawa, largely in journalism. Secondly, employment was influenced by academic cliquism as manifested in networks of alumni of the same school. For example, Masuda Takashi invited many graduates from Tokyo Commercial School (Tokyo Shōgyō Gakkō, formerly Shōhō Kōshūjo, later Tokyo College of Commerce) to Mitsui Trading Corporation (Mitsui Bussan).

These ties between school and industry were exceptional because in the early decades of this century, the most capable students preferred to seek employment in government, and only growing enterprises could afford to employ graduates from institutions of higher education. For example, Yasuda Hozensha, the central agency of Yasuda zaibatsu, started a training system (renshū-sei seido) in 1907. Its purpose was to train candidates for managerial roles,

TABLE 4   Keiō Gijuku Graduates Employed by Mitsui, by Years of Employment before Entry, 1891–96.

Years	3	4	5	6	7	8	9	10	11	12+
Number	2	0	3	1	1	2	2	0	1	6

Source: Sakamoto Fujiyoshi, Nihon Koyōshi, Chūō Keizaisha, Tokyo, 1977, pp. 176–82.

screening applicants by interview and examination. Yasuda Hozen-sha advertised in newspapers for graduates of middle schools. Admission was highly selective: one in 15 to 30 applicants was chosen. After a year, trainees (*renshū-sei*) were evaluated by examination, they were assigned to one of three ranks, and their salaries were determined accordingly. This system was carried on by Yasuda Zenzaburō, the vice-president, until his departure in 1918.[14]

By the end of the Meiji era in 1912, the public educational system was fairly well consolidated both at the secondary and advanced levels. The curricula and accreditation of technical and commercial schools at the secondary level were integrated in 1894 by the Ordinance of Industrial Education (Jitsugyō Kyōiku Rei). As to technical education at the secondary level, the central government promulgated the Decree of Apprentice Schools (Totei Gakkō Kitei) in 1894 in order to regulate the training institutions that had already established themselves. Most of these schools were local and dealt with such crafts as pottery, lacquerware, and wood-working. Initially, their purpose was to modernize traditional industries by introducing new technology and new apprenticeship systems. Those established after the Decree of 1894 added courses dealing with such subjects as machine engineering, electrical and chemical engineering, and architecture. These schools were included in the Technical School (*kōgyō gakkō*) system in 1899 at the level of secondary education by the Ordinance of Vocational Education (Jitsugyō Gakkō-rei). This ordinance also awarded official standing to the system of commercial and agricultural schools.

In post-secondary education, professional schools of medicine, foreign languages, arts, music, agriculture, technology, and commerce appeared in the late 19th century. They were authorized in 1901 to issue college diplomas by the Ordinance of Colleges (Semmon Gakkō-rei). Private universities excluded from the Ordinance of Imperial University also grew gradually. Most were established in the 1880s, except for Keiō Gijuku University, founded in 1858. Though Keiō emphasized the study of economics, others from their beginnings established departments of law and political science, adding economics and commerce and, later, science and technology.

In the early stages of development light industries, and later heavy industries, developed and expanded rapidly. They had to recruit large numbers of non-manual workers as well as manual workers and to employ people of varying backgrounds. However, the employment of graduates of secondary and post-secondary institutions was irregular. One reason for this is that job titles and descriptions were not clearly defined, especially in non-manual positions, a characteristic persisting to the present day. Consequently, the ladder system replaced the system of status hierarchy in which employees were placed according to their educational backgrounds. This is the origin of "degreeocracy in industry," an aspect of the Japanese management system. Another cause of the irregularity in employment of educated manpower was due to war booms and depressions, which made it difficult to pursue a coordinated personnel policy.

Occasionally, there was a glaring lack of balance between schools and industry. Since educational institutions could not supply appropriate manpower to industry in the requisite numbers, some companies had to create training programs. Mitsubishi Technical Preparatory School (Mitsubishi Kōgyō Yobi Gakkō) at Mitsubishi Nagasaki Shipyard was founded for this purpose in 1899, as was the Yawata Training School for Young Workers (Yawata Yōnen Shokkō Yōseijo) at Yawata Iron Works in 1908. Both schools were pioneers in the private sector's alternative to public technical education at the secondary level. It is generally accepted that these private institutions played a role in forming the so-called lifetime employment system, another important factor in the Japanese management system. But for at least a decade they contributed to neither the lifetime employment system nor development of the internal labor market, both of which were basic characteristics of Japanese management.

3. Bureaucratic Organization

In the Taishō period, after 1912, the economy made great strides, with extraordinary advances after the take-off phase in the chemical and heavy industries. To manage these growing organizations, companies diversified departments and sections by differentiated functions and multiple levels of control and management. Bureaucratic systems thus emerged in these large organizations,[15] and they were able to employ graduates of both secondary and higher educational institutions.

The growth of universities altered the supply of educated labor. Between 1886 and 1897, the Imperial University in Tokyo had been the sole university. By the end of the Taishō period, only four other imperial universities had appeared. On the recommendation of the Special Conference on Education (Rinji Kyōiku Kaigi), founded in 1917, the University Ordinance (Daigaku-rei) was promulgated in the following year, resulting in the upgrading of many private post-secondary institutions to university status. This ordinance also strengthened the research and education functions of the imperial universities by adding departments, chairs, and independent research institutes. Moreover, the conference announced a six-year plan to expand the number of students at professional universities to 20,000, including a project to increase the number of colleges of technology from eight to eighteen and colleges of commerce from five to twelve.

Reforms in technical and commercial education at the secondary level were also implemented after deliberations at the conference and other meetings. The Ordinance of Vocational Education in 1910 ended the apprentice schools and amalgamated them with technical schools. The commercial schools became equivalent to the level of the middle schools for general studies, with respect to required length of attendance and qualifications for admission. But political leaders and public officials made a point of downgrading graduates of secondary vocational schools, saying that they ought not to be proud of their educational achievements. These statements were typical of a situation in which those with academic achievements and skills were more highly regarded than those with skills learned in on-the-job training after completing compulsory education. In fact, the revised Ordinance of Vocational Education emphasized the importance of moral cultivation and civic education, reflecting current nationalistic ideology, as did a recommendation by the conference to introduce military training in vocational schools.

Educational opportunities expanded during the 1910s and 1920s. The attendance rates in higher education of comparable age cohorts rose from 0.5% in 1900 to 2.5% in 1920, while they rose from 2.9% in 1900 to 32.3% in 1925 for secondary education. Considering males only, these figures increased to 4.7% for higher education and 39.6% for secondary education.[16] These increases in attendance at post-compulsory educational institutions after 1925 changed both the labor market and the staffing of business organizations.

For a short period after World War I, prosperity continued, and the private sector could absorb graduates of these schools. Talented manpower with higher education levels found employment even in large companies. The attendance rate of male students in higher education was 3.0% in 1920, but graduates were fewer than 2.0% in the same year. The abrupt depression of 1929, together with a steep rise in prices and many bankruptcies, resulted in unemployment and poverty among both white- and blue-collar workers. The oversupply and underemployment of college and university graduates thus became a serious problem in the late 1920s and into the 1930s.

As a result of the complicated ladder system set up by the educational reforms recommended by the Special Conference on Education, the social strata of society came to be centered on educational careers. "Degreeocracy," or educational credentialism, as a means of evaluating people—in terms of length of school attendance and institutions attended—gradually came to prevail both in business and government. The first criterion of evaluation was length of attendance at school, reflecting the level of education attained. The second was the nature of the schools attended. Even at the same educational stage, those from the most distinguished school were regarded as an elite group and received not only prestige but higher salaries. For example, in the late Taishō era, the initial monthly salary at a Sumitomo company varied in terms of educational achievement (see Table 5).

Furthermore, multiple levels in the management organization developed along with detailed job status. Ōji Paper Mills (Ōji Seishi) had a rank-and-file system with five levels of manual workers, four of formal employee (shain), two of foreman, and six of manager. Qualifications for promotion were in terms of years of service at a given level, with further differentiation by educational background.

TABLE 5   Initial Monthly Salary by Educational Background.

State universities and colleges of engineering	¥90
State universities and other colleges	¥80
Colleges of Commerce of Tokyo and Kobe, Tokyo College of Technology, Waseda University, College of Science and Technology	¥70
Colleges of commerce other than Tokyo, Keiō Gijuku, and Waseda universities	¥65
College of Foreign Languages, Meiji University, Tokyo University of Agriculture	¥60
Kansai, Hōsei, Chūō, Rikkyō, and other private universities	¥45–55
Secondary education	¥35

Source: Magota Ryōhei, ed., *Nenkō Chingin no Ayumi to Mirai* (History and Future of Seniority Wage), Sangyō Rōdō Chōsajo, Tokyo, 1970, p. 92.

We must be cautious in analyzing the origins and meaning of the formation of the Japanese management system. The establishment of educational and training facilities in companies spread in the Taishō era. They certainly played a role in forming the Japanese management system. But these facilities, previously mentioned, that appeared in the late Meiji era at Mitsubishi Nagasaki Shipyard and Yawata Iron Works could not sustain a lifetime employment system, at least not in the early decades. Documents clearly record that these craftsmen's schools aimed at training skilled workers, foremen, and even technicians (*gijutsu-in*). The status of technician, though not clearly defined, was regarded as that of a white-collar worker. In the case of Yawata, newspaper advertisements for applicants stated that they could be promoted to technician after finishing these schools, appealing particularly to applicants who had just graduated from six years of primary school. At that time, four years of ordinary primary education were compulsory; the period of required education was extended to six years in 1907.

Those who completed the courses at these company schools left the factories after a few years because they realized that they could not be promoted to technician. In 1919, the dissatisfaction of students and alumni of these schools in Yawata exploded in labor unrest. In the Taishō era, educational and training facilities at Yawata and Nagasaki changed the system from an in-house school to train primary school graduates to agencies to train workers already employed who had worked for some years.[17] The lifetime employment system and the wage system (based on the length of service of manual laborers) gradually took shape in the 1920s. Yawata was one company that initiated such a system. Former Yawata employees in military service were invited to return to the company; their salaries were based on the length of their service in Yawata prior to their military service.[18]

White-collar workers (those appointed as officials or *kan'in*) in the public sector and formal employees (those who were salaried full time, and permanent, or *sei-shain*) in the private sector, were given privileges including promotion and salary increases. Those whose status was not yet permanent, the "semi-employees," were excluded from these privileges (this is a rough translation of the word *jun-shain* or *kōin* in the prewar private sector). However, the increase of semi-employees, many among them from secondary schools, gave impetus for a change in the personnel system and an improvement in their treatment.

In the course of the development of personnel administration designed for a wide range of employees, a clear distinction was gradually established between white-collar jobs and blue-collar jobs, primarily allocated by educational background. The type of school attended after compulsory education became very important at the starting points of their careers. After a few years of service, graduates from secondary schools could obtain jobs as *shain* even in large companies in the period at the turn of the century.

IV.   Changing Patterns of White-Collar Employment

We can trace the rise, growth, and change of white-collar workers in modern Japan from its industrialization to the 1930s as follows: At the early stage of the development of white-collar employment, a distinction existed between organizational procedures in the private sector in selecting, appointing, allocating, and promoting employees and those in public organizations. In public organizations, a status ladder of positions was linked to the stratified wage system with a broad range of hierarchical structure. In general, the wage system was composed of ranks from senior (number one) to junior (number fifteen). An upgrading within the same status group generally accompanied an increase in salary. Transfer from one status to a higher status within a company similarly caused inter-class mobility in society (like the change of the quasi-standing, *mibun*). Full-time salaried employees in government were stratified according to their social origin, capability, and length of service. Some of them could acquire the status of management through promotion. As organizations expanded, those who took the role of supervisor and of lower-management executed jobs designed to control manual workers. Subdivision of jobs and stratification of statuses accompanied the rise and growth of white-collar workers.

In the private sector, slow growth delayed the development of the size of the work force, division of labor, and the range of a hierarchical structure. Most of the companies were too pressed for capital to hire new employees, and the hiring of young people with post-compulsory school education helped to cut down costs. But some of them had the same wage system as the government had. For example, one of the representative companies of a former zaibatsu established a system with a ranking from number one to number fifteen from its start in 1875.[19]

The existence of a stratified wage system did not necessarily explicate the growth of white-collar workers. However, as the wage system with ranks extended to manual workers, this hierarchical structure of status and job required a concomitant growth in the organization's administrative function. In the process of bureaucratization of organizations, the administrative function to control rank-and-file employees became inevitable. The appearance of white-collar jobs could be the result of systematizing the maintainance of order in the workplace. Furthermore, clerical jobs became important as the process of diversification of functions in companies continued.

The pattern of white-collar employment changed in various aspects through industrialization. During these stages, the characteristics of white-collar workers gradually shifted from tradition-oriented to rationality-oriented. These characteristics seem to be tolerably vague and are difficult to clarify because, on the one hand, the combination of tradition and rationality developed during a period of transition and, on the other hand, the influence of modern tradition shaped this particular phenomenon. I will trace some aspects of changing patterns of white-collar employment from this viewpoint.

First, the attributes of white-collar workers changed during the process of industrialization. By the middle of the Meiji era, around the 1890s, the power and authority of the ex-samurai class continued to be strong, and those who were descendants of the warrior class had more opportunities to secure white-collar jobs as well as senior status in government and in private companies, and to be eligibile for and have access to higher education. This monopoly over opportunity in terms of one's social status changed as equal opportunities became available to other groups. The modern school system inaugurated in 1872 played an important role in equalizing the occupational opportunity as well as educational opportunity available to all people. Although the opportunity for higher education was limited to those from relatively wealthy families, academic achievement became an important prerequisite to enter post-primary schools.

In modern times, educational achievement has replaced the dominance of the ex-samurai class, because graduation from institutions of secondary and tertiary education has begun to recognize the efforts and capabilities of the individual. Careers in education have been reevaluated from the standpoint of meritocracy; especially careers in higher education have been regarded as the "royal road" to acquire not only the status of higher civil service but also of senior management in the private sector. At the first stage in organizing the school system, those who graduated from universities and colleges were conferred the highest value by virtue of their scarcity. But in the course of expansion of educational opportunity, the scarcity value of higher educational background gradually diminished, except perhaps for the graduates of the Tokyo and other prestigious imperial universities. The hierarchical structure of educational institutions, including both the prestige at the same educational level (as in the ranking of universities) and at different educational levels (the stratum from university to college, professional school and secondary school), matched the status of companies. For example, while graduates from the more prestigious universities were eligible for the highest initial salaries, graduates from secondary vocational schools had to work as semi-employees, paid on an hourly basis, for several years to become even the lowest white-collar workers. This kind of match between type and level of education and its resulting status within companies developed in the 1910s. This phenomenon has been called "degreeocracy," or "educational credentialism," in industry.

Secondly, as the number of white-collar employees expanded and the range of statuse broadened, white-collar workers were divided into a couple of sub-groups. Those with managerial roles received positions in upper white-collar employment, and those in clerical jobs were placed in lower white-collar employment. The division of white-collar workers into separate sub-groups created the stratified organizational structure we see today.

This situation accelerated during the 1910s when Japanese companies were involved in the world-wide business cycle during and after World War I. The growth of big companies enabled them to absorb a large number of graduates from higher education when enrollment had expanded due to the new University Ordinance in 1918. During the period of business revival, higher education graduates could find jobs, but they lost their privileged status during the business recession, and even their standards of living went down. Unemployment among college graduates, due to over-supply and reduction of the work force of bankrupt firms became a serious social problem. Educated white-collar employees organized themselves into a white-collar union, primarily to raise their standards of living. The Council of White-Collar Unions, or Union of Salaried People in Tokyo (Tokyo Hōkyū Seikatsu-sha Dōmei Kyōgikai) started in 1919. The terms "middle class" (*chūsan kaikyū* or *chūtō kaikyū*) and "intellectual class' (*chishiki kaikyū*) appeared in the 1910s and were diffused in the 1920s in journalism. In a report by Tokyo City Office, "A Survey on Living Costs of the Middle Class" (Chūtō Kaikyū Seikei-hi Chōsa), a warning of the serious situation was issued. The middle class was in jeopardy of being differentiated into sub-classes. This report implied that the situation affected over-educated people. Subsequently, the government embarked on a plan to reorganize and recover from the business recession as a part of the nationwide economic policy of industrial rationalization.

Thirdly, companies did not describe the content of white-collar jobs in detail, and the division of labor in white-collar jobs did not develop in a strict sense. The distinction of the tasks of university and college graduates and those of secondary school graduates was not explicitly clear. Graduates of prestigious universities started in autonomous clerical positions. And, in accordance with company policy, even those from engineering colleges might have to perform tasks which were not directly related to engineering. The personnel policy usually required the assignment of employees to various jobs; they were reassigned several times throughout their careers. In the process of changing jobs, they might be assigned to a position in management. This is why the companies did not develop detailed job titles, job classifications, and job descriptions, which became the basis of the uniqueness of the Japanese management system, especially of the personnel management for white-collar employees. Such a system of modern tradition developed by the 1920s and has continued on even in contemporary Japanese companies.

NOTES

1. Unesco, *Technological Development in Japan*, Paris, Unesco, 1971, p. 107.
2. Ryoichi Iwauchi, "Institutionalizing Technical Manpower Formation in Meiji Japan," *The Developing Economies*, Vol. 9, No. 4 (1977), p. 424.
3. Ogata Hiroyasu, *Seiyō kyōiku inyū no hōto* (The Introduction of Western Education), Tokyo, Kōdansha, 1961, pp. 64–65.
4. Uchida Hoshimi, "Shoki ryūgaku gijutsusha to Ōbei no kagaku kyōiku kikan" (The engineers who studied abroad at the early stage and European and American institutions for techonological education) in *Tokyo keizai daigaku jinbun shizen kagaku ronshū*, 1985, pp. 116–19.
5. Tokyo Institute of Technology, *Tokyo kōgyō daigaku 60 nenshi* (A history of 60 years of the Tokyo Institute of Technology), Tokyo, 1940, p. 56.

6. Unesco, *op. cit.*, p. 107.
7. Tokyo Institute of Technology, *op. cit.*, p. 132.
8. Shōwa Dōjin-kai, *Waga kuni chingin kōzō no shiteki kōsatsu* (A historical study of wage structure in Japan), Tokyo, Shiseidō, 1960, pp. 343–45.
9. Nagai Michio, ed., *Nihon no kyōiku shisō* (Thoughts on education in Japan), Tokyo, Tokuma Shoten, 1967, p. 67.
10. Kobayashi Masaaki, *Nihon no kōgyōka to kangyō haraisage* (Japanese industrialization and the disposal of government enterprises), Tokyo, Tōyō Keizai Shinpōsha, 1977, pp. 240–41.
11. *Ibid.*, p. 273.
12. Sano Zensaku, *Nihon shōgyō kyōiku 50 nenshi* (50 years of commercial education in Japan), Tokyo University of Commerce, 1925, pp. 10–11.
13. Sakamoto Fujiyoshi, *Nihon koyōshi* (A history of employment in Japan), Vol. 1, Tokyo, Chūō Keizaisha, 1977, pp. 175–82; Nihon Keieishi Kenkyūjo, *Nakamigawa Hikojirō denki shiryō* (Biographical data on Nakamigawa Hikojirō), Tokyo, Tōyō Keizai Shinpōsha, 1969, pp. 299–304.
14. Sakamoto, *op. cit.*, pp. 80–81.
15. Hazama Hiroshi, *Nihon rōmu kanrishi* (A history of labor management in Japan), Tokyo, Diamondsha, 1964, pp. 194–95.
16. Ministry of Education, *Japan's Growth and Education*, Tokyo, 1962, p. 181.
17. For more details, see Ryoichi Iwauchi, "Industrial Training in Japan, 1890–1930," Parts 1 and 2, *Bulletin of Tokyo Institute of Technology*, No. 111 (1972) and No. 114 (1973).
18. Fujita Wakao, *Nihon rōdō kyōyaku-ron* (A theory of labor contracts in Japan), University of Tokyo Press, 1961, pp. 72–73.
19. Shōwa Dōjin-kai, *op. cit.*, p. 420.

Comment

Hoshimi Uchida
Tokyo Keizai University

Professor Iwauchi emphasized three points about the origin and development of middle managers or white-collar workers in modern Japan. First, the successively founded higher or secondary schools almost exclusively supplied the industry with these personnel. Second, the rank-and-file system in the government sector, which originated in the early Meiji period, was imitated by private companies to form a "ladder system" to rate and promote staff by school career and seniority, treating them as generalists rather than as specialists, which is one of the characteristic features of Japanese management. Thirdly, the "mismatch" between the supply and demand of manpower made peculiar organizations within the private firms in different generations.

The first and the third points are interrelated, and I essentially agree with Iwauchi. Table 1 shows the exponential growth of the employment of engineers who graduated from universities and technical colleges between 1880 and 1920.

By 1920, the industry had hired ten thousand graduate engineers, a number comparable to those in the contemporary advanced industrialized nations. And between 1890 and 1910, when the first fever for founding modern firms arose, we notice a mismatch in the excess in demand and scarcity of supply of technical personnel. But after 1920, when schools were supplying increasing numbers of graduates and when the industry fell stagnant, a reverse mismatch might easily have occurred.

The historical trend in the employment of school graduates also seems to support the second point of the report. Employment of engineers by the public sector apparently preceded the private

TABLE 1   Distribution of Engineers in Government and Private Industry.

Graduated from	Employed by	1880	1890	1900	1910	1920
University	Government	79	133	474	1,075	1,795
	Industry		90	385	846	3,230
	Total	79	223	859	1,921	5,025
Technical	Government		39	263	1,160	1,806
College	Industry		17	389	1,963	6,731
	Total		56	652	3,123	8,537
Total	Government	79	172	737	2,235	3,601
	Industry		107	774	2,809	9,961
	Total	79	279	1,511	5,044	13,562

Sources: Uchida H., "Shoki ryūgaku gijutsusha to Ōbei no kōgaku kyōiku kikan" (The engineers who studies abroad at the early stage and European and American institutions for technological education), *Tokyo keizai daigaku jinbun shizen kagaku ronshū* 71 (Dec. 1971); Uchida H., "Meiji kōki minkan kigyō no gijutsusha bunpu" (Employment of engineers in Japanese industry, 1900–1910), *Keiei shigaku* 14, No. 2 (Oct. 1979); Uchida H., "Taishō chūki minkan kigyō no gijutsusha bunpu" (Distribution of engineers in the changing business, 1920), *ibid.* 23, No. 1 (April 1988).

sector, and it is reasonable to suppose that the private firms introduced the same system of rating as established within the government, offering equivalent treatment to the technical elite who would switch from public service to private business.

Large-scale employment of executive personnel was, of course, a prerequisite to their grading by career within companies. Table 2 shows the increase in the employment of graduate engineers at individual zaibatsu enterprises.

From the table, we find that as early as 1900, mining companies or shipyards employed 20 to 30 technical staff, and by 1910 the number had tripled or quadrupled. Therefore, we can assume the "ladder system" in the private sector was ready in these firms some time between 1900 and 1910, and it is reasonable to suppose that the system had spread to every industry, at least in the zaibatsu groups, by 1920, earlier than Iwauchi's proposal, which identified the date as late 1920s.

His second point has other shortcomings: If the companies had copied the "ladder system" from the government, why did it work

TABLE 2   Number of Engineers Employed in the Zaibatsu Business.

	1900			1910			1920		
	U	C	T	U	C	T	U	C	T
Mitsui									
Trading	3	6	9	6	35	41	57	95	152
Mining	14	6	20	28	40	68	112	191	303
Shibaura	8	6	14	15	46	61	24	141	165
Ōji Paper	0	4	4	6	21	27	15	30	45
Nihon Steel				0	15	15	30	50	80
Kanebō	2	5	7	14	33	47	19	81	100
Total	27	27	54	69	170	239	247	588	835
Mitsubishi									
Mining	24	4	28	41	32	73	132	129	261
Shipyard	10	14	24	53	66	119	195	211	406
Paper				1	7	8	14	24	38
Asahi Glass				0	5	5	28	41	69
Ironwork							20	24	44
Total	34	18	52	95	110	205	389	429	818
Sumitomo									
Mining	11	7	18	17	30	47	35	56	91
Copper Rolling				0	4	4	26	43	69
Steel Foundry				4	11	15	18	22	40
Total	11	7	18	21	45	66	79	121	200
Furukawa	27	8	35	33	34	67	81	132	213

Notes: U=university graduates; C=college graduates; T=total.
Sources: Same as Table 1.

as well as other systems in other nations? How did imitation of the public system and mismatch in the personnel market lead to the generalistic service of white collars rather than to job specification? He did not address these questions, and we still have much research to do on the origin of Japanese management.

REFERENCE

H. Uchida, "Japanese Technical Manpower 1890–1930, a Statistical Survey," Report to the Second Anglo-Japanese Business History Conference, London, 1988.

Instead of Management: Internal Contracting and the Genesis of Modern Labor Relations

W. Mark Fruin
California State University, Hayward

The origins of 20th-century or modern management and its relationship to previous business practices in Japan are issues that seem to hinge largely on the character of labor relations during the latter half of the 19th century when internal or inside contracting was the main form of industrial relations. There is widespread agreement that the capital and technology supporting industrialization were for the most part newly created and recently imported and thus were not the critical indigenous catalysts in Japan's industrial development. This suggests the importance of labor and the management of labor as the crucial domestic factors for explaining Japan's notable adaptation to the factory system and modern management.

Two hypotheses have been offered concerning the importance of traditional labor in Japan's industrial modernization. Expansion of output in the traditional work force, both by a natural increase in numbers and by a willingness to work harder, longer, and better, is said to explain a good deal of Japan's initial increase in economic activity from the 17th to 19th century. However, this position, which might be labeled "the industrious revolution" hypothesis, stops short of asserting that expansion of the traditional economy had a direct effect on the establishment of a modern factory and managerial system. The two were complementary but not causally interrelated developments.

A second hypothesis is that traditional labor practices became the basis of modern industrial relations. This assertion has been considered and argued on two levels: institutionally and ideologically/interpersonally. Institutionally, it is asserted that the bureaucratic work structures of Meiji Japan, themselves often the stepchildren of Tokugawa institutions, laid the foundations for such labor practices as lifetime employment and seniority-based compensation. Ideologically/interpersonally, it is argued that the authority patterns of traditional, 19th-century labor relations continued during the 20th century in the form of feudal, authoritarian work relations. Together, institutional and ideological continuities from the past form the kernel of 20th-century industrial management practices.

It is the second of these hypotheses, namely that traditional labor practices became the basis for modern industrial relations, that concerns me. This position might be termed "the industrious restoration" hypothesis because it posits a return to, or, a continuation of traditional values long after the time of their origin.

Traditional labor practices might become the basis for modern practices in two ways. They could provide the root for modern practices without disappearing themselves, such as when modern practices branch off or are grafted onto traditional practices. A second possibility is for modern practices to originate in, but overwhelm and replace, traditional ones.

However, the fact that such practices as lifetime employment and seniority-based compensation were adopted widely only during the 20th century makes this hypothesis problematic for me. The possibility, therefore, that traditional labor practices did not become the foundation for modern practices should be considered as well. In this paper, I argue for a fairly sharp break from traditional sorts of work relations, including internal contracting, to more direct forms of labor management designed to cope with the new forms of technology and production that were appearing by the early 20th century.

These new forms were only weakly connected with past practices, even though a considerable degree of interaction occurred between them. This is not to say that traditional practices were unimportant. They provided an important foundation for the appearance of modern practices, and, even more importantly, it was through the

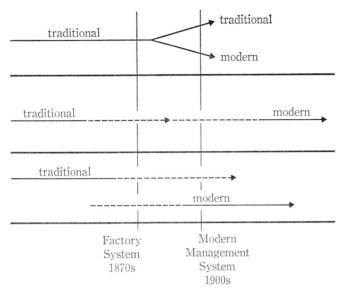

traditional

traditional

modern

traditional

modern

traditional

modern

modern

Factory
System
1870s

Modern
Management
System
1900s

FIG. 1

clash and combination of the old and the new that alternative forms of labor relations arose to deal with new industrial opportunities. This kind of dynamic interaction characterizes a transitional period in industrial management, something between traditional and modern, and it is especially pronounced from the 1870s to the 1920s. The three most likely pathways from traditional to modern labor practices during the course of what is known as the Industrial Revolution may be schematically represented in Figure 1.

I.   Method

In order to assess the degree to which traditional labor practices actually provided the institutional and ideological bases of modern industrial relations, and in order to characterize the nature of that process, the qualities of industrial management are examined in mining, shipbuilding, the food and beverage industry, and cotton textiles from the latter half of the 19th century to the early part of the 20th century.

All of these industries were amidst dizzying technological and organizational experimentation during this time. In terms of the style of industrial management, the scale and internal structure of work place organization, the nature of production technology, as well as the means of on-site energy generation and transmission, this period was clearly one of transition—something between what is generally called "traditional" and "modern." An underlying theme of this paper is that the models and paradigms that have been developed to analyze the institutions and practices of either the traditional or modern period do not reveal clearly the character of this transitional era where the processes of forming new practices in labor relations, rather than definitive and fully evolved structures, were crucial.

The nature of the transactions which bind employers and employees together is fundamental to this analysis. Labor historians who worry only about workers and business historians who concern themselves solely with managers miss the centrality of employment transactions as the key to understanding labor management. Employment transactions weld together labor's and management's separate interests, forcing each side to accommodate the other in the crucible of a common interest, that is getting the job accomplished.

An examination of 19th-century employment transactions and practices suggests that business enterprises chose indirect methods of labor employment because of the difficulties of concluding and enforcing direct labor contracts. Neither workers nor managers were accustomed to continuous employment in privately held enterprises, and neither had the skills, experiences, or attitudes suitable for industrial production. In the language of Professor Oliver Williamson's transaction cost approach, the costs of internalizing labor costs as an integral part of a firm's overall costs were too high.

II. Internal or Inside Contracting

Traditional labor practices in these four industries will be measured by the degree to which internal contracting was prevalent. Internal contracting, known in Japanese by a variety of phrases, such as *naya seido*, *shōya seido*, and more generally *naibu ukeoi*, was a system of management where persons other than the owners of the manufacturing or processing plant were hired to complete a cycle of work using the owners' premises and tools. Organizationally, internal contracting juxtaposed labor intermediaries between workers and owners. Intermediaries, with the knowledge and connections to get the job done, such as the ability to procure technical specialists, raw labor, and materials, contracted directly with owners for work and then hired and supervised those who actually did the work. In this way, owners and workers were kept apart, and the intermediaries profited from the separation.

Although other measures of traditional or modern might be employed, this paper's focus on labor relations and industrial management, motivates consideration of internal contracting as the crucial measure of a traditional or, at least, a transitional approach to employment transactions. Another advantage to this approach is that it allows a comparative treatment of these matters to be considered at some future point in time, because internal contracting was a widespread practice in Western industry at about the same time. But, in Japan as in the West, by the early 20th century, internal contracting had all but disappeared in most industries, and this finding leads me to assert that as the factory system matured, as owners and managers gained experience with newer methods of production and organization, and as technology required closer and more consistent coordination in the steps of production and distribution, "modern" practices clearly became dominant.

Internal contracting contributed in many ways to the appearance of these modern practices. It eased the difficult passage between traditional and modern, it allowed time for invention and experimentation in industry, it contributed experience and know-how to what came after. In these ways, traditional and transitional practices contributed to what we call modern without assuming a direct link between them.

Inside contracting had clear-cut advantages and disadvantages for manufacturers. The most important advantage was that work supervision was the responsibility of outside specialists. These men were presumably highly skilled in their respective fields, and they were able to directly supervise work in their areas of responsibility, including the hiring of workers of their own choosing. Owners had no need to hire, fire, train, and reward. In most ways, owners were not yet "managers," and for these manufacturers, industrial management was made easy.

But there were disadvantages to inside contracting. Most significantly, owners had little involvement with and even less control over the manufacturing process. Cost management, technological choice, work process, and worker supervision were all delegated. Such a system worked well only where there was considerable slack in the manufacturing process, so that the crucial role of coordination, which is contemporary management's principal role, was less important.

Such disadvantages, however, were not especially discouraging for owners of industrial enterprises in the late 19th century. Internal contracting allowed them to initiate manufacturing enterprises without the technical, organizational, and managerial skills needed to run them. Extreme decentralization of authority and organization could continue as long as labor-saving initiatives remained unimportant and insofar as coordination of delivery, quality, and quantity between various stages of production was relatively unimportant.

In each of the following industries, it is possible to follow the process by which owners become managers, that is, the process by which owners gradually broadened the range of industrial activities for which they were responsible and for which they sought means and other capable men to help them manage. But until then, internal contracting flourished instead of management.

III. Mining

Mining is more an extractive industry than a manufacturing industry, yet the energy and metal resources that were dug from the ground, refined, reworked, and introduced downstream into the manufacturing process were the core materials of industrial development. Likewise, many of the labor and management practices which appeared first in the mining industry became models for emulation in later manufacturing endeavors.

Coal mining provides one of the best-known examples of the

internal contracting system. In western Japan, internal contracting went by the name *naya seido*, while in the Tōhoku region *hanba seido* was more common. Because there has been less research on *hanba seido*, it is not clear how systematized (*seidoka shite iru*) the *hanba* system was relative to the *naya* system. In the metals mining industry, the *tomoko* system of labor mobilization, management, and oversight was the functional equivalent of the *naya* and *hanba* system in coal mining.

It is useful, therefore, to distinguish several different types of labor intermediaries or, at least, several different kinds of labor intermediation in the extractive industries. There were skilled technicians or craftsmen, like *tōryō*, who specialized in different production techniques or processes. They were distinct from labor recruiters, from those who provided room and board for miners, and also from those who functioned in a middleman role in coal sales and distribution. Additionally, there were labor managers, sometimes referred to as bosses, who supervised work conditions and who might oversee the work environment by managing the *naya* or worker lodging/labor hall.

At the turn of the 20th century, the functions of internal contractors in the coal mining industry were detailed as follows:

(1) Recruiting and engaging coal miners.
(2) Guaranteeing the proper degree of respect by coal miners to mine owners and operators.
(3) Providing needed clothing, room, board, equipment, and all necessary items.
(4) Supervising miners in the work place to ensure their effort and a proper return to mine owners and operators.
(5) Providing miners who are not married with appropriate housing, food, and care.
(6) Taking care of all matters relating to miners who die, are injured, or fall ill.
(7) Ensuring that workers do an honest day's work and do not flee the work place.
(8) Following the directions of mine owners and operators as to what work should be done and when.

(9)   Providing miners with the daily necessities.

(10) Redistributing wages received from mine owners to the coal miners.

(11) Mediating among miners during disputes and guaranteeing harmony among miners.

(12) Providing for the flow of information from outside the mine to the miners and vice versa.

    (Sumiya, p. 1087)

Obviously, the obligations of labor intermediaries like *tōryō* (production specialists) or *oyakata* (labor recruiters) were comprehensive and central to the provision, supervision, and compensation of workers. Owners and operators had little to do with what went on inside and even outside the mines. Virtually all matters, from where coal miners would be lodged to the very work that they performed, fell under the supervision of inside contractors.

Around 1900, however, the global responsibilities of *tōryō* in the larger mines began to diminish. Companies moved either to manage miners directly or to hire subcontractors who were themselves directly responsible for their employees. These developments occurred as mining became more mechanized, as mineral resources were integrated more swiftly into manufacturing processes, and as mining skills began to replace simple brawn in the pits.

Although the use of subcontractors may appear to be a continuation of indirect contracting in the mines, there are several notable differences. First, mine owners and operators specified more clearly the nature of the work to be done: how much coal of what quality and grade should be dug by when. Owners had not been so demanding or invasive previously. Second, subcontractors were no longer responsible for all facets of their workers' lives. The nature of the work contract was more formalized, specialized, and delimited. Work relationships became less diffuse and more specific. The growing particularization of work relations between subcontractors and workers was tied obviously to the more constrained contractual relations between subcontractors and owners. The growing use of subcontracting underlines the process of transition between traditional and modern practices in industrial management.

By the early 20th century, the larger mining companies had all but abandoned internal contracting in favor of more direct methods of labor management. Economies of scale in the larger mines demanded a close coordination in the steps of production in order to realize the benefits of capital-intensive improvements in mining and transportation technology. Smaller mining firms, however, tended to continue past practices, especially in those cases where markets for coal were not certain. In these circumstances, loose arrangements between labor contractors and mine owners favored the owners because they could quickly and relatively easily reduce their overhead expenses by severing relations with contractors. The lack of integration between mining and manufacturing operations in these cases allowed considerable leeway in labor practices and industrial management.

IV. Shipbuilding

In shipbuilding, the legacy of government projects from the late Tokugawa and early Meiji periods provided a model of shipyard organization, work supervision, training, promotion, and compensation that became the basis for subsequent efforts in the industry. Although a traditional shipbuilding industry flourished in Japan during the Tokugawa period, the newly imported technology of shipbuilding and rigging which appeared during the 1860s differed sharply from traditional designs and methods.

In order to assimilate and cope with so much that was new, shipyard owners and operators clearly improvised. In the area of labor organization, various skills associated with fairly discrete steps of production, which had not been so clearly differentiated previously, were separated. As a result, work structures and labor supervision in different specialities evolved independently. Metal fabricators were separated from metal fitters, riveters from plate workers, woodworkers from wood caulkers. To some degree, such occupational specialization was a function of the size of the shipyard: the larger the yard, the greater the degree of specialization. But more fundamentally, occupational specialization was a reflection of the inherent specialization in the work itself. The division of work grew along with the introduction of new designs and methods of shipbuilding.

Because each skill was rather different from the others, and because distinct work processes were not highly integrated (in the sense either of the timed sequence of production or of the degree of interrelatedness in production steps), each stage of production remained separate. Separation led to distinct work cultures, modes of operation, and different patterns of work-related interaction.

In spite of the evolving functional specialization of work, which aimed to match appropriate work to persons of appropriate skill, turnover was the major problem of labor relations at this time. Once workers became skilled in their area of activity, they often left to take work elsewhere. The specialization of work, itself a result of the growing division of labor, was apparently not a sufficient curb to turnover. Craftsmen, proud, independent, and known as "traveling journeymen," were a common sight during the Meiji period. (Gordon, 1985).

It is unclear, however, whether traveling journeymen should be considered part of what Osamu Saitō calls the growing casualization of labor which began to appear by the mid-18th century. (Saitō, 1985). This resulted in the shortening of the average length of a work contract and the corresponding increase in the frequency with which such contracts were concluded. Traveling journeymen in this sense may reflect simply the buoyancy of the traditional casual labor market. Alternatively, traveling journeymen may reflect an upheaval of late 19th-century labor markets as a result of new working circumstances during the late Tokugawa and early Meiji periods. My own research suggests the former was more important than the latter, although both may be true during this transitional phase of industrial development.

The incessant mobility and unwillingness of skilled workers to stay put with any employer for too long were constant frustrations to labor contractors and enterprise owners alike. Companies, at least, could attempt to corral them by offers of high wages, attractive living conditions, and possibilities of promotion. Labor bosses, because they themselves were subject to fluctuating cycles of demand for labor, were unable to offer similar inducements to skilled journeymen. In short, bosses lacked the organization to internalize incentives for reducing turnover.

Companies devised training programs as well as intricate wage and promotion systems in order to build and retain a skilled work force. Companies were reluctant to make such human resource investments unless they had some certitude of benefiting from their investments. This was more likely when they directly controlled workers and the organization of labor. Internal contracting grew less attractive as enterprises invested more in hiring, training, motivating, and retaining a skilled work force. For these reasons, inside contracting diminished in direct proportion to the growing sophistication of Japanese-managed shipyards in the late 19th century.

As early as 1890 in the Mitsubishi Nagasaki Shipyard, an apprentice (*minarai*) system in the various functional specialities was established which paid daily wages based on past experience and skill attainment (*Nagasaki Zōsenjo Rōmushi Daiichihen*, pp. 9–10). The apprentice system was part of the company's efforts to master the complex technology of shipbuilding and corporate management without relying on internal contracting. By the early 20th century, the company could proudly proclaim that

> all workers in shipyards are dealt with directly. Supervision, wage determination and disbursement are all handled directly without the intervention of any other party. This differs from employee relations in the coal and metals mining divisions of our company . . . . In these areas, inside contractors (*bushitsu-nushi* and *shōyagashira*) intermediate between employers and employees, being in charge of supervision to some degree and handling wage collections and disbursements. (*Rōdōsha Toriatsukaikata ni kansuru Chōsa Hōkokusho*, p. 5).

The *minarai*, or apprentice, system represents a clear step in the direction of establishing an internal labor market for the Mitsubishi Shipyard. But the Mitsubishi Shipyard and other major firms did not establish a pure internal labor market system until World War II or thereafter. It was then that new employees were hired only at the bottom of the organization and that all openings were filled internally through training and the scheduled creation of new or replacement positions. These would appear to be necessary conditions for the establishment of a pure internal labor market.

Minarai were not always hired at the bottom and they did not always fill vacancies that were created by internal transfer, but they do represent an attempt to hire, train, and promote from within. *Minarai* were a break with the internal contracting system: they were not traditional labor resources, and they heralded a discontinuation of traditional labor practices in favor of an entirely new approach to labor recruitment, training, and promotion.

In 19th-century Japan, direct management of labor in shipyards could not satisfy minimal conditions of profitability, and various sorts of internal or inside contracting systems were the result. However, only those companies that were able to replace or supersede internal contracting with more modern forms of labor management were successful in the 20th century. An example of this was the contrast between the Mitsubishi and Yokosuka shipyards. The success and profitability of the Mitsubishi Shipyard into the 20th century was largely the consequence of the development of the apprentice system as a more modern alternative to internal contracting. Yokosuka Shipyard on the other hand attempted to manage labor indirectly through the use of traditional *naya* intermediaries under French engineers. Yokosuka lost money until the government rescued the shipyard, making it the principal naval base of the Japanese Imperial fleet in eastern Japan. This points out the success of internal contracting as a transitional system of industrial management as well as its limitations in an increasingly industrial modern world.

V. Food and Beverage Industry

This essay will focus on the soy-sauce manufacturing industry as representative of the food and beverage industry in the late 19th and early 20th centuries. This was another industry where the internal contracting system was the primary mode of labor recruitment, organization, and supervision, until more modern, that is, more capital-intensive, more continuous, and more interconnected, methods of manufacture came to characterize the industry. Nevertheless, in smaller soy-sauce producing plants as well as in many rice wine (*sake*) enterprises where large-scale, integrated facilities were not the rule, internal contracting practices continued to the middle of the 20th century.

In the case of Noda Shōyu (Kikkōman), workers were recruited and paid through master brewers (*tōji*) and labor contractors (*oyakata*) during the 19th century and until the second decade of the 20th century. Workers were organized by teams or groups subordinated to *tōji*, *oyakata*, and *oyabun* (work group foremen). They received a cash advance for their labor services (often paid to their parents, guarantor, or someone else), a subsistence monthly wage, room and board, as well as training in a skill or craft. (Fruin, 1983).

The traditional wage system did not provide continuing incentives to work. Wages, other than the cash advance, were abysmally low, and wages were geared to length of service rather than to skill, motivation, and experience. Such a wage system encouraged turnover, and because turnover was high, wages were low. A vicious low income–low performance trap was the result.

At Noda city, where Kikkōman has been located for more than two centuries, the collection of family entrepreneurs who engaged in soy-sauce manufacture decided to modernize their plant and equipment and their methods of operation in the early 1920s. This necessitated an overhaul of labor organization and factory management. This was accomplished primarily through the creation of a personnel office in 1922 to reorganize factory production teams and methods of manufacture, to cut turnover, to better train and reward workers, and to properly house, feed, and socialize them.

As a prelude to the establishment of a personnel department in 1922, the company formed the Noda Placement Company in 1919. This enterprise brought together the five labor contractors (*oyakata*) in Noda and required them to cooperate with the company in considerations of how best to hire, train, retain, and reward workers. In addition, the work process itself was exposed to a strong dose of Taylorism—work was carefully observed, measured, and weighed relative to total work flow and product. As a consequence, a fair and equitable wage system was composed.

In Noda in the 1920s, therefore, a vision of a new way to make and distribute soy sauce prompted the company's owners to involve themselves directly in management, to eliminate inside contracting in favor of direct supervision of labor, and to construct an entirely new framework of labor organization, management control, and even corporate philosophy. A thousand-year-old product and a decidedly traditional way of work gave ground to conditions of mass production and mass distribution. Until the 20th century, however, the food and beverage industry could be characterized as one which made traditional products with traditional technology, employing traditional or transitional labor practices.

VI. Cotton Textiles

The first modern industrial enterprises were textile firms engaged in cotton spinning and weaving and in the manufacture of wool, linen, and hemp goods. These enterprises were modern because they developed an organization which incorporated the factory system of operation with managerial methods of cost control and production coordination. In doing so, they relied little upon the past, and instead incorporated Western machinery, technology, organization, and management into Japan.

All of the above, of course, had to be adapted to local circumstances, but unlike the shipbuilding, mining, and food and beverage industries, the modern factory system in textiles rushed into Japan and for the most part swept aside former practices. The new, high-thread count cotton textiles which began to appear in the 1880s were quite different from the low-thread count, low-quality goods that were common before the introduction of the modern factory system in textiles. High-quality textiles were a new product, requiring a new technology and a new form of industrial organization.

The new spinning and weaving operations, using European and American technology and machinery, employed hundreds of personnel—a scale of production quite unlike that of the earlier textile operations. The steps of production were closely integrated and carefully monitored in the new mills. The size and sophistication of textile firms led to the development of a functionally specialized but closely interrelated organization incorporating purchasing, sales, finance, engineering, power supply, employee recruitment and training, and plant inspection and maintenance.

These changes represent a conscious choice on the part of textile owners to move away from small (2,000–3,000 spindles), water-powered mills which lost money in the 1860s and 1870s, to larger (>10,000 spindles), steam-powered mills which achieved some economies of scale later. But technological choices, such as these, demanded both better-educated engineers and workers. Technological sophistication led to the creation of an internalized labor market where firms hired, fired, and trained directly rather than rely on labor intermediaries to perform such functions.

Close coordination between functional specialities demanded that managers actually manage. They could not delegate responsibility and be certain that the appropriate amount of work would be carried out at the right time and in the right way. In 1895, in a show of entrepreneurial leadership, Mutō Sanji of Kanegafuchi Spinning (now Kanebō) established a separate company headquarters with factories in Tokyo and Kobe. He put the chief works engineer and other general specialists in staff positions at the headquarters while university and technical school graduates were assigned specific functional responsibilities in the two plants. Mutō designed the plant and machinery for the factories, established an engineering department for each site, and created a labor department to recruit, train, oversee, and even provide housing for workers.

Textile firms like Mutō's Kanebo were large, multifunctional organizations with a developing managerial hierarchy which reached down to the shop floor and extended up to the head office. Foremen in textile plants were generally not *oyakata* or traditional labor bosses as they were in shipyards, mines, and other less centralized manufacturing establishments. Traditional foremen were unfamiliar with the machine technology on which modern cotton textiles were based. They lacked the experience, skill, and insight necessary to deal with this technology, and they could not effectively lead others working in such circumstances.

Modern textile enterprises did not look to the past. They developed new organizational, technological, and managerial methods to cope with a distinct system of production and a new type of product. The owners of such plants recruited, trained, and managed their employees directly; they themselves learned how, or hired those who knew how, to install, repair, and maintain textile machinery and power supply systems. They developed their own capabilities rather than rely on those of others, for the simple reason that traditional skills and methods of work organization were inappropriate to the new system of production. The internal contracting system never took root in the cotton textile industry.

VII. Discussion

These examples of what the Japanese call internal contracting (*naya seido*) are evidence of a much larger realm of organizational decentralization and labor intermediation than is generally considered when the history of internal contracting in Japan is discussed. It is more useful, however, to consider the history of *naya seido* within the larger perspective of organizational structure and labor market theory rather than to examine specific historical instances of the *naya* system divorced from a wider framework. Without a broader perspective, one is left with a number of different examples of *naya seido* operating in different industries at different times, and these specific examples make it extremely unwieldly to construct a general model of internal contracting in the course of industrial development. It is also difficult to propose a model of the process by which modern systems of labor relations emerge and mature out of traditional and transitional experiences.

Today or in the past, firms have two choices when hiring: to hire or fill vacancies from within, and to hire or fill vacancies from without. Japanese firms in the 19th century chose the latter in its most extreme form. Labor recruitment, labor contracting, and labor supervision were all delegated to labor intermediaries on a short-term basis. Enterprise owners chose indirect methods of labor contracting because it was too difficult and expensive to do otherwise.

Owners and managers of the newly established firms of the late-19th century were not experienced at managing workers. This was not something for which Tokugawa society had prepared them, and workers did not have the skills companies could easily convert to profitable endeavor. Workers were not accustomed to long-term service with one employer, and often their skills were not sufficiently developed to make employers feel a need to create compensation and promotion schemes to reward long service. In short, the costs of direct labor management, that is, the costs of finding, training, and supervising workers for employers and the opportunity costs of offering long-term employment for workers, were too high. It was for such reasons that the internal contracting system flourished in the 19th century but not in the 20th.

The rationale of internal contracting stands in contrast to both human capital theory and internal labor market theory, the two major models of labor markets in contemporary economic theory. Modern labor market theory does not deal effectively with the transition period between preindustrialization and industrialization because the theory assumes that human resource investment is marginally effective. However, this research has demonstrated that it was not economically rational during the transitional period to invest in labor resources, whether in the workers themselves (as human capital theory would have it) or in the organizations which employed workers (as internal labor market theory would have it). Turnover was too high, the level of skills formation too low, and the costs associated with internalizing technological competence too great.

Another way to consider the issue is to ask when and under what conditions it is desirable to have someone other than owners manage production and salaried managers supervise labor. The simplest answer, I think, is when labor intermediation is less expensive. Labor intermediation or inside contracting is less expensive when:
  –labor markets are undeveloped and unstable,
  –labor costs and skills are low,
  –asset-specific investments in physical and human resources are low,
  –quality control and product reliability are not very important,
  –coordination between steps in production is limited,
  –market uncertainty is high.
In short, internal contracting is viable when investment in coordinated, integrated manufacturing is low and when quality production and timely delivery are relatively unimportant.

It is important to recognize, moreover, that internal contracting in the sense that the term is used in this paper is distinct from two related forms of industrial management, namely subcontracting and manufacturing by affiliates. What distinguishes internal contracting from these others is that both labor and managerial transactions are indirect. There is a double delegation of authority: owners engage in neither production nor supervisory management.

In subcontracting, by contrast, there is direct control over what to buy, when to buy it, and at what price. These decisions are a matter of managerial authority. But in most instances of subcontracting, there is no attempt to extend managerial control over labor transactions, and labor market transactions are indirect in this sense. Under such circumstances, subcontractors are faced with a certain amount of risk due to the fluctuating demand for their services, and they depend to a large extent on part-time and temporary workers. Such a situation, as we saw earlier, characterized many of the subcontractors in the coal industry after large mines became more mechanized and capital-intensive in their operations.

In the case of manufacturing by affiliated enterprises, there is a distinct and separate managerial hierarchy, that is the manage-

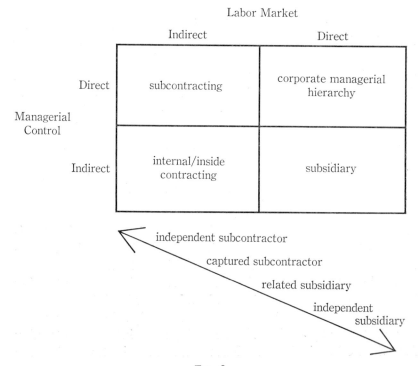

Fig. 2

ment of the subsidiary. The contracting/parent company, therefore, does not interfere directly in the internal affairs of its affiliate. The affiliate depends on the recurrent business of its parent and related companies, and it hires a permanent work force over which it has direct control. It is necessary to point out, however, that a parent enterprise may choose to interfere in the affairs of an affiliate for financial, technological, and organizational reasons as well as for issues related to the nature of labor transactions. Manufacturing by affiliated enterprises did not become a significant feature of Japan's industrial organization until the interwar period, long after most instances of internal contracting had disappeared from major enterprises in Japan.

The 2×2 table in Figure 2 disaggregates the possibilities of direct and indirect control in production and management. It is meant to be suggestive rather than exhaustive for, in actual fact, there are an infinite number of possible combinations of direct and indirect production and managerial supervision.

VIII. Conclusion

Internal contracting (*naya seido*) was a central component of industrial management in 19th-century Japan. It was the primary mode of labor recruitment, organization, and supervision in the food and beverage, mining, and shipbuilding industries. It was common in a host of other industries as well, although they have not been considered here. Internal contracting was much less important, one could even say unimportant, in the cotton textile industry, however.

The two principal forces acting upon the internal contracting system in the late 19th century were the introductions of the factory system of production and the joint-stock form of enterprise organization. But in the late 19th century, the full impact of these innovative institutions was not yet felt due to the small size and the very speculative nature of the market. Thus, at first, the limited spread of the factory system and the incipient character of organized capitalism allowed traditional institutions and values to continue. At best, transitional institutions like the *naya* system appeared to bridge the gap between what was traditional and inadequate and what was necessary but not yet clearly defined.

The prevalence of internal contracting until the early 20th

century suggests that human capital theory is an inadequate framework for explaining industrial management before this time. Human capital theory is not pertinent when the level of education of most workers is low and when the level of technology makes it unlikely as well as unprofitable for companies to invest in educating labor resources. In short, it was not economical for firms to attempt the creation of a trained and motivated work force, as human capital theory would have it.

The internalized labor markets which characterize Japanese companies today represent 20th-century adjustments to 19th-century problems of such low levels in production and distribution technology and in worker education, skills, and motivation. However, before these 20th-century adjustments could be realized, enterprises attempted to overcome these problems with the internal contracting system. This worked for a while but not for too long, because of inherent limitations in the system.

The decline of internal contracting was directly related to ongoing industrial change. As the nature of Japan's industrial development moved from products of the First Industrial Revolution, such as iron, steel, and textiles, to the products of the Second Industrial Revolution, namely, electrical and non-electrical machinery, sophisticated chemicals, cars, trucks, and railroad equipment, the comparatively decentralized mode of work organization in earlier industries and the delegation of production responsibility to outside contractors declined. Greater scale in production, vertical integration of the steps in production, the technological sophistication of production, and the drive to coordinate organizational resources more closely, all mediated against internal contracting.

In this analysis, I part company with those who argue in favor of the social continuity of Japanese labor institutions from traditional to modern times. Instead, I argue that the industrial revolution introduced new forms of energy, management, and organization in the production process, and the converging conditions of industrial competitiveness at the end of the 19th century created a clear and considerable rupture with past practice. Moreover, as the initial tentative efforts at industrialization during the last quarter of the 19th century were replaced by more significant and confident efforts during the 20th century, the first fissures with past practices opened even wider, introducing a genesis of entirely new forms of labor organization and management.

As the units of production grew in size and as the degree of coordination between steps of production became more important, traditional, decentralized systems of production diminished and eventually disappeared in favor of greater interdependence and management in the stages of production. This appeared most often in the factory in the guise of adopting, adapting, and sometimes co-opting traditional labor leaders into the roles of company men. Inside contractors were given a choice: either become foremen within expanding corporate hierarchies or be forced out of firms altogether.

Cotton-textile companies, however, were the exception. They established more direct methods of industrial management from the beginning. Nevertheless, not everything associated with the management of textile companies was modern. Their methods of labor recruitment were traditional in the sense that non-company, labor recruiters were employed. Compensation was not modern in that large advance lump sum payments indentured workers to mills for long periods of time. And textile firms were among the first to develop paternalistic philosophies of interaction between workers and managers.

These textile industry practices may represent a continuation of Tokugawa wage payment practices, or, more likely, they suggest ways in which certain traditional labor practices helped bridge the transition between the past and the future. But in the crucial sense of labor management, as the concept is applied in this paper, textile enterprises were more modern because they employed more direct forms of labor management and more comprehensive philosophies of management almost from the start.

Finally, change in the nature of industrialization itself—from products of the First to those of the Second Industrial Revolution—was more important than changes in industrial organization and management within the same cycle of industrialization. The requirements of close coordination in production and the drive to control variable costs, largely labor costs, during the expensive process of

adding plant and equipment for capital-intensive manufacture after
the turn of the century forced management much more directly
into the processes of hiring, training, motivating, and supervising
the work force during the 20th century. Tradition was not accommodated in labor relations. Most simply put, the internal contracting system was no longer needed, and indeed, could become an
impediment to effective production and management control.

Traditional as well as transitional forms of labor management
and the ideas associated with them—the ideal of the independent
industrial craftsman and traditional concepts of work, authority,
and autonomous work-place groups under *naya* supervision—were
supplanted by more direct and more modern labor employment
practices. In these ways, qualitative change in technology and
a concomitant shift in education and performance levels were more
significant than the mere passage of time. Thus, intercyclical change
was more important than intracyclical change in explaining the
decline of inside contracting.

Nevertheless, even without a break in industrial technology,
a shift away from the traditional internal contracting system to more
direct methods of managerial and production control can be observed within the food and beverage, mining, and shipbuilding
industries by the eve of the 20th century. Accordingly, even within
the cycle of the First Industrial Revolution, inside contracting grew
less important, although it continued in many industries for a long
time.

In short, in industries with a predominantly traditional character,
like mining, soy-sauce manufacture, and, to a degree, even shipbuilding, the methods of organization which tolerated a great deal
of slack between the stages of production and the different functional components of corporate operation permitted the internal
contracting system to continue while technology, the market, and
management matured. By the 20th century, however, modern institutions were clearly supplanting traditional practices in all industries.

As the factory system grew in importance, as industrial business
values and customs matured, as the average level of education rose,
and, most importantly, as modern management principles and

practioners flourished, traditional institutions, like the internal contracting system, declined, were absorbed, or disappeared. As this
was happening, during the transitional period between traditional
and modern, interaction between what was needed and what was
known, as opposed to what was available and what was traditional,
created a kind of dialectical tension that allowed new possibilities
to emerge in the arena of employment transactions and industrial
relations. A second wave of industrialization, associated with newer
products and more capital-intensive methods of production, however, pushed this process even further along and finally ended a
dependence on internal contracting (Fig. 3).

In conclusion, from the late 19th to early 20th century—a transitional phase of industrial development before the takeoff to heavy
industry and manufacturing preeminence—internal contracting
functioned instead of management in labor relations and the labor
market in Japan. Internal contracting accommodated tradition
while allowing sufficient change in tradition to fuel a process of
industrial maturation which led ultimately to the replacement of
internal contracting with direct labor management. Once this occurred, however, internal contracting quickly diminished in significance and thereby contributed little to the genesis of the specific

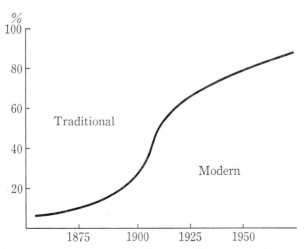

Fig. 3   Character of Industrial Management System.

forms and practices which generally characterize modern labor relations in Japan.

REFERENCES

I would like to thank Professors Eisuke Daitō, Thomas C. Smith, Koji
Taira, and Christena Turner for help with earlier drafts of this paper.

L. A. Clarkson, *Proto-Industrialization: The First Phase of Industrialization?*,
London, Macmillan Publishers, 1985.
Daniel Clawson, *Bureaucracy and the Labor Process*, New York, Monthly
Review Press, 1980.
Eisuke Daitō, "Management and Labor: The Evolution of Employer-
Employee Relations in the Course of Industrial Development," in
K. Nakagawa, ed., Proceedings of the Fuji Conference, *Labor and
Management*, Tokyo, University of Tokyo Press, 1979.
W. Mark Fruin, *Kikkoman*, Harvard University Press, 1983.
———. "The Family as a Firm and the Firm as a Family in Japan,"
The Journal of Family History, Vol. 5, No. 4 (Winter 1980).
———. "Peasant Labor Migration in Nineteenth Century Japan," Ph.D.
dissertation, Stanford University, 1973.
Andrew Gordon, *The Evolution of Labor Relations in Japan*, Cambridge,
Mass., Council on East Asian Studies, Harvard University, 1985.
Tadashi Hanami, *Labor Relations in Japan Today*, Tokyo Kodansha Inter-
national, 1979.
Tetsuya Hashimoto, "Miike Kōzan to Shūjin Rōdō" (Miike mines and
convict labor), *Shakai keizai shigaku*, Vol. 32, No. 4 (1967), pp. 44–64.
Hazama Hiroshi, *Nihon ni okeru rōshi kyōchō no teiryū* (Currents in Japanese
labor-management collaboration), Tokyo, Waseda University Press,
1978.
Heibonsha, *Sekai daihyakka jiten* (World encyclopedia), 1981, p. 64.
Ken'ichi Iida, "Origin and Development of Iron and Steel Technology
in Japan," Tokyo, United Nations University, 1980.
Ishihara Ryōhei and Tanaka Mitsuo, "Tankō naya seido no hōkai" (The
decline of the *naya* system in mines), *Nihon rōdō kyōkai zasshi*, Vol. 6,
Nos. 5, 7, 8 (1964), pp. 9–17, 25–34, 17–22.
Takeo Izumi, "Transformation and Development of Technology in the
Japanese Cotton Industry," Tokyo, United Nations University, 1980.
Kashiwa Shobō, *Nihonshi yōgo daijiten* (Dictionary of Japanese historical
terms), 1978, p. 517.

Kawade Shobō Shinsha, *Nihon rekishi daijiten* (Dictionary of Japanese history), Vol. 14, 1959, p. 151.

Shogo Koyano, "Technology of Traditional Industry and the Role of Craftsmen," Tokyo, United Nations University, 1979.

Solomon Levine and Hisashi Kawada, *Human Resources in Japanese Industrial Development*, Princeton, Princeton University Press, 1980.

Matsushima Shigeo, *Tomoko no shakaigakuteki kōsatsu* (Sociological observations in the *tomoko* system), Tokyo, Ochanomizu Shobō, 1978.

Mitsubishi Kōgyō Semento Shashi Hensanshitsu, *Mitsubishi Kōgyō Semento shi* (A history of Mitsubishi Mining and Cement Corporation), Mitsubishi Kōgyō Semento K.K., 1976.

Mitsubishi Nagasaki Zōsenjo Shokkōka, "Nagasaki Zōsenjo rōmushi (A history of labor management in Nagasaki Shipyard), mimeograph, 1930.

Mitsubishi Zōsenjo, *Rōdōsha toriatsukaikata ni kansuru chōsa hōkokusho* (Report on the treatment of workers), Mitsubishi Zōsen Shomubu Chōsaka, 1914.

Miyamoto Mataji, "Ono-gumi no kōzangyō ni tsuite" (On the mining business of Ono-gumi), *Shakai keizai shigaku*, Vol. 32, No. 2 (1966), pp. 1–25.

Murakushi Nisaburo, "Technology and Labour in Japanese Coal Mining," Tokyo, United Nations University, 1980.

Nakamura Hachirō, *Denki jigyō no ranshō to tenkai katei* (The emergence and development of the electrical industry), Tokyo, Kokusai Rengō Daigaku, 1982.

Nakanishi Yō, *Nihon kindaika no kiso katei* (Foundations of Japan's modernization), 2 vols., Tokyo, University of Tokyo Press, 1982.

Daniel Nelson, *Workers and Managers*, Madison, University of Wisconsin Press, 1975.

Osamu Saitō, *Puroto kōgyōka no jidai: Seiō to Nihon no hikakushi* (The age of proto-industrialization), Tokyo, Nihon Hyōronsha, 1985.

Harley Shaiken, *Work Transformed*, New York, Holt Reinhardt & Winston, 1984.

H. A. Simon, "A Formal Theory of the Employment Relationship," *Econometrica*, Vol. 19 (1951), pp. 293–305.

Tokyo Sōgensha, *Nihonshi jiten* (Dictionary of Japanese history), 1960, p. 384. Sumiya Mikio, "Naya seido no seiritsu to hōkai" (The development and decline of the *naya* system), *Shisō*, Vol. 8 (1960), pp. 102–12.

Koji Taira, *Economic Development and the Labor Market in Japan*, New York, Columbia University Press, 1970.

Tokida Y., " 'Sangyō kakumei izen ni okeru tankō kōgyo no keisei"

(The formation of the mining industry before the industrial revolution),
Ritsumeikan keizaigaku, Vol. 15, No. 2 (June 1966).

Patricia Tsurumi, "Female Textile Workers and the Failure of Early
Trade Unionism," *History Workshop*, Vol. 18 (Autumn 1984), pp. 1–26.

Oliver E. Williamson, *Markets and Hierarchies: Analysis and Antitrust Implications*, New York, The Free Press, 1975.

Yamakata Heiuemon, ed., *Hakushika komonjo* (Archives of Hakushika),
Kobe, Hakushika Shuzō Kabushiki Kaisha, 1978.

Fumio Yoshiki, "How Japan's Metal Mining Industries Modernized,"
Tokyo, United Nations University, 1980.

Comment

Hideki Yoshihara
Kobe University

Generally speaking, good papers stimulate the reader to ponder many issues. Professor W. M. Fruin's paper satisfies this condition as it made me consider several interesting points. As the substance of the first part of my comments, I would like to present, in the form of questions, a number of these issues that came to mind as I read this paper. Next, good papers should make original contributions. Does Fruin's paper fulfill this condition? An inquiry into this point constitutes the second part of my comments.

1. *Several Questions*

(1) The Extent of the Diffusion of Internal Contracting in Japan. Fruin seems to think that internal contracting was practiced at many Japanese firms in many industries. However, can we deny the possibility that it was practiced at a relatively small number of firms in a few industries? I can mention three reasons that support this possibility. First, as Fruin points out in his paper, firms engaged in spinning and weaving cotton textiles did not adopt internal contracting. Second, in England, internal contracting was only observed in a limited number of firms. This is a point that was analyzed by Suzuki Yoshitaka (Tōhoku University). Third, in the United States, internal contracting was also not widely diffused across all industries. This was pointed out by Shiomi Haruhito (Nagoya City University) and other scholars.

(2) Reasons for Not Having Adopted Internal Contracting in Cotton Spinning and Weaving Textile Firms. Internal contracting was not adopted in the cotton spinning and weaving textile industry, a new leading industry at that time, and this is an important fact.

It is expected that an investigation of the reasons for not having adopted internal contracting would contribute towards an understanding of the nature of the internal contracting system. Relative to other industries, why did internal contracting have fewer advantages in the cotton spinning and weaving textile industry? Or, from the opposite perspective, why did direct employment have more advantages? Why did direct employment have lower costs?

(3) A Comparison of Internal Contracting, Subcontracting, and Subsidiaries. There are a number of questions regarding Fruin's classification (See Fig. 2). First, the managerial control of subcontracting is thought to be direct. Second, employment at subsidiaries is considered direct. In reality, there is a variety of internal contracting systems. In order to make the classification of these systems more distinct, it is necessary to detail clearly and precisely the characteristics of internal contracting, subcontracting, and subsidiaries.

(4) An International Comparison of Internal Contracting. Since this is an international conference, I expected a comparison between the features of Japanese internal contracting and American and British internal contracting. What are the common points shared by the Japanese, American, and British systems? What are their respective singularities? What are the reasons that gave origin to these singularities?

(5) Relationship with Prior Research. Research on internal contracting has been previously conducted in England, the United States, and Japan. The consideration of the relationship that Fruin's paper has with the existing body of research on the subject seems to be insufficient. This problem relates to another question that I would like to address in these comments, namely, what is the original contribution of Fruin's paper?

2. *Original Contribution of the Paper*

(1) Novelty of the Subject. Does the novelty of Fruin's contribution lie in having addressed for the first time the subject of internal contracting in Japan? The answer is no. Regardless of whether their works were thorough enough or not, research on Japanese internal contracting has already been conducted by C. R. Littler, Chokki Toshiaki (Hōsei University), and other scholars.

(2) Novelty of the Theoretical Framework. Fruin analyzes internal contracting from the standpoint of the theory of transaction costs (economics of internal organization, theory of internalization). Is this a new approach? The answer is also no. O. E. Williamson refers to internal contracting in his development of the theory of transaction costs. Suzuki Yoshitaka adopted the theory of transaction costs as his basic theoretical framework when he discussed internal contracting in England.

(3) The Transition Period Point of View. Does this paper's originality stem from the fact that it looks at internal contracting as a phenomenon specific to the transition period from a traditional period to modern times? In regard to this point as well, our answer has to be no. For example, G. C. Allen analyzed internal contracting as a phenomenon related to the transition period.

(4) The Point of View of an International Comparison. Is the novelty of Fruin's paper related to having addressed the problem of internal contracting from the perspective of an international comparison? This point too has to be answered in the negative. For example, Littler deals with the subject of internal contracting in his comparative research on British, American, and Japanese labor relations.

(5) New Facts, New Historical Documents. In his paper, does Fruin present new facts relating to Japanese internal contracting? Does he uncover new historical materials? Since I am not a business historian well versed in internal contracting, I am not prepared to answer this question with complete confidence, but, as far as I know, a negative answer is probably appropriate here as well.

I have presented above a number of questions relating to Fruin's paper. I have also expressed a negative evaluation of several aspects regarding the originality of his research. However, I want to place a high value on the following aspect of the paper. Fruin attempts to investigate internal contracting on the basis of a well-defined theoretical framework. Given the prevalent general tendency to write descriptive business history that attaches great importance to finding facts and discovering historical documents, I want to highlight the value of this approach. In this regard, and in spite of my posing several questions and negative criticisms, Fruin's paper deserves to be evaluated basically as a highly positive contribution.

Response

W. Mark Fruin

There are several points of disagreement between Professor Yoshihara and myself concerning the place of the internal contracting system in the enterprises of an industrializing, 19th-century Japan. First, contrary to Yoshihara's suggestion that the system of indirect labor management was not widespread, the internal contracting system was extensively practiced in most industries at the turn of the 20th century in Japan. I have studied and written about four examples only, in shipbuilding, food and beverages, mining, and textiles (with textiles being the exceptional case of not typically employing a *naya* system of labor relations), but the practice of internal contracting was nearly universal at this time.

Second, internal contracting is not a particularly Japanese solution to problems of labor management during the course of industrial development. Among others, Sydney Pollard has written of the practice in Great Britain, Daniel Nelson and Oliver Williamson in the United States. While the timing of internal contracting may vary according to the onset and stage of the industrialization process, there appears to be little doubt as to general significance of the phenomenon.

Third, given the importance of internal contracting across many industries and in any number of countries, it is not possible to overemphasize the pivotal character of this system of labor-management relations in the transition from protoindustrial to industrial society. This transitional importance rests not only on the matter of continuity but also on the issue of discontinuity. Traditional labor practices and institutions provided an important foundation for the appearance of modern practices, and in this sense continuity may be emphasized. At the same time, however, it was through the clash and combination of old and new practices that alternative forms of industrial structure and management were created. The significance of discontinuity should not be minimized. Clearly, the transitional period of industrial development deserves more attention and study in Japan as well as elsewhere.

Finally, Oliver Williamson's transaction-cost analysis, while not conceptually original with me, had not been applied previously to problems of internal contracting and labor management in Japan at the close of the 19th century. I believe the use of transaction-cost analysis helps one predict when and under what circumstances internal contracting systems will be employed, and, just as importantly, when and why more direct forms of labor management may eventually emerge. Perhaps Yoshihara has missed the point of my use of transaction-cost analysis.

Innovation and Business Strategy in the Prewar Chemical Industry

Barbara Molony
Santa Clara University

Modern Japanese industrial development is synonymous with high technology. Yet a little more than a century ago, Japan's agrarian society and economy were largely unaffected by sophisticated industrial technology. Indeed, as recently as the immediate postwar years Japan's economy lay in ruins, and few in the West had the imagination to predict it would make an astounding recovery—a recovery due, in no small part, to the innovation and importation of technology. During the 1980s, a spate of scholarly work has appeared to explain Japan's apparent successes. These studies assume a variety of approaches: analyses of the government's guidance in applying industrial policy;[1] accounts of the techniques of Japanese management;[2] discussions of development of technology;[3] analyses of commercial application of technology;[4] new insights into the development of labor-management relations;[5] and studies emphasizing entrepreneurial firms rather than firms associated with the prewar zaibatsu as innovators in high technology companies.[6]

These approaches highlight significant components of Japan's modern technology-intensive industrial economy. But none focuses specifically on an equally important subject—the highly skilled entrepreneurs who pioneered investment in technology as early as the Meiji period. These adventurous businessmen were the beneficiaries of 19th- and early 20th-century public policies encouraging the development and diffusion of both basic science and process technology. It was these investors whose concentration on technology spawned further innovations. Diffusion of their innovations created

an increasingly technology-intensive economy. The prewar entrepreneurial pioneers of technology, then, contributed significantly
to the postwar high tech environment. They also fashioned an
effective relationship between innovative technology and business
strategy which was replicated in postwar high tech firms. That is,
the availability of new technology in various forms—newly understood basic science which could be commercially applied, new products which could be marketed to technology-attuned customers,
new processes which could be used both to make existing products
more efficiently and to invent unknown ones—was a major factor
in prewar managers' decisions to invest and expand.

The most sophisticated technologies of the pre-World War II era
—both in processing and in basic science—were developed in the
West and Japan in the electrochemical industry. Electrochemical
manufacture can be said to have contributed to technological
sophistication in several ways: farmers, whose methods had epito-
mized traditional technology, became accustomed to using the
fertilizer products of the technologically advanced electrochemical
industry; entrepreneurs with a good foundation in science and
technology were sufficiently knowledgeable to take advantage of
the high tech production methods originally developed for other
products; and researchers in Japan, narrowing their lag behind
European (and sometimes North American) scientists, were able to
import, understand, and adapt complex technology. The electrochemical industry was certainly an archetypal high technology
industry. Moreover, the industry was both commercially successful
because it produced, among other things, fertilizers for Japan's
largely farming economy, and militarily significant because it manufactured explosives. The industry was destined to grow, so it is small
wonder that the effects of its technological advances would multiply
as they diffused throughout the economy. This article, therefore,
focuses on the electrochemical industry in its analysis of innovation
and business strategy.

The connection between business strategy and innovation is
critical and is particularly conspicuous in countries like Japan in
the 20th century and the United States in the 19th century. It is
less evident in the case of Germany, however: whereas scientists in

countries at the "cutting edge" of chemical technology like Germany were noted for their greater interest in producing new basic knowledge than in developing innovative products or manufacturing old products more efficiently,[7] scientists in the United States and, later, Japan were known for their interest in exploiting the practical applications of the new technology. Americans were particularly noted for their "Yankee ingenuity," a term referring to their ability to take basic science, usually first developed abroad, and improve it to lower manufacturing costs. This was hardly a unique ability, the beliefs of contemporaries notwithstanding, but merely the best strategy for new American firms to attain competitiveness with European innovators.

Prewar Japanese scientist-entrepreneurs generally resembled the American more than the German type. Neither the Americans nor the Japanese, however, may be said to have lacked creativity or skill in development of electrochemicals. "Imitation"—first use of a technology after its innovation elsewhere—required a level of competence virtually equal to that of the innovator, particularly if the imitator were to improve the process. Indeed, there is a strong correlation between ability to innovate and brevity of lag in imitation: the most innovative chemical firms in the West were also most readily able to imitate their competitors' technology.[8] Imitation and innovation were two ends of a continuum of creativity. In Japan and the United States in the late 19th and early 20th centuries, mastery of borrowed technical application was rapidly followed by innovation, particularly in production technology.

The emphasis on developing production technology to become competitive with the Europeans was most appropriate to the electrochemical industry. That is, the industry itself was originally one of process—electrochemical methods were used for such tasks as plating metals and "fixing" atmospheric nitrogen so it could be used as fertilizer. Neither plated metals nor nitrogenous fertilizer were novel products. In time, the industry developed more basic science, but process technology remained at its core.

The importance of process technology should not be underestimated. It is important to remember that the world's two current leaders in high technology manufacturing, the United States and

Japan, got their starts by focusing on "making it more cheaply, making it more efficiently." Innovative process technology was significant on the microeconomic level, too, as both a determinant of and a response to leading chemical firms' competitive strategies.

Entrepreneurial strategies are vital to an understanding of technological innovation. Technology is rarely advanced without some purpose for the innovation. Creative scientists and engineers produce novel ideas all the time, but many of these are never commercially produced (or, analogously, supported by patronage or government grants in lieu of market demand), and therefore never engender a derivative line of technological innovations. And ideas must be not only useful, but also practicable. Consider, for example, the ball-point pen. Designed in the 19th century, it had to wait 60 years until process technology was sufficiently developed to allow its production. Moreover, someone must recognize the usefulness of new products and technologies; in modern industrial societies, that role is filled by entrepreneurs (except in the case of non-commercial technology with potential strategic applications which enjoys government support). Thus, entrepreneurs deciding to commercialize new ideas which they either generate themselves or else acquire from another imaginative thinker are integral to the process of technology development. Moreover, new ideas are usually a refinement of existing knowledge, which must be available and widely disseminated as already developed technology for imaginative minds to be able to base new ideas on it. Thus, entrepreneurs in technology-intensive fields have to have adequate technical training.

Electrochemical technology in the prewar period was advanced by a handful of Japanese companies with unusual interest in innovative technology as an aspect of business strategy. The best example of an electrochemical company with a "high-tech consciousness" in its strategic planning was also the first, Japan Nitrogenous Fertilizers Inc. (Nippon Chisso Hiryō KK, hereafter Nitchitsu), founded in 1908 by scientist-entrepreneur Noguchi Jun (1873-1944).

Other companies demonstrated interest in advanced technology, too, but not so dramatically. Electrochemical Industries Inc. (Denki Kagaku Kōgyō KK), founded in 1915 by ¡Noguchi's former partner, Fujiyama Tsuneichi, was approximately contemporaneous with Nitchitsu. But Fujiyama was less successful in pioneering new technologies, and so his company remained less competitive technologically. A second wave of electrochemical producers emerged in the 1920s. These included an established producer of superphosphate fertilizer, Dai Nihon Artificial Fertilizer (later Nissan Chemical), which diversified to synthesize ammonia in 1925, and a producer of iodine and electricity who established Shōwa Fertilizer to branch into electrochemicals in 1929. A third wave included the electrochemical enterprises established in the 1930s by the Mitsui, Mitsubishi, and Sumitomo zaibatsu. All three zaibatsu had technicians interested in electrochemicals, but they were late developers. Organizational changes during and after World War I gave these innovative leaders greater latitude to research new processes, but it was the discovery of electrochemical methods using coal, a resource the zaibatsu already possessed, that inspired their investment in innovative technology in the 1930s. Thus, business strategy affected whether the zaibatsu would innovate, while innovations helped determine Noguchi's company strategy.

I. Diffusion of Technological Research and Education

The guiding spirits of these enterprises were all creative men who recognized the importance of technological innovation to furthering their business interests. Whether as entrepreneurs or as top managers employed by large zaibatsu, all were scientifically literate. Most were schooled in scientific subjects; the government had stressed education since the beginning of the Meiji period. Dissemination of scientific knowledge through schools and research institutes was arguably the most important macroeconomic policy until mobilization for war began in 1937.[9]

Technology cannot be developed without scientists to develop it. The Meiji leadership recognized that domestic production of the desired tools of economic and military strength depended on the diffusion of knowledge through educational and research institutions. Technical education was quite limited before the Meiji Restoration, so the government formalized the system of scientific education in the 1870s with several specialized training schools and two schools of higher technical education, the Kaisei School and the College of Technology (Kōbu Daigakkō), both later part of Tokyo Imperial University.[10] Foreign instructors and foreign research trips supplemented students' exposure to international knowledge.

The Japanese technical education system was modeled on the German and thus had a three-tier structure: lower vocational schools for a skilled work force; higher-level technical colleges for future managers of companies; and imperial universities for researchers in pure science. Only the highest-levels were set up immediately, however. In the event, there was little need for skilled workers in the chemical industry before the turn of the century, but had there been, government schools could not have produced them. The emphasis was on the development of managers and researchers. By the end of the Meiji period, universities in Kyoto, the Tōhoku, and Kyushu taught both pure and applied sciences.[11] Students clearly opted for the latter type; graduates in engineering outnumbered those in science four to one. Indeed, most early chemical manufacturers had degrees in engineering rather than in chemistry.

Furthermore, there was a high degree of occupational mobility for technology graduates. Almost two-thirds of the pre-1905 graduates of the College of Technology and the Tokyo Imperial University Faculty of Engineering moved from government to private sector employment, or vice versa, by 1920. This high rate of inter-sectoral mobility increased the speed of diffusion of technical information.

Research institutes were the other of Japan's two major methods of dissemination of technology. Most Western countries established nationally funded research laboratories under the crisis conditions of World War I; for Japan, the need to catch up with Western scientists was justification enough to set up facilities. Regional agricultural stations carried out chemical fertilizer research as early as the 19th century. In June 1900, after a series of conferences involving government officials, businessmen, and academics, the government founded the Tokyo Industrial Experimental Laboratory (TIEL), which was charged with assisting research requested by private entrepreneurs.[12] TIEL's leading researchers were among the top scientists in Japan. In 1909, an electrochemical division was set up, and during World War I, a special section devoted to nitrogen was added. TIEL laid the groundwork for systematic research and, together with the teaching of science in the new educational institutions, created the infrastructure for innovation in Japan's chemical industry.

II. Electrochemistry's Pioneer, Noguchi Jun

Noguchi, an 1896 graduate in electrical engineering from Tokyo Imperial University, combined a creative scientific mind with good business and marketing instincts. Even as a student, he displayed a talent for identifying promising technologies. A part-time student job at a silk spinning company's electric generating plant permitted him to observe the problems of long-distance transmission, which the company proposed as a way of profitably using its surplus electricity. He also contemplated, apparently for the first time, manufacture of the electrochemical calcium carbide (used at that time in lighting) to use unneeded capacity.[13] This was the same year (1895) that Niagara Falls was harnessed and its power first transmitted "long distance" (20 miles) to Buffalo.[14] Japan's technology lag behind the West, as shown in the activities of this creative undergraduate, was clearly narrowing. This anecdote also highlights the success of Japan's educational system in producing young scientists able to use their knowledge of existing technology to come up with commercially viable applications. More than a decade before Noguchi owned and directed his own firm, then, his work exemplified the connection between innovative technology and development of commercial uses for it.

Noguchi's technological learning did not end when he left school. He joined another Tokyo University graduate, Fujiyama Tsuneichi, in researching calcium carbide, then worked as a service engineer for the Japanese branch of the German Siemens company where he learned about advanced machinery.[15] A series of other jobs and foreign travel ended in 1906 when Noguchi established his first electric plant, Sogi Electric in Kyushu. Like the silk spinning plant a decade earlier, Sogi Electric generated surplus electricity, which Noguchi hoped to use to produce calcium carbide.

By 1907, he was ready to use the new carbide technology to further his company's interests. He had all the requirements for investment in new applications of technology: access to resources, especially his own sources of electricity; access to capital, borrowed from friends; availability of good, skilled managers, especially Fujiyama, who rejoined him in Kyushu, and Ichikawa Seiji, a college classmate; a market for his product through import substitution; a benign business climate fostered by government policies; and above all, access to the appropriate technology. Access to technology, resources, labor, skilled managers, and capital and the absence of factors outside the firm impeding investment, such as discouraging public policies or adverse market conditions, are necessary and sufficient conditions for investment in innovative technology. Moreover, failure to expand and innovate when new technologies are available lessens a company's competitiveness.

No sooner had Noguchi begun producing calcium carbide than he heard of an innovative use for it. Calcium carbide was first used as a raw material for calcium cyanamide (a nitrogenous fertilizer) at Piano d'Orta in Italy in 1906. By 1908, Noguchi and Fujiyama were already en route to Europe to negotiate a production license. Negotiators from Mitsui and Furukawa also vied for the license, but Noguchi's successful track record with calcium carbide plus his friendship with Siemens officials from his earlier employment (as its largest shareholder, Siemens could influence the Italian company) won the day.[16] At ¥400,000, however, the license was prohibitively expensive for the tiny Kyushu company, so Noguchi solicited aid from Mitsui. Mitsui's unattractive terms drove Noguchi to seek help from relatives, who put him in contact with Mitsubishi. Fortunately for Noguchi, access to sufficient capital with minimal intervention from Mitsubishi permitted him to meet the above conditions for investment in innovative technology. Nitchitsu was thus founded to produce calcium cyanamide fertilizer in August 1908.

Within months of its founding, production and marketing problems encouraged Noguchi and his partners to upgrade their technology to produce ammonium sulfate (a fertilizer preferred by Japanese farmers) using calcium cyanamide as a raw material. The technology was available, having been pioneered in 1900 by Germans Adolf Frank and Nikodem Caro, the discoverers of calcium cyanamide.[17] In 1909, no one in Japan yet produced ammonium sulfate from calcium cyanamide. But not to advance the technology domestically would have jeopardized Nitchitsu's survival in a fertilizer market dominated by imported ammonium sulfate.[18] It made little sense to compete in the fertilizer market with a less desirable product. Thus the availability of new technology pushed Nitchitsu to innovate.

The technology for calcium cyanamide itself had to be improved before it could be used as the foundation for ammonium sulfate. To upgrade the technology, Noguchi invested in a new plant in Niigata prefecture. The plant, which was close to good transportation and sources of raw materials, was ideal as a pilot production facility. But a freak flood destroyed it in 1912. Nevertheless, Noguchi skillfully nurtured his financial and scientific resources and continued to develop his company and its technology.

Innovative technology was indeed the basis for Noguchi's successful business strategy. In 1911, Fujiyama Tsuneichi, who was soon to leave Nitchitsu, had developed the world's first continuous (flow) method of production to replace the old batch method of Frank and Caro.[19] Fujiyama's innovation of a new process had important implications. First, it was one of the earliest cases of significant refinement by a Japanese engineer of a widely used commercial process. Fujiyama's profound understanding of the original technology, including its faults, permitted him to rethink the method and improve it. Adolf Frank's son Albert even traveled to Japan in 1911 to inaugurate the new process at Nitchitsu in recognition of its international importance.[20] And second, the hallmark of technological advancement in the international chemical industry in the first half of the 20th century was the improvement of process technology; in the United States, for example, the development of "unit operation" was hailed as America's unique contribution to international technology.[21] Unit operation was the process of bringing the necessary components of production together in one place to facilitate manufacture without interruption. This was essentially what Fujiyama accomplished with his continuous method of production.

During World War I and the immediate postwar years, Noguchi continued to use the technology developed by 1912. Both the absence of European competition during the war and some unintended assistance from the Japanese government made Nitchitsu sufficiently profitable to slow its pace of innovative research and development.[22] (When old methods are profitable, there is less incentive to innovate to cut costs.) Higher productivity was once again required as the Europeans, recovering after the war, began to raise their own standards of technology. Fortunately for Noguchi, the profits earned and saved during a half decade of weak competition and little reinvestment in R and D were then available for innovation in the 1920s. And the innovative new technology for synthesizing ammonia under high temperature and pressure accorded well with the company's orientation to electrochemistry. That is, the new process technology Noguchi introduced shared more than its end product—ammonium sulfate—with the old technology; it also shared its high demand for electricity and some electrochemical production techniques.

The differences between the cyanamide and synthetic methods were more significant than the similarities. The former process did not encourage development of spun-off technology (that is, diversification); the latter did. Company strategy was best served in the former case by maximizing profits through increased production when profit margins were high, as during World War I. Nitchitsu increased production at that time by increasing plant space dedicated to the same products. The cyanamide process installed at Kagami in 1914 was replicated at Noguchi's Minamata plant in 1915.[23] Similar facilities making the same products did not foster the creative cross-fertilization of scientists' ideas which spawned innovations, however; that would come only with the diversified, multiunit, vertically integrated organization of the following decade. Nevertheless, the cyanamide process was important because it was profitable and because it represented a noteworthy incremental advance in technology. Indeed, Nitchitsu's incremental absorption and development of new technology bespeaks its scientific maturation. Extraordinary leaps in levels of sophistication of licensed technology often indicate a frantic effort to catch up from an inferior position; gradual advances, on the other hand, imply that the purchasing company's ability to apply the technology is almost on a par with the industry leaders'. Such was the case with electro-chemicals, including cyanamide and synthetic ammonia, at Nitchitsu.

By contrast, most contemporaries saw Nitchitsu's pioneering of synthesis of ammonia in Japan in 1922 as a kind of great leap forward. To be sure, the importance of this technology should not be underestimated: it permitted more efficient fixation of atmos-pheric nitrogen, with all its economic and strategic implications; it induced, by the 1930s, a reorganization of Nitchitsu's management corresponding to the extensive diversification in manufacture of products spun-off from ammonia and its process technology; and it made expansion to Japan's Korean colony profitable and perhaps inevitable given the technology's resource requirements. These are certainly adequate justifications to consider the synthesis technology epoch-making. But this technology, like that for cyanamide, repre-sented many years of study and refinement of existing knowledge.

Methods of synthesis were understood in Japan, at least by a handful of scientists and entrepreneurs, as early as the World War I period. Noguchi wrote an article in 1914 which revealed his under-standing of European advances in ammonia synthesis and of Japanese and Western shortcomings in production of machinery able to withstand high temperature and pressure. Noguchi was not the only Japanese scientist or entrepreneur keen on ammonia synthesis. Several studied or attended conferences in the United States or Europe, and in 1913 they formed a Society for the Investi-gation of Ammonium Sulfate (Ryūan Chōsakai). This diverse group of scholars included champions of French, German, and Italian methods. They had just settled on a French method as desirable for licensing when World War I interrupted their negotiations. The more enthusiastic members of the society then began research to develop their own methods.[24]

During World War I, these private research attempts all encoun-tered the same stumbling block: inadequate machinery for com-mercial production. Machinery able to withstand the high pressure of ammonia manufacture was produced only by the German arms maker Krupps, but it was unavailable during the war.[25] The Japanese Navy was working on high-pressure machinery, but had not yet perfected it. Process technology clearly lagged behind Japanese scientists' and entrepreneurs' understanding of basic science.

The government, therefore, felt compelled to assist researchers to delve into the mysteries of high-pressure, high-temperature production. Like governments in the West, it invested in research in ammonia synthesis for strategic reasons during the war. (Explosives required fixed nitrogen.) World War I, a government-sponsored group of academics reported, was a "chemical war."[26] Accepting this definition, the government established the Institute of Physical Chemistry in 1917 and the Special Nitrogen Research Laboratory at TIEL in 1918. The latter was particularly successful, patenting its own method of ammonia synthesis in 1922; this Japanese method would be used by a major producer, Shōwa Fertilizer, by the end of the decade.[27]

Noguchi's efforts as Japan's first successful producer stand out amid these attempts. In 1922, he had just one potential rival in commercial synthesis of ammonia, Suzuki Shōten (a trading company known for its aggressive expansion of business activities), which began planning early synthesis under a license it acquired in 1922. But Suzuki Shōten's electrochemical production encountered numerous problems with explosions and faulty equipment during the early 1920s, and eventually the company went bankrupt in 1927 (for reasons unrelated to its chemical manufacture). By contrast, Nitchitsu's progress was successful.

Britain's resumption of exports of ammonium sulfate in 1919 led to a competitive battle for the Japanese market among European producers. The price of fertilizer began plummeting in the fall of 1920;[28] by February 1921, Noguchi had arrived in Europe to study and possibly acquire a more profitable synthetic method. Moreover, his license for use of the cyanamide method was about to expire and would either have to be renewed or replaced. Worsening market conditions pushed Noguchi to choose a synthetic method. He settled on one developed by an Italian, Luigi Casale. Other Japanese entrepreneurs initially interested in the license failed to see how Casale's limited experimental setup could be expanded to commercial proportions.[29] Noguchi, by contrast, had the scientific training to assess the merits of the work Casale did in his tiny laboratory and pilot plant. After paying a 10% deposit (¥100,000) to hold Casale's license, Noguchi took a quick trip to Germany to investigate rayon production before returning to Japan.

Back at home, Noguchi discussed with his Nitchitsu colleagues how the new Italian technology would serve company strategy. The Nitchitsu managers analyzed how their facilities could be modified. They inspected various plant sites. They dealt with politicians to get a favorable ruling permitting them to retain most of the electricity they generated for company use. They then left for Europe, stopping in New York to get American Cyanamid to relinquish its license for Casale's process, in London to acquire yen with the help of Mitsubishi Bank, and in Berlin to reexamine rayon manufacture (closely related to ammonia production) before arriving in Rome in December 1921.[30] There they concluded their negotiations with Casale, arranging payment of the balance and acquiring the license.

Noguchi and his colleagues returned home quickly and in the next few months began construction of a new plant at Nobeoka. Some members of the Board of Directors had hoped to convert existing facilities at Kagami to the new method, but Noguchi persuaded them that the requirements of the new technology, particularly for increased supplies of energy, dictated construction of a new plant at Nobeoka. Besides, he said, the Nobeoka area was preferable because it was not surrounded by farmers and fishermen who would protest plant construction, as was Kagami.[31] The plant was ready within 18 months, and Casale himself threw the switch to start production at Nobeoka in September 1923. In the next five years, Nitchitsu built five new electricity generating plants to supply Nobeoka and upgraded the technology at Minamata to use the synthetic method. Technical employees trained at Nobeoka joined the work force at Minamata. These highly skilled recent graduates with state-of-the-art training averaged just 28 years of age and in later years helped foster a sense of company interdependence as they moved to higher managerial positions in the diverse Nitchitsu subsidiaries.

By the spring of 1927, Minamata was producing 20 tons of ammonia daily. The success of the synthetic process drew attention to the inefficiency of the cyanamide process. Nitchitsu had already begun to dismantle its old technology by then. Even a subsidiary—Shin'-etsu Nitrogenous Fertilizer (Shin'etsu Chisso Hiryō KK)—set up in 1926 to produce calcium cyanamide with the machinery Nitchitsu no longer needed, dropped that line in 1928 in favor of other chemicals.[32] Less efficient technology, even when used by a subsidiary, did not serve company interests. What did serve Nitchitsu's interests at Nobeoka was diversification in areas related to ammonia synthesis.[33] Rayon, a new fiber which required ammonia in its manufacture, became the first of an ever-widening circle of closely related products made by Nitchitsu or its subsidiaries in Japan and Korea.

Diversification led to numerous subsidiaries being created, each making one or more products spun-off from the technology of ammonia manufacture, and each having a complementary relationship with some other subsidiaries or the parent company.[34] The existence of complementary subsidiaries, in turn, encouraged their researchers to be creative in planning new products using techniques or materials developed by themselves or by their counterparts in other subsidiaries. Some of these creative scientists were particularly innovative: at Minamata, Murayama Kyūzō developed an internationally patented method of oxidizing ammonia to produce nitric acid (for explosives), and Hashimoto Hikoshichi made significant innovations in carbide-based organic synthetics. Although Hashimoto's discovery represented a scientific breakthrough, it also eventually caused the residents of Minamata extraordinary suffering from poisoning by the mercury used in the production process.[35] Minamata Disease, like the notorious electrochemical pollution cases at Love Canal, New York, and Hopewell, Virginia, is a sobering reminder that innovations that serve company interests do not always serve the public interest.

Nevertheless, innovations in these processes and products, together with Nitchitsu's pioneering development of synthetic ammonia within Japan, indicate that Noguchi and his colleagues had a bold entrepreneurial spirit and solid scientific training. They anticipated spinoffs and interrelated uses of new technology. By the end of the decade Nitchitsu was Japan's quintessential technology-driven chemical company.

The pace of research, development, and commercial production of new products accelerated with Nitchitsu's expansion to Korea after 1925. Resources, particularly electricity, were abundant and accessible to Chōsen Chisso Hiryō, Nitchitsu's Korean subsidiary, because of the company's cooperative relationship with the officials of the Government General. The cost of labor was cheaper in the colony. Many of Noguchi's skilled technicians and managers were sent to Korea, so there were experienced white-collar employees with a sense of company identification. A good market for Chōsen Chisso's products, especially fertilizer, was right at hand in Korea, and additional output was sent to Japan. And capital for investment in innovative techniques and products was available through governmental and semi-governmental banks in Japan and Korea. Thus, Chōsen Chisso met the conditions for investment in new technology, and failure to invest would have been unprofitable. Indeed, investment in innovation was as much a part of Noguchi's business strategy in Korea as it had been in Japan. His Korean sites were not simply factories for cheap off-shore manufacture of products developed back home; they were the heart of Noguchi's program of innovation and diversification.

Noguchi's initial investment in Korea in 1925 followed years of interest in the colony. Before 1920, there had been insufficient incentive to invest there, as the Corporation Law of 1911 severely restricted investment opportunities. The law was lifted in 1920, but Noguchi was busily acquiring and installing the Casale method at Nobeoka and Minamata in the early 1920s. By mid-decade, and increasingly into the 1930s, the Government General in Korea had changed its policy and was actively encouraging investment.[36]

It was at that time that Noguchi was enticed to Korea by two engineers: a college classmate, Morita Kazuo, and a much younger Tokyo University graduate, Kubota Yutaka. These two had drawn up plans for developing hydroelectricity in northern Korea and had applied to the Government General for permission to build. The Governor General, who had received another application, asked the two to find guaranteed customers for their anticipated generation. Kubota and Morita decided that electrochemical manufacture would probably be the best use of the huge planned capacity, and they could find no better customer than Noguchi, whom they each knew in a separate context.[37] Noguchi replied enthusiastically to the invitation to join the two engineers and quickly made the project his own. The Government General was impressed with Noguchi's track record in Japan and gave him the right to develop the Pujon River, one of the largest in the north.[38]

Chōsen Hydroelectric (Chōsen Suiden) was formally established in January 1926 and began generating electricity in 1929. The Pujon River's capacity of 80,000 to 90,000 kilowatts made it the largest in the Japanese empire at the time. (Noguchi's later hydroelectric plants would dwarf even the Pujon.) Construction itself played a significant role in the advance of technology in Japan, as stages two, three, and four of dam construction used sophisticated machinery designed and built in Japan, one of the first such uses on a large scale. By the end of 1929, the manufacturing complex—Chōsen Chisso at Hungnam—which accompanied the Pujon electrical plant, was ready for operation. Chōsen Chisso had recently merged with Chōsen Hydroelectric, and the new company (called Chōsen Chisso) was capitalized at ¥30 million.[39]

In January 1930, the first ammonium sulfate came off the line, just as world fertilizer prices were heading toward their nadir. Such adverse market conditions demanded that Noguchi concentrate most of his fertilizer production where it was cheapest—at Hungnam—and accelerate diversification of his product line to lessen the impact of market fluctuations. The former strategy was carried out quickly. In 1932, Hungnam produced 225,000 tons of ammonium sulfate, while Minamata produced 99,100 tons. By 1935, Hungnam's output had grown to 341,000 tons, while Minamata's and Nobeoka's had dropped to 49,000 and 9,500 tons, respectively. Hungnam was on its way to becoming Asia's largest and the world's third largest electrochemical facility. Diversification was also quickly advanced. By 1935, the firm had greater sales volumes—although, interestingly, not profits—in products other than fertilizers.[40]

As the decade of the 1930s opened, however, Chōsen Chisso was facing serious problems: revived dumping of European fertilizer, drought in Korea which depleted the Pujon reservoir, and adverse international conditions due to the Great Depression. Noguchi and his closest colleagues supported expansion of investment in production, diversification, and innovative research, which required increased generative capacity.[41] To gain access to additional rivers in Korea, Noguchi approached Governor General Ugaki Kazushige at an appropriate moment. During 1931 and 1932, Ugaki had conferred with Mitsubishi Gōshi about the company's pursuing its interest in developing the Changjin River; the zaibatsu replied that it had no immediate plans to do so.[42] But Noguchi did have plans and applied to Ugaki for development rights. Noguchi was granted the right to the Changjin, but at great cost. His expansion of investment at the height of the Depression bothered his benefactors at Mitsubishi Bank, and they demanded repayment of the ¥25 million loan. Thus, Noguchi became alienated from Mitsubishi Bank, though Iwasaki family members continued to have extensive shareholdings. To be sure, the repayment terms were easy,[43] and Noguchi had a comfortable cushion of profits to draw on.[44] Moreover, Noguchi benefited from his connection to Ugaki, who expedited contacts with bankers at the government-managed Bank of Chōsen, the Industrial Bank of Japan (Kōgyō Ginkō), and the Industrial Bank of Korea (Shokusan Ginkō). Interestingly, the connection with the Government General (and the loss of Mitsubishi support) accelerated diversification because the officials particularly encouraged development of products like synthetic fuel and explosives which were otherwise too expensive to develop.

The Bank of Chōsen contributed the largest loans of the three banks. The bank's president, Katō Keisaburō, strongly endorsed companies which manufactured strategic products; thus, Bank of Chōsen loans were often earmarked for subsidiaries of Chōsen Chisso making such products.[45] Because new product lines were often produced in specially created subsidiaries after an initial period of development in an existing entity of Chōsen Chisso,[46] it is possible to infer, by studying loans, which product lines the authorities and the semigovernmental banks wished to encourage. Before

1937, Chōsen Chisso, which itself concentrated on fertilizers, received most loans from the Bank of Chōsen. Of course, many new products eventually manufactured by their own subsidiaries had been developed at Chōsen Chisso, so loans to the parent company might represent the bank's support of research in these new products and/or expansion of fertilizer production; the specific uses of these loans cannot be unbundled. Loans to newly created subsidiaries tell us more about the intent of the lender. For example, it is possible to note that Chōsen Artificial Oil, a strategically important subsidiary, received large loans after 1937.[47]

The most costly investments for Chōsen Chisso were in electrical generation. Here, too, government involvement played a significant role. When the massive 340,000 kilowatt Changjin Hydroelectric (Chōshinkō Suiden) was established in May 1933, the Governor General required creation of Chōsen Electricity Transmission (Chōsen Sōden) to transmit power to Seoul and Pyongyang.[48] Later, generating plants built at the Hochon and Yalu Rivers were similarly required to transmit a large part of their output to customers outside the company.

But it was in investment in specific types of manufactures that public policy most affected business strategy. Production of explosives, for example, had not been permitted in Korea, yet Noguchi had an excellent source of both glycerine and nitric acid. Ugaki permitted Noguchi to make explosives after 1934 because the government encouraged industrialization, construction, and mining, all of which needed explosives. Innovative research in explosives, in turn, fostered greater intrafirm cooperation, as the Changjin project contributed electricity; Hungnam supplied ammonia, oxygen, glycerine, and nitric acid; the Pon'gung plant sent glycol; and Nobeoka sent skilled technicians and scientists.[49] The large variety of explosives was marketed by Chōsen 'Mite (Chōsen Maito, or dynamite), an early example of the company's vertical expansion into new types of industries. Vertical integration was later a most significant feature of Noguchi's operations, encouraged by the colonial government's support of innovation and diversification of production in the company's multisubsidiary organization.

The technology for synthetic oil, which was produced from coal tar, was another area researched and commercially developed with government encouragement. There was no market in Japan or Korea for synthetic fuel in the early 1930s. Its advanced technology, which used many of the principles of ammonia synthesis, was not cost effective because real oil was still cheap. But the Navy had a strategic interest in a source of oil independent of potentially hostile foreign producers and therefore undertook research on its own while engaging Noguchi's assistance in carrying out original research. Noguchi put scientists to work on fuel synthesis, and in 1935 set up a subsidiary, Chōsen Coal Industries (Chōsen Sekitan Kōgyō KK, later renamed Chōsen Artificial Oil [Chōsen Jinzō Sekiyu]).[50]

In 1941, Noguchi opened the world's second largest hydroelectric dam on the Yalu River. Abundant electricity permitted exceptional growth in capitalization of Chōsen Chisso Explosives and Chōsen Artificial Oil. It also permitted accelerating diversification. But this diversification was different from that of the first half of the 1930s. That is, many of the new products developed did not represent research in innovative science and did not specifically serve company interests. As mobilization for war intensified, company strategy took a back seat to national strategic needs. The company was encouraged to expand territorially to China, Hainan Island, Indonesia, and elsewhere in East Asia. Nitchitsu innovated and produced according to government requests. The company began to stress supplying products like ball-bearings and resources like silver, gold, nickel, and sulfur which were both unprofitable and unable to stimulate scientific creativity.[51] Indeed, Nitchitsu's principle until that time—profitability and growth through innovation, diversification, and reinvestment in related research and development—had to be modified. Company strategy came to reflect service of the national interest as well as the need for solvency and profitability. During the company's first three decades, however, Nitchitsu did indeed manifest a close tie between innovation and business strategy.

III. Conclusion

Nitchitsu offers a particularly good example of the relationship between innovation and business strategy because it indicates both sides of the innovation-strategy equation during its three prewar decades. That is, a study of Nitchitsu shows unambiguous cases in which the availability of new technology induced innovative commercialization and cases in which, conversely, commercial necessity inspired the search for innovative technology.

Students of innovation frequently favor one side over the other. Advocates of science emphasize the technology-push theory of innovation; those oriented toward economic interpretations tout the market-pull theory. Either theory is insufficient by itself, as Nitchitsu's case shows us empirically. To be sure, there are cases of technological breakthroughs producing new ideas and products which have no prior demand, but which nevertheless succeed in creating their own market (e.g., space satellite research, originally undertaken for strategic reasons, has revolutionized communications by telephone, fascimile, and other methods). And there are cases where market demand brings forth technological innovation, as in the development of plastics as substitutes for rare natural products. But, though "necessity may be the mother of invention, . . . procreation requires a partner."[52] Indeed, scientists and engineers with great ideas have to sell them, either to a funding agency (the government or an enthusiastic wealthy patron) or to the marketplace in the form of successful products. Only then can the technology be the foundation of further innovation. Similarly, entrepreneurs must understand science in addition to having a good understanding of the market because they must maintain competitiveness at the "cutting edge" of technology.

Noguchi Jun was successful because as a scientist-entrepreneur he understood both technology and the market—both innovation and business strategy. He linked the two in his Nippon Chisso Hiryō. Moreover, he understood that neither was static, that technology continued developing and the market always changed. The permutations and combinations of changing technology and business conditions were complex and subtle and demanded conscientious linking of business strategy with innovation. This was best achieved in a company like Nitchitsu whose scientist-entrepreneur founder multiplied his talents with a strong cadre of scientifically well-trained managers who understood new technology and knew how to apply it.

NOTES

Place of publication is Tokyo unless otherwise noted.

1. Studies representative of widely differing interpretations of the efficacy of industrial policy include Chalmers Johnson, *MITI and the Japanese Miracle: The Growth of Industrial Policy, 1925–1975*, Stanford, Stanford University Press, 1982; Edward J. Lincoln, *Japan's Industrial Policies*, Washington, D.C., Japan Economic Institute of America, 1984; and Daniel I. Okimoto, "Regime Characteristics of Japanese Industrial Policy," in Hugh Patrick, ed., *Japan's High Technology Industries: Lessons and Limitations of Industrial Policy*, Seattle, University of Washington Press, 1986.
2. Studies representative of this approach include William Ouchi, *Theory Z: How American Business Can Meet the Japanese Challenge*, Reading, Mass., Addison-Wesley, 1981; and Richard Tanner Pascale and Anthony G. Athos, *The Art of Japanese Management*, New York, Simon and Schuster, 1981.
3. See, for example, Toshio Shishido, "Japanese Technological Development," in Toshio Shishido and Ryuzo Sato, *Economic Policy and Development: New Perspectives*, Dover, Mass., Auburn House Publishing, 1985; and Sheridan Tatsuno, *The Technopolis Strategy: Japan, High Technology, and the Control of the Twenty-first Century*, New York, Prentice Hall, 1986.
4. For an informative treatment of the historical dimensions of the adaptation in Japan of technology developed elsewhere, see Ryuzo Sato, "Nothing New? An Historical Perspective on Japanese Technology Policy," in Shishido and Sato, *Economic Policy and Development*.
5. An excellent historical exposition of this subject is in Andrew Gordon, *The Evolution of Labor Relations in Japan: Heavy Industry, 1853–1955*, Cambridge, Mass., Council on East Asian Studies, Harvard University, 1985.
6. James C. Abegglen and George Stalk, Jr., *Kaisha, the Japanese*

Corporation, New York, Basic Books, 1985, pp. 189–90; and Tatsuno, *op. cit.,* p. 58, find the greatest dynamism among Japanese companies not related to "groups," some of which were prewar zaibatsu.

7. Paul M. Hohenberg, *Chemicals in Western Europe: 1850–1914,* Chicago, Rand McNally and Company, 1967, p. 82; Martha Moore Trescott, *The Rise of the American Electrochemicals Industry, 1880–1910: Studies in the American Technological Environment,* Westport, Conn., Greenwood Press, 1981, p. 127.

8. Christopher Freeman, *The Economics of Industrial Innovation,* Harmondsworth, England, Penguin Books, 1974, p. 92.

9. Except from 1937 to 1945, when the government actively purchased strategic products, Japanese industrial policy has generally tended to encourage efficiency, quality, and scale of production. Before the war, extensive government "targeting" or selecting of promising industries was rare; the common practice was to elevate the factors of production and expect competent firms to rise accordingly, a kind of "supply side" assistance. And the government in Japan, as in the Western industrialized countries, got the best return on its investment by promoting education.

10. For more extensive treatment of scientific education and research during the Meiji period, see Watanabe Tokuji, *Gendai Nihon sangyō hattatsushi: kagaku kōgyō* (The development of modern Japanese industries: chemical industries), Gendai Nihon Sangyō Hattatsushi Kenkyūkai, 1968, pp. 182–89; Nakamura Chūichi, *Nihon sangyō no kigyōshiteki kenkyū* (A business historical study of Japanese industry), Yūkonsha, 1965, Chs. 1 and 2; *Meiji kōgyōshi: kagaku kōgyō* (Industrial history in Meiji Japan: chemical industry), Meiji Kōgyōshi Hakkōjō, 1925, pp. 1117–37; Nihon Kagakukai, *Nihon no kagaku 100 nenshi: kagaku to kagaku kōgyō no ayumi* (A 100-year history of Japanese chemistry), Nihon Kagaku Dōjin, 1978, pp. 92–113; Nihon Kagakushi Gakkai, *Nihon kagaku gijutsu shi taikei,* Vol. 21, *Kagaku gijutsu* (A history of Japanese technology: chemical technology), Daiichi Hōki Shuppan, 1964; Yuasa Mitsutomo, *Kagakushi* (Science history), Keizai Shinpōsha, 1961, passim; Miyoshi Nobuhiro, *Nihon kōgyō kyōiku seiritsu no kenkyū* (A study of the establishment of industrial education in Japan), Kazama Shobō, 1979, pp. 269–70; Ryōichi Iwauchi, "Institutionalizing the Technical Manpower Formation in Meiji Japan," *Developing Economies,* Vol. 15, No. 4 (Dec. 1977), pp. 420–39; and an interesting series of articles in English in *Journal of World History,* Vol. 9 (1965).

11. Nihon Kagakukai, *op. cit.*, p. 99; Watanabe Minoru, "Japanese Students Abroad and the Acquisition of Scientific and Technical Knowledge," *Journal of World History*, Vol. 9 (1965), pp. 278–82; Nakayama Shigeru, "The Role Played by Universities in Scientific and Technological Development in Japan," *Journal of World History*, Vol. 9 (1965), p. 348.

12. Watanabe, *op. cit.*, pp. 184–85; *Tokyo Kōgyō Shikenjo 60 nenshi* (A 60-year history of Tokyo Industrial Experimental Laboratory), Tokyo Kōgyō Shikenjo, 1960, p. 1.

13. Kamata Shōji, "Waga kuni saisho no kābaido jigyō; Kōriyama Kābaido seizōjo" (Japan's first carbide enterprise), in Kamata Shōji, ed., *Nippon Chisso shi e no shōgen*, Vol. 24, Tokyo Shinkū Sābisu-nai Nippon Chisso Shi e no Shōgen Henshū Iinkai, 1985, pp. 75–76.

14. Trescott, *op. cit.*, p. 36.

15. Kābaido Kōgyō no Ayumi Iinkai, *Kābaido kōgyō no ayumi* (Development of the carbide industry), Kābaido Kōgyōkai, 1956, p. 31. Canadian Thomas Willson discovered calcium carbide in 1892 and began producing it commercially in 1895. Japan began importing it in 1896, and Fujiyama perfected the production process in 1901. For more on the Siemens company, see Sigfried von Weiher, "The Rise and Development of Electrical Engineering and Industry in Germany in the Nineteenth Century: A Case Study—Siemens and Halske," in Akio Okochi and Hoshimi Ushida, eds., *Development and Diffusion of Technology: Electrical and Chemical Industries*, University of Tokyo Press, 1980, p. 39.

16. Denka Rokujūnenshi Hensan Iinkai, *Denka 60 nenshi* (A 60-year history of Denka), 1967, p. 91; Nihon Ryūan Kōgyō Kyōkai, *Nihon ryūan kōgyōshi* (A history of the ammonium sulfate industry), 1963, p. 50; Katagiri Ryūkichi, *Hantō no jigyō-ō Noguchi Jun* (Noguchi Jun: entrepreneurial king of the peninsula), Tōkai Shuppansha, 1939, pp. 184–85; L. F. Haber, *The Chemical Industry 1900–1930: International Growth and Technological Change*, Oxford, Clarendon Press, 1971, p. 88.

17. Nihon Kagakukai, *op. cit.*, p. 92.

18. Japanese farmers used 69,364 tons of imported and 3,534 tons of domestic ammonium sulfate in 1910. Watanabe, *op. cit.*, Appendix, pp. 27–35.

19. Freeman, *op. cit.*, p. 43, discusses the importance of the flow method.

20. Denka Rokujūnenshi Hensan Iinkai, *op. cit.*, p. 92.

21. Trescott, *op. cit.*, Ch. 6.

22. In 1912, as Nitchitsu was suffering a cash flow crisis, the Railroad Board, hoping to electrify the railroads, purchased the company's facilities in Kyushu for ¥1,570,000. But the government agency was unable to use the facilities right away, so Noguchi continued to use his facilities to produce electricity and electrochemicals for a small payment to the government. Three years later, the government decided to sell the facilities back to Noguchi. By then the company had rebounded.

23. Yamamoto Tomio, *Nippon Chisso Hiryō jigyō taikan* (Nitchitsu company survey), Osaka, Nippon Chisso Hiryō, 1937, p. 451.

24. Noguchi's article, published in 1914 as part of the series *Denki hyōron*, was entitled "Kōgyōjō yori mita kūchū chisso kotei hō" (Commercializing the fixation of atmospheric nitrogen), Yamamoto, *op. cit.*, p. 457; Nihon Ryūan Kōgyō Kyōkai, *op. cit.*, pp. 123–27.

25. William J. Reader, *Imperial Chemical Industries: A History—The Forerunners 1870–1926*, London, Oxford University Press, 1970, p. 350.

26. Watanabe, *op. cit.*, p. 242.

27. Nihon Kagakukai, *op. cit.*, pp. 146–47; Nihon Ryūan Kōgyō Kyōkai, *op. cit.*, pp. 130–31.

28. Hashimoto Jurō, "1920 nendai no ryūan shijō" (The market for ammonium sulfate in the 1920s), *Shakai keizai shigaku*, Vol. 43, No. 4 (1978), p. 386.

29. Yoshioka Kiichi, *Noguchi Jun*, Fuji Intānashonaru Konsarutanto, 1962, pp. 125–26; Yamamoto, *op. cit.*, p. 458.

30. Yoshioka, *op. cit.*, pp. 133–36; "Nippon Chisso 30 nen kinen zadankai" (Round-table talk on the 30th anniversary of Nippon Chisso), in Kamata Shōji, ed., *Nippon Chisso shi e no shōgen*, Vol. 14 (1981), p. 57; Yamamoto, *op. cit.*, p. 459.

31. Yoshioka, *op. cit.*, pp. 137–38.

32. Yamamoto, *op. cit.*, pp. 464–65; Shimotani Masahiro, "Nippon Chisso Hiryō KK no takakuka no tenkai" (On the diversification of Nippon Chisso), *Osaka keidai ronshū*, Vol. 112 (1976), p. 109; Takeoka Kōji, "Kagami kōjō to Shin'etsu Chisso no kaiso" (Kagami factory and Shin'etsu Chisso), Kamata Shōji, ed., *Nippon chisso shi e no shōgen*, Vol. 9 (1980), p. 68.

33. The pattern of diversification after acquisition of the license for ammonia synthesis was repeated at Du Pont, American Cyanamid, and Union Carbide in the United States in the mid to late 1920s as well. Graham D. Taylor and Patricia E. Sudnik, *Du Pont and the International Chemical Industry*, Boston, Twayne, 1984, pp. 80–82.

34. Sugimoto Toshio, "Ōtsu, Nobeoka kōjō no kaiko: Noguchi-san no jinken kōgyō kaihatsu e no kōken" (A memory of Ōtsu and Nobeoka factories), in Kamata Shōji, ed., *Nippon Chisso shi e no shōgen*, Vol. 5 (1978), pp. 5–99.

35. Fukumoto Kunio, *Noguchi wa ikite iru: jigyō supiritto to sono tenkai* (Noguchi lives on: the development of his entrepreneurial spirit), Fuji Intānashonaru Konsarutanto, 1964, p. 46; Shibamura Yōgo, *Kigyō no hito Noguchi Jun den: Denryoku, kagaku kōgyō no paionia* (Biography of Noguchi), Yūhikaku, 1981, pp. 77–78.

36. Kobayashi Hideo, "1930 nendai Nippon Chisso Hiryō Kabushiki Kaisha no Chōsen no shinshutsu ni tsuite" (On Nippon Chisso's advance into Korea in the 1930s), in Yamada Hideo, *Shokuminchi keizaishi no shomondai*, Ajia Keizai Kenkyūjo, 1973, p. 141.

37. For further information, see Chōsen Denki Jigyō Shi Henshū Iinkai, *Chōsen denki jigyō shi* (A history of Korean electrical companies), Shadan Hōjin Chūō Nikkan Kyōkai, 1981, pp. 249–50.

38. Yoshioka, *op. cit.*, pp. 164–65; Nagatsuka Riichi, *Kubota Yutaka*, Denki Jōhōsha, 1966, pp. 130, 175; Chōsen Denki, *op. cit.*, p. 133; Suzuki Tsuneo, "Nihon ryūan kōgyō no jiritsuka katei" (The autonomous development of the ammonium sulfate industry), *Shakai keizai shigaku* Vol. 43, No. 2 (1978), p. 74; Ōshio Takeshi, "Nitchitsu kontserun to Chōsen Chisso Hiryō" (Nitchitsu *konzern* and Chōsen Chisso Hiryō), *Keizai kenkyū*, Vol. 49–50 (1978), pp. 68–69; Ōshio Takeshi, "Chōsen Chisso Hiryō Kabushiki Kaisha no shūeki ni kansuru ichikosatsu" (On the profits of Chōsen Chisso), *Keizai kenkyū*, Vol. 72 (1985), pp. 117–23; Kobayashi, *op. cit.*, pp. 180, 171.

39. Noguchi Jun, "Nihonkai ni kiriotoshita Fusenkō no suiden jigyō" (The hydroelectric enterprise on the Pujon River), in Shinogi Itsuo, ed., *Chōsen no denki jigyō o kataru*, Seoul, Chōsen Denki Kyōkai, 1937, p. 117; Yoshioka, *op. cit.*, p. 167–70.

40. Shimotani Masahiro, "Nitchitsu kontserun to gōsei ryūan kōgyō," (Nitchitsu *konzern* and the synthetic ammonium sulfate industry), *Osaka keidai ronshū*, Vol. 114 (1976), p. 73; Kobayashi, *op. cit.*, p. 163.

41. Parallels with Du Pont are instructive here. The American firm used diversification as a business strategy to survive the Depression. Impoverished American farmers did not buy fertilizers, so new uses for ammonia technology had to be found. Taylor and Sudnik, *op. cit.*, p. 144.

42. Yoshioka, *op. cit.*, p. 233.

43. Apparently, Nitchitsu paid back about half the amount in 1933;

the rest was deferred until later. To be sure, ¥13 million was a large sum, but Nitchitsu had large internal reserves from profits in Korea and access to short term loans from other banks. Ōshio Takeshi, "Nitchitsu kontserun no kin'yū kōzō (Financial structure of Nitchitsu *konzern*), *Keizai kenkyū*, Vol. 75 (1986), pp. 142–43.

44. Ugaki Kazushige, "Noguchi Jun o omou" (Recollections of Noguchi), Takanashi Koji, *Noguchi Jun o tsuikairoku*, Osaka, Noguchi Jun Tsuikairoku Hensankai, 1952, pp. 45–46; Ichikawa Homei, *Ichikawa Seiji den* (Biography of Ichikawa Seiji), Osaka, Bunshindo, 1974, p. 104.

45. Katagiri, *op. cit.*, pp. 84–85; Chōsen Ginkō, *Chōsen Ginkō Shōkeisanshō*, (General accounts of Bank of Chōsen), 1930–43, unpaginated, Seoul, Chōsen Ginkō.

46. Nitchitsu or its subsidiary Chōsen Chisso frequently created wholly or partially owned subsidiaries rather than merely setting up a factory that was owned by the parent corporation. These subsidiaries were separate corporate entities for tax reasons.

47. *Chōsen Ginkō shōkeisanshō.*

48. Yoshioka, *op. cit.*, p. 240.

49. Kariya Susumu, "Kayaku kōjō" (The explosives factory), *Kagaku kōgyō* (Jan. 1951), p. 80.

50. Kamoi Yu, *Noguchi Jun*, Tokosha, 1943, p. 327; Hoshiko Toshiteru, "Chōsen ni okeru sekiyu jigyō" (The petroleum industry in Korea), in Shibuya Reiji, *Chōsen no kōgyō to sono shigen*, Seoul, Chōsen Kōgyō Kyōkai, 1937, pp. 364–67; Ōshio, *op. cit.*, p. 105.

51. Ōshio, *op. cit.*, pp. 182–86, 192.

52. Freeman, *op. cit.*, pp. 165–66.

Comment

Akira Kudō
University of Tokyo

Professor Molony's paper deals with the contributions of the "highly skilled entrepreneurs" who are overlooked in all approaches to the causes of Japan's apparent economic successes. She takes the entrepreneurial activities of Noguchi Jun (or Shitagau), founder of Nitchitsu, as a case. Noguchi is described not merely as a speculative or adventurous businessman, but as the embodiment of entrepreneurship with scientific and technological knowledge—the "scientist-entrepreneur." Molony finds in Noguchi an ideal combination of a creative scientific mind with good business instincts, a bold entrepreneurial spirit with solid scientific training. She gives us a brief and well-balanced description of Noguchi's entrepreneurial activities, exploiting primary literature as well as the most recent studies, of which Ōshio Takeshi's papers are representative.

A more vivid picture of Noguchi can be obtained by comparing Noguchi with other founders of newly risen zaibatsu, such as Aikawa Yoshisuke of Nissan and Mori Nobuteru of Shōwa Denkō, as Udagawa Masaru did in his book *Shinkō zaibatsu* (Newly risen zaibatsu, 1983), with entrepreneurs of a different type, such as Kaneko Naokichi of Suzuki Shōten and his contemporary entrepreneurial counterparts in the United States.

Criticizing a generally accepted understanding, she characterizes Nitchitsu's absorption and development of new technology, including its introduction of Casale's process led by Noguchi, as "incremental." It is true that Nitchitsu moved into ammonia synthesis after succeeding in producing ammonia through the calcium cyanamide process, so that its development was more incremental than those of, for example, Suzuki Shōten and Nippon Tar Kōgyō (later Mitsubishi Kasei). But her criticism is somewhat overstated; it seems to me that the common interpretation still has validity. Nitchitsu's introducing the Casale process was a kind of great leap forward in both a technological and a managerial sense: in a technological sense because the process required basic ability in chemistry as well as in chemical engineering and went beyond the so-called electrochemistry; in a managerial sense because Noguchi bought the Casale license for the enormous sum of about one million yen and attempted its immediate commercialization on the large scale of over ten thousand tons per year at Nobeoka. In order to make the difference between the calcium cyanamide process and the synthetic process clear, Noguchi himself used the metaphor of the steamship and airship. Noguchi's understanding of this differentiated him from Fujiyama Tsuneichi. Certainly, we need a more detailed analysis of the process of Noguchi's introduction of the Casale license, from the negotiations through contracting for the license to the establishment of operations, as Wakimura Yoshitarō and Ōshio did for the case of the Frank-Caro process.

It still seems to me that Noguchi's activities consisted of continuous leaps of various magnitudes. How could he overcome almost all types of troubles caused by his many leaps? Under what circumstances could he practice his enormous entrepreneurship? The answers to these questions, which Molony gives us in her paper, are somewhat obscured by her denial of discontinuities in Noguchi's activities. Entrepreneurship is more than an ideal combination of scientific mind and business sense.

My next comment concerns the failure of Noguchi's last leap: that in fuel synthesis or coal hydrogenation. In 1935, immediately after the Navy had announced the success of the "Navy process" of coal hydrogenation independent of IG Farben, Noguchi decided to launch fuel synthesis by using the Navy process. For this, he established new plants in Korea and later in Manchuria. This was one of his leaps, too, in both a technological and a managerial sense, although it was a kind of diversification related to ammonia synthesis referred to by Molony. According to my research, he started this project not under apparent pressure from the Navy or other sections of the government, but voluntarily because of his strong confidence in Nitchitsu's abilities due to its success in controlling the high-temperature and high-pressure chemical reactions of the Casale process. His self-confidence, however, was excessive. The technical staff of Nitchitsu failed to overcome serious problems accompanying control of coal under high temperature and high pressure. They suffered commercially from cheap oil entering Japan from the Southeast Asian areas under Japanese military occupation. But their failure to earn profits was mainly due to technical problems. This case seems to me to be crucial in analyzing Molony's "incrementalism" hypothesis as well as her "scientist-entrepreneur" model.

Of course, we cannot attribute Noguchi's failure in oil synthesis only to some limitations in his entrepreneurship. Nitchitsu was a leader in technological innovations in oil synthesis in Japan, but, unlike in Germany, synthetic oil, in the strict sense of the word, was not produced in Japan at all. Chemistry and chemical engineering in Japan had not matured sufficiently to succeed in coal hydrogenation, as the United States Strategic Bombing Survey pointed out in one of its final reports as early as in 1946. Nevertheless, Noguchi's investment in synthetic oil should still be characterized as an error.

The case of synthetic oil suggests a few additional points concerning our theme "Japanese Management in Historical Perspective."

One point concerns the need to reexamine the meaning of the introduction of American technology and management after World War II. Only through this process could some barriers which Noguchi also had to confront be removed. It is true that Noguchi's activities were continued by his colleagues and followers and that successor enterprises of Nitchitsu, such as Asahi Kasei, Sekisui Kagaku, Sekisui Hausu, and Nippon Kōei, are well known for their innovativeness. But there is no simple continuity. What was abandoned and what was added? These questions are still open for study.

Another point which the case of oil synthesis suggests relates to the general character of entrepreneurship in Japan. I agree with Molony that imitation is an indispensable part of innovation. But it cannot be denied that more secondary innovations prevailed than original ones. How did entrepreneurship in Japan relate to this phenomenon? Molony's reference to the technological education system gives us suggestions, especially in her presentation of the German-model hypothesis. In this regard, recent papers by Uchida Hoshimi concerning technical education and training during the early stages of industrialization in Japan are informative.

Response

Barbara Molony

Professor Kudō's incisive comments address several significant aspects of technology and entrepreneurship in Japan. He suggests the appropriateness of comparing Noguchi Jun with his contemporaries in Japan and the United States. Noguchi had few peers in Japan before the war. Indeed, he had few among scientist-entrepreneurs in the United States as well. To be sure, historians of American management like Alfred Chandler (or Martha M. Trescott, more specifically for the electrochemical industry) cite numerous young men and women scientists with entrepreneurial spirit. But only a few, like DuPont, Dow, and Hooker, founded companies which have become household names. How these men differed from their less commercially successful contemporaries is an interesting story; more research remains to be done on how Noguchi may have differed from other young scientists of his day in Japan.

Kudō questions my stress on incrementalism in the adoption of new processes. I agree with him that entrepreneurialism involves risk-taking and therefore may be said to require "leaps." But these are leaps in a managerial sense; technologically, large leaps in licensed technology indicate a lack of scientific maturity. The technology for ammonia synthesis was not conceptually difficult, and Noguchi's own article on the method clearly indicated that he understood it years before adopting it. For him, adoption of the method after World War I represented a small technological leap but a large entrepreneurial leap. Kudō cites the case of coal hydrogenation; here Noguchi might even be said to have "leaped before he looked!" This case is particularly interesting because the involvement of the state unbalanced the more or less dyadic relationship of technology and business strategy characteristic of Noguchi's enterprise before the 1930s. Nevertheless, it is important to note that Noguchi did not believe the technology of coal hydrogenation represented an insurmountable leap.

Kudō also raises the important point of postwar continuities. There are two ways in which this issue can be addressed. One is the study of the successor companies to Noguchi's enterprise. The other is an analysis of the "demonstration effect" of Noguchi's experience on postwar entrepreneurial firms. Noguchi showed the feasibility of scientific-entrepreneurship. What effect this had on postwar firms deserves further study.

Araki Tōichirō and the Shaping
of Labor Management

Andrew Gordon
Duke University

I. Introduction

Araki Tōichirō founded a management consulting firm in Tokyo in the mid-1920s. He offered to help clients increase efficiency and adopt scientific management practices. He was one of the first successful professional business consultants in Japan. In a career that spanned six decades, he advised hundreds of businesses, including some of Japan's major public and private industrial enterprises, pushing his particular blend of engineering and human motivation techniques. Araki was a flamboyant personality, obsessed with the goal of efficiency in all matters, large and small, and devoted to Japan's national glory. Although historians of Japanese management have generally overlooked him, his impact was considerable.

I first came across Araki's name a decade ago while studying a labor dispute at the Yokohama Dock Company in 1929. Curious about his role in the incident, I sought more information on him, with little success. Several years later, I happened to meet one of his daughters in Boston, Massachusetts, and I discovered more about the man.[1] In this paper, I will introduce Araki's major contributions in the field of labor management, focusing only on the period before World War II.

Aside from the intrinsic interest of Araki's unusual career (he had an astonishing knack for placing himself at the center of the action), his story sheds light on a critical issue in the history of Japanese business: the nature and the origins of so-called Japanese-style labor management. Put simply, Araki exemplified and reinforced a managerial attitude toward labor motivation and efficiency in Japan that played a major role in the history of corporate control of labor.

A triad of purported key features of Japanese labor management is well known in the West by now, inside and outside the academic world: permanent employment, seniority wages, and cooperative company unions. A number of influential scholars of labor and business history accept these practices as characteristic of the Japanese system, with various qualifications, of course, and search for the roots of this "employment system" in the creative manipulation or transformation of past traditions by business managers.[2]

Hazama Hiroshi is perhaps the Japanese historian of labor management practice working in this tradition best known to Western scholars, for two reasons. First, because he does not write in a Marxist tradition (a rarity among labor historians in Japan), American scholars allergic to Marxism do not sneeze at his work. A second, closely related factor is that a condensed version of one of his books was translated and published in the *Journal of Japanese Studies*.[3] In it, Hazama argues forcefully but, I feel, unpersuasively that "the 'creative' use of tradition in Japan" on the part of management lies at the heart of labor-management history.[4] By tradition he means "paternalism, groupism, feelings of dependency, and a high regard for harmony and cooperation."[5] He maintains that managers in the interwar era perfected a method of "treating workers warmly," which he calls "systematic paternalism," and he asserts that incentive programs "in a Tayloristic vein" were *not* part of this management strategy.[6]

In both his book and the English-language article version, Hazama draws these conclusions from consideration of the career of Uno Riemon, a self-proclaimed specialist in "industrial education."[7] Hazama does make clear that Uno indeed espoused a kind of "systematic paternalism." What he fails to show is that Uno had significant impact. The strongest positive evidence offered concerning his impact was that one of his major publications was distributed to 316 "distribution outlets" in 1915.[8] But surely any company with a personnel office, and their numbers increased sharply during

World War I, would subscribe to a variety of publications on labor management. The simple fact of wide distribution tells nothing about the response of the readers. More telling evidence of his limited impact is Uno's failure to convince large numbers of business-men to pay for his advice:

> Uno was extremely active as the author of a variety of works, as a labor consultant, in lecturing societies and research associations, and in inspection tours of factories and related facilities. However, he lacked business talent, and was unable to develop the Industrial Education Society into a business resembling a present-day manage-ment consulting firm. Although the need for such organizations was already beginning to be felt as industrialization progressed, the Society was unable to take advantage of this golden opportunity and was continuously plagued with deficits. Since Uno in fact ruled the Industrial Education Society like an autocrat, it broke up when he died.[9]

The case of Araki Tōichirō sharply contrasts to that of Uno in three crucial regards. Araki developed a successful consulting business in the very years that Uno floundered; he helped create several management institutions which survive to this day; and his approach drew significantly upon ideas of industrial efficiency and industrial psychology gaining popularity after World War I in the United States.[10] Some of the differences in their fates may stem from Araki's greater business acumen, but surely the readier appeal of his advice to managers was a crucial factor. Araki's career and his hardly paternalistic "system" for managing labor offer a different perspective on the nature of interwar labor relations.

II. A Management Consultant in Prewar Japan

Araki Tōichirō was born in Tokyo in 1893, son of a bureaucrat in the new Meiji government, grandson of a *kendō* master from Kuma-moto *han*. From his family he absorbed a tremendous sense of national pride and personal mission. After obtaining a degree in applied chemistry from Tokyo Higher Industrial Institute in 1916, he worked two years with the Fujikura Electric Wire Corporation. In 1918 he took and passed the examination for study abroad given by the Ministry of Agriculture and Commerce and went to Akron Ohio to study the chemistry of rubber manufacture.[11]

He enrolled as a student at Akron University. Within one year his supervising professor had him working as an assistant instructor for $20 a week "because I am busy with my writing."[12] The arrangement greatly displeased Araki, certainly neither the first nor the last graduate student to feel exploited by a professor at some cost to his own research agenda. He remained in the United States four years, and after receiving a master's degree from Akron, he switched his focus away from chemical engineering and spent roughly a year pursuing a deepening interest in industrial engineering and scientific management.

Araki's timing was excellent. He managed to meet and study with two of the most prominent industrial engineers and industrial psychologists in America, Lillian Gilbreth and Harrington Emerson, as well as the followers of Frederick W. Taylor (d. 1915) at the Taylor Society. By the early 1920s, the field of industrial engineering in the United States had moved beyond Taylor's single-minded emphasis on monetary motivation and minute job analysis.[13] The philosophy of industrial efficiency and engineering which Araki absorbed and later sought to implement in Japan reflected an extremely recent broadening of American concerns to encompass what we now call personnel management: such practices, for example, as group production contests and systematic promotion and transfer plans.[14]

Beyond good timing, Araki's feel for an exciting new professional field in the era of managerial capitalism was astute. He claims to have decided that Japan at the time lacked a rigorous *method* for analyzing and solving human and technical problems of industrial management, rather than lacking any specific industrial skills.[15] His later consulting practices did use time-and-motion efficiency studies and some short-term wage incentives, but he also insisted that simple piecework wage stimuli alone were inadequate to motivate labor; he advocated a variety of more complex incentive plans and longer term group motivation tactics. This emphasis reflected the influence of his American experience to a considerable degree. We will also discover that the reluctance of Japanese workers to accept his early wage programs shaped his consulting strategy.

Upon his return to Japan in 1922, Araki quickly secured a position in the Industrial Efficiency Research Institute just initiated within the fledgling Kyōchōkai, a research institute for the study and solution of social (especially labor) problems founded in 1919 by government officials and corporate sponsors. In 1923 he also took on his first private client, a small pharmaceutical firm in Tokyo. Collaborating with a German psychologist also retained by the firm, he helped devise psychological tests for employees, train workers, and redesign both the factory layout and work flow. The earthquake of 1923 then intervened to temporarily end this job and permanently close the Kyōchōkai's Efficiency Institute. The latter had failed to establish a secure place for itself within the Kyōchōkai, and the earthquake apparently offered a convenient excuse to shut it down.[16]

Araki remained firm in his resolve to spread the new gospel of industrial efficiency, and he decided that the position of outside consultant offered the greatest potential for exerting influence and retaining his independence. After the earthquake he rented space in the Kyōchōkai building and founded his own Araki Efficiency Center. For two years he and a staff of two young assistants struggled to keep the enterprise afloat, but by 1925 Araki boasted an expanding list of clients and a stable consulting business.[17] In addition to seeking corporate clients in these years, Araki also played an active role in founding and promoting several organizations concerned with industrial efficiency. By 1928 he was an executive director of the new Japan Federation of Efficiency Associations, and in 1929 he proudly welcomed a delegation of American efficiency experts to Japan, including his former mentors Gilbreth and Emerson.[18]

Araki's decision to start his own business, rather than enter a company and serve as an in-house efficiency or personnel expert, reflected his personality as well as a strategic insight; impetuous and confident to the point of arrogance, Araki was a prototypical Japanese "one-man" (*wan man*), far better at giving orders than taking them. Throughout his life, he took delight in flamboyant displays of skill or opinion, ranging broadly from personal to political.

In 1928, for example, the *Jiji* newspaper announced it would sponsor two Japanese in a race around the world, seeking to break the current record of 35 days held by an American. Araki was selected as one of the contestants, and he turned the trip into a showcase for his "scientific management" techniques. He mobilized his staff to research the logistics of the trip, applying to his travel schedule the principles he used to eliminate wasted work time. A surviving photograph shows an intent Araki standing behind his staff of nine young men, all seated at a long desk piled high with timetables and papers, the walls behind them plastered with maps and charts.[19] Not surprisingly, he broke the American record by two full days.[20]

Araki applied similar zeal to the organization of his home life. His children recall constant admonitions to button their blouses from the bottom up because it was "more efficient": it reduced the number of false starts due to misalignment. Boasting to his wife of the potential for his methods at home, he had his kitchen torn up and redesigned as an "efficiency kitchen," every object in the best possible location within easy reach of the cook. But, as the size of his family grew, so did the number of servants, and the kitchen turned out to be an unpopular failure: far too small, conducive not to efficiency but to constant collisions.[21] And Araki's single-minded devotion to efficiency carried over to leisure activities as well. Upon detecting inefficiency in the operations of a restaurant or store, he would pull aside the manager for some impromptu free advice, to the endless embarrassment of his wife and children.[22]

Araki served as management consultant to the Southern Manchurian Railway from March 1931 to 1935, making several trips each year to Manchuria. His first job involved redesigning the docking and loading process for ships calling for coal at Dairen. He significantly reduced the turnaround time for the ships, but was puzzled that business in Dairen subsequently declined. Asking around among shippers and seamen, he learned that short stays were a disincentive to sailors looking forward to several days shore leave and visits to the brothel quarters. He decided the solution was to make Dairen a more exciting "play spot" (*asoberu machi*) for the sailors. He urged the Japanese authorities there to build a red light district, and when they refused, he went to the Russian quarter and supervised the renovation of a dance hall. He also brought his family along on one trip to Manchuria in the summer of 1931. He insisted on showing all the sights, to the point of visiting an opium den *en famille*. His second daughter, then four, to this day remembers her shock at the sight of the listless addicts sprawled in the den.[23]

The Dairen story does strain credulity, and cannot be verified independently of Araki's memoir, but two later instances of certified public boldness complete our picture of a brash and fearless loner. Araki viewed the Pacific War with considerable misgivings; he was no pacifist, but he felt Japan was ill-prepared and the economy inefficiently managed. By 1944, he was certain of defeat and he began to speak out in public, denouncing Tōjō as a "traitor" in a speech at the Railroad Association (Tetsudō Kyōkai). Soon the military police were watching him, and in May 1945 he was arrested. He remained in Sugamo (overlapping Yoshida Shigeru's brief imprisonment) and other detention centers until the war ended.[24]

The experience in no way demoralized him. Soon after the war he was back on a soapbox, this time to protest the death sentence imposed on General Yamashita Tomoyuki for ordering the Bataan Death March. Against the advice of most of his staff, he and one assistant tore down the curtains in his home to make banners and set up a stand in the Ginza to gather petitions to "Save Yamashita." He maintained that Yamashita, lauded as a great national hero in 1942 for taking Singapore from the British, was simply following orders. He could not abide the spectacle of the press and people, who had supported the war and acclaimed Yamashita with such fervor, simply standing by and accepting his death.[25]

If Araki had been all bluster and self-promotion, and a champion of lost causes, of course, his business career would not have gone far. In addition to these traits, he possessed an uncanny aptitude for anticipating trends, seeking out powerful allies, and advancing his cause effectively. This was true of his initial conclusion that the American movements for industrial efficiency and psychology in the 1920s offered much to Japan, and during the "rationalization" boom of the 1920s he found himself very much in the mainstream of business and government thinking. Araki both reflected and sought to influence the nature of rationalization,

Japanese-style. In 1930 the Ministry of Commerce and Industry created a Production Management Committee (Seisan Kanri Iinkai) within its Industrial Rationalization Bureau, and Araki served on this body. Although he later wrote that this committee accomplished rather little, it did represent one of the bureaucracy's first attempts to define "rationalization" in the Japanese context.[26]

In the 1930s he turned his attention to efficiency at the macro-economic level and decided that the Nazi system had the most to offer. Again, he moved successfully with, or slightly ahead of, the current. In 1933 Nakajima Chikuhei (founder of Nakajima Aircraft) donated a part of his fortune to establish a private think-tank he called the National Economic Research Center (Kokka Keizai Kenkyūjo), with Araki as a director. Araki convinced rising young economic bureaucrats Kishi Shinsuke and Yoshino Shinji to serve as advisors and attend twice monthly meetings. Over the next two years the Center produced a wide range of position papers advocating economic controls in various sectors—coal, fertilizer, raw silk, electric power—as well as the creation of what Araki called an "Economic General Staff" (Keizai Sanbō Honbu) to coordinate the economic functions of various ministries and orchestrate private economic activity as well.[27] In all these proposals, some of which anticipated eventual policies rather closely, the group drew heavily upon fascist economic thinking. It even invited to Japan as advisors two European government economists, one German Nazi and one Italian Fascist. Araki, however, recognized no contradiction in his activities in the 1920s and 1930s or thereafter. He believed that "American-style rationalization" was most effective at the level of the firm, while "German rationalization," apparently a mix of Weimar and Nazi initiatives in his mind, eliminated inter-firm inefficiencies and offered the best model for national economic policy.[28]

III. Araki Tōichirō's System of Wage and Labor Management

Araki's memoir describes in more or less detail his work for 33 businesses between 1924 and 1945. He summarizes some cases briefly, in a paragraph or less, while he offers considerable detail on others. He dealt with a wide range of problems, ranging from control of the work process (placement of machinery, work flow design, inventory control: 14 cases), to wage systems and personnel management (12 cases), to market analysis and sales strategy (4 cases), to advice on incentive programs for the sales force (3 cases).[29] His best-known clients included several major Kantō area firms—Nippon Kōkan, Asano Cement, Yokohama Dock, Union Beer—as well as the Southern Manchurian Railway, Kawasaki Aircraft Company, and Nippon Gakki (maker of Yamaha Piano). He also consulted for numerous smaller firms, mainly in the Keihin area, in a wide variety of industries: chemical, textile, machinery, printing. In the postwar era he came to focus his efforts primarily on smaller business, but prominent clients also included Yamaichi Securities, Furukawa Electric, Meiji Chocolate, and Japan Travel Bureau.

The dozen labor-related cases documented in his memoirs reveal that Araki gradually arrived at a coherent strategy for labor motivation and control in the 1920s and 1930s through a contentious process of trial, error, and retrial. He first undertook to reform a company's wage practices, in one of his earliest cases, with a small Tokyo printing company in 1924. He reports meeting with what he characterized as a very assertive, anticapitalist union at the company and convincing it to accept a Halsey-type premium plan. (The Halsey system originated in the United States in the 1890s. It set standard times for specific jobs. A worker who beat the standard time would receive a premium calculated as the product of his hourly wage multiplied by the amount of time saved, and then divided by two.) In 1926 this union apparently did lead a dispute of some sort at the printing company, but no details are available and any connection with Araki's intervention is unclear.[30]

The following year, however, Araki engaged in a more ambitious and controversial effort. He remade the wage system at Nippon Kōkan (NKK), Japan's largest private steel maker. NKK in the mid-1920s needed to lower costs to compete with less expensive foreign steel entering Japanese markets, and between 1925 and 1929 the company sought Araki's advice on a variety of matters. He changed the layout of machinery to speed the production flow. He convinced management to shift from 12- to 8-hour days, reducing day wages in proportion, since the longer day resulted in exhaustion and less efficient work.

He was also responsible for NKK's infamous double premium

plan, said by contemporaries to be so complex that not even managers were sure how wages were calculated. In it, a worker's first "premium" was actually a fixed multiple of the day wage intended to insure prior income levels. The second premium was a combination group and individual incentive in which a worker first received an individual monthly point total calculated as the product of days worked, an overtime multiplier, a status multiplier, a responsibility multipler, and an attendance multiplier. Next, an entire work group, at a given furnace, for example, received a monthly premium reflecting the extent to which the group bested a standard job time. Finally, individuals divided this premium in proportion to their point totals.[31]

Through the NKK system Araki aspired to promote both group solidarity (work group speed determined the premium total) and encourage individual exertion (attendance and overtime influenced the individual share). From a management perspective, the system was a great success. By the time he finished his work in 1928, productivity per worker had increased 38%, and costs per ton had fallen 25%.[32] NKK executives were so pleased that they reportedly continued to send Araki a monthly "honorarium" even after the consulting contract had expired, although Araki did no further work for NKK.[33]

Problems remained with the wage reforms, however. The system was so cumbersome and opaque that its short-run incentive effect was questionable. Even so, the premium portion of a worker's pay lacked the predictability of a daily or hourly wage. And the system was also subject to management manipulation of standard rates.

NKK experienced several labor disputes in the late 1920s, and at least two were related to Araki's efforts. The predictability problem led to dispute while Araki was still under contract with NKK in 1927, when the steel mill local of Sōdōmei, the national union federation, led a successful movement to revise the new pay system and place a satisfactory floor on wage levels. In 1931, the depression led managers to cut unit prices in the incentive program by 12%, and the union led an unsuccessful strike to prevent this.[34]

The NKK case set a pattern for Araki's labor management consulting, for labor resistance accompanied or followed his efforts in

6 of the 12 labor-related cases discussed in his memoirs. Concurrent with his work at NKK, he advised Asano Cement Company and found himself embroiled in a labor dispute pitting foremen and sub-foremen against regular workers. He earned the ferocious enmity of the former for openly castigating them for their poor labor management skills, and he recalls the Asano case as one of his major failures.[35] Similarly, the opposition of the foremen at Nippon Gakki in 1931 forced him to abandon implementation of a wage incentive plan based on his successful intervention at Yokohama Dock Company two years earlier.[36] And at the Konishiroku Camera Company in the late 1930s, resistance to his proposed incentive pay system came from the Army inspector on the scene, who maintained that "one should not motivate people with money" and prevented its implementation.[37]

Araki gradually altered his approach to labor management. He came to balance his initial concern with incentives and efficiencies with attention to the security of worker income and the promotion of labor commitment to the goals of the firm. The critical point is what by the 1930s he would call simply the "Araki system" of incentive wages and personnel management evolved through a succession of difficult confrontations with resistant workers who had their own ideas about how to organize factory life. The turning point in this evolution came in 1929 during his work for the Yokohama Dock Company (nicknamed Yokosen). In the wake of a bitter strike precipitated by his proposed reforms, he sat down with management, the union, and Kyōchōkai mediators to design a so-called rational wage. The result not only furnished the model for the "Araki system," which he then applied in numerous wartime and postwar cases, it also furnished a model to bureaucrats regulating wage practice during the war.[38]

Labor-management relations at Yokosen had been turbulent since before World War I. In the late 1920s the company found itself in a difficult business situation, forced to take on work below cost in a soft shipbuilding market to maintain employment and market share. At the same time, a formerly meek company-sponsored union, the Kōshinkai, was beginning to show signs of independence and a readiness to act on worker discontents. Into this tense situation stepped Araki in early 1929, enjoined to lower costs and raise productivity. He initially worked together with a work inspection team composed of supervisors and technicians to reform the incentive pay system. The union, led by a newly elected slate of officers, resisted. In early March a meeting of 238 workshop representatives voted to present a carefully worded petition to the company, and the union made preparations for a strike in the likely event of its rejection. The company offered a compromise, the union repeated the initial petition in more forceful language, to be rejected again, and a ten-day strike resulted.[39]

The petition had stated the union's support for rationalization to increase efficiency and strengthen the nation's industry, but it stated that a "secure psychological environment for the workers" was needed to win labor cooperation. To create such an environment the union called for several reforms: higher severance and retirement pay, promotion of temporary workers to regular status, an end to overtime work, and higher pay. But the negotiations to end the strike revealed that the critical issue for workers and managers was precisely the matter of wage structure that Araki was addressing: the balance between a worker's fixed daily wage and his incentive wage payment. The union wanted a guaranteed average daily income of ¥3.05, with three-fourths of this derived from a fixed day wage, the remainder from incentive pay. Management from the start was ready to grant ¥3 per day, already a ¥0.52 increase over existing average pay, but it refused to admit the day and incentive proportions as bargaining issues.[40]

The dispute aroused intense emotions. According to Araki's memoir, on one occasion he addressed the workers, urging them not to strike. Someone in the crowd threw a stone which hit him in the face and left a permanent scar.[41] His eldest daughter was just five years old at the time, but to this day she vividly recalls the traumatic evening in the spring of her fifth year (1929) when a tattooed leader of the union ("a gangster," as she retells it) barged into the Araki home in Tokyo and sat down on the tatami-floored receiving room. He took out a dagger, and drove it into the floor, announcing his intention to remain until Araki returned home and shouting "Bring me Araki!" [Araki o dase!]. Araki's wife managed to sneak both the maid and her daughter out the back door, the former to warn her husband, the latter to seek refuge with a neighbor, and she eventually convinced the worker to leave.[42]

The unofficial mediation of the Kyōchōkai resulted in an unusual resolution which placed Araki at the center of the action. The company and the union each agreed to place 9 representatives on a Rational Wage Committee, although the company chose the slate of 18 from which the workers elected their 9 representatives. Araki, too, would be a member of the group.[43] The committee was charged to *decide* upon a new, "rational" wage structure.

The committee began with a survey of living costs of Yokosen workers, and it also studied cost-of-living data compiled by the Kyōchōkai. It redesigned the wage curve to reflect the standard living expenses of the workers. The average day wage was set at ¥2.21, said to be sufficient to meet an average worker's basic necessities. Of this sum, 65% was to derive solely from age and seniority.[44] For management to agree that wages ought to reflect worker needs was a major concession granted in recognition of the union's strength, although the company still retained important discretion. It calculated the remainder of each man's day wage by offering rank and work point increments. Workers received work points based on their skill, the difficulty of their jobs, their attendance, and their diligence. The points were assigned monetary value, and this was added to the wage. In addition, the committee agreed that future raises would be given every six months to only 30% of the work force, based upon management evaluations of skill, diligence, and job difficulty.[45]

For their part, workers had from the start agreed to rely in part upon incentive wages to bring their total income up to the ¥3.05 daily average they had demanded. But in the system devised by Araki and the committee, the workers gained an important concession to bring predictability to the incentive payments. Rather than offer premiums only when a work group exceeded a standard output, payments began when the group reached just 70% of this standard. In essence, a portion of the incentive wage was guaranteed even if workers fell well short of the output mark. In exchange for this, the rate at which the premium increased when workers exceeded 100% of the standard was low compared to other systems.[46]

The settlement at Yokohama Dock received much attention at

the time and subsequently. A major survey of labor management on the "home islands" carried out by the research bureau of the Southern Manchurian Railway in 1930, for example, devoted an entire chapter to the Yokosen case. The researchers identified the just-implemented Yokosen wage system as one of four innovative models for the railway to consider adopting.[47] During World War II, labor management experts in the state bureaucracy, private corporations, and the academic world engaged in a prolonged debate on how to reform wages and personnel management to maximize labor-capital harmony and industrial productivity. The plans they discussed invariably combined fixed day wages conceived as livelihood guarantees with incentive additions based on various premium systems, in a fashion clearly similar to the Yokosen model. At least one important participant in these debates, Mori Kiichi, explicitly recognized the 1929 Yokosen plan as a forerunner of wartime plans.[48]

Araki himself came to regard his work at Yokosen as a turning point in his consulting practice. At ten pages, his recollection of the Dock Company episode is the longest single case description in the prewar section of his memoirs.[49] In the final five pages of the account, he presents the essence of the "Araki system" he created on the basis of his experience at Yokosen. His system, he wrote, eventually came to involve three parts: a fixed day wage, the incentive wage, and some form of profit-sharing bonus. Its goal was to exact diligent service to the enterprise and increase productivity by offering employees a carefully designed balance of security and incentive, with the incentive paid only insofar as existing production norms were exceeded. He justified bonuses as ways to share the fruits of productivity gains with workers. He concluded that "I came to call these related wage policies the Araki-style (*Araki-shiki*), and as a result of experimenting with them at a variety of companies, they today form a system (*taikei*)."[50] Subsequent cases presented in the memoir support this conclusion. He applied the "Araki-style incentive wage" in 1935 at the Ebisu Bulb Company.[51] During the war, he consulted with the Teikoku Chemical Corporation, where he "naturally" implemented an integrated reform of personnel and wage practice, and he took similar steps for Kawasaki Aircraft.[52] After the war, he continued this approach.[53]

IV. Conclusion

Araki Tōichirō made important contributions to the management of labor and the structure of wages in 20th-century Japan both through his intervention at specific companies and through the importance of some of these companies as models to others. In conclusion, we must note three aspects of his work.

An obsession with efficiency and productivity lay at the core of Araki's consulting philosophy. These two words occur over and over in his memoirs. In every case his goal was to produce more while expending less time, material, or energy. By contrast, he barely mentioned the word profits. We cannot conclude that he saw profit as a minor goal of business activity. Rather, he apparently saw it as a natural reward for efficient business practice. If one looked after the latter, the former would follow. Araki's success suggests that numerous businessmen in that era, and more recently, maintained a similar attitude.

Second, the great irony in Araki's career is that his "system" of labor management in fact emerged through his struggles with workers reluctant to go along with his plans. From his earliest consulting projects, he experienced labor resistance directly, from daggers in his living-room floor to stones to the head. Moved by a nationalistic and pragmatic spirit, Araki quickly decided that for the sake of the nation's industry, it was critical to win the hearts of workers away from unions and build a shared community of interests within the enterprise. Repeatedly in his memoirs he wrote of the futility and foolishness of oppositional unions and the need for managers and workers to cooperate. With this concern, too, Araki found himself in the mainstream of Japanese (and other nations') business thinking.

Finally, rather than stress "warm paternalism," systematic or not, as the way to motivate labor, Araki insisted his clients use a combination of the carrot and stick. He did come to agree that a portion of the day wage be secure, tied to objective factors of age and seniority. But, he also repeatedly emphasized that another portion of even this fixed wage must reflect ongoing managerial evaluation of the skill and diligence of each worker, as with the work point system devised at Yokosen. Further, in the Yokosen settlement he explicitly *rejected* the idea of a universal seniority wage, which might encourage complacence. Instead, only 30% of the workers would receive wage increases each semi-annum.

This does not mean that Araki repudiated the idea that a worker ought to identify his goals with those of the company. To the contrary, he insisted repeatedly that workers and managers had common interests and that employees should devote themselves to the company. To this extent, he and Uno Riemon stood on common ground. Yet their means to this end diverged fundamentally. Uno felt that systematic programs of benevolence, such as company welfare, periodic pay increases, retirement payments or factory beautification, should be at the heart of any program to elicit diligent, productive labor. Araki sought to create a community of interest by systematically returning a portion of productivity gains to labor through premium systems and bonuses. This was the heart of the Araki wage and personnel management system. It was a creative adaptation less of "Japanese tradition" than of American scientific management and industrial psychology, which took place in a context of labor-management contention. To deepen our understanding of Japanese business and labor history, we must study this context rather than seek to extract from the past an elusive traditional foundation of Japanese-style management.

NOTES

1. It turned out that one of my wife's good friends was Araki's daughter.
2. Robert Cole, "The Theory of Institutionalization: Permanent Employment and Tradition in Japan," *Economic Development and Cultural Change*, Vol. 20, No. 1 (Oct. 1971). Ronald Dore, *British Factory-Japanese Factory*, Berkeley, University of California Press, 1973, Ch. 12. Hazama Hiroshi, *Rōshi kyōchō no teiryū* (Currents in labor-management collaboration), Tokyo, Waseda daigaku shuppankai, 1978. For a summation of this literature through 1978, Mark Fruin, "The Japanese Company Controversy," *Journal of Japanese Studies*, Vol. 4, No. 2 (Summer 1978).
3. Hazama Hiroshi, "Japanese Labor Relations and Uno Riemon," *Journal of Japanese Studies*, Vol. 5, No. 1 (Winter 1979).
4. *Ibid.*, p. 104.

5. *Ibid.*
6. *Ibid.*, pp. 90, 92.
7. *Ibid.*, p. 78.
8. *Ibid.*, p. 82.
9. *Ibid.*, pp. 78–79.
10. These institutions include the Nihon Keiei Shi Kai, Nihon Keiei Nōritsu Kenkyūjo, Kigyō Keiei Tsūshin Gakuin.
11. Araki Tōichirō, *Nōritsu ichi dai ki*, Nihon Nōritsu Kyōkai, 1971. This memoir (the first in a series of two) covers Araki's career through 1955. It is the principal source of the information on Araki introduced in this paper. Any autobiographical source must be approached with caution, including this one. In a number of the cases he describes, however, 1 have been able to check the basic facts against both the recollections of his daughters and other documentary sources. While this procedure reveals that Araki exaggerated the centrality of his role in places, crosschecking also shows that the memoirs present an accurate chronology of his travels and the cases he handled and a fair representation of his general attitude and consulting style. For our purposes, the memoirs are a reliable guide in two crucial respects: they demonstrate his success in convincing numerous owners and managers to seek out and pay for his advice, and they convey a sense of his overall strategy for dealing with issues of labor management.
12. *Ibid.*, p. 1.
13. Sanford M. Jacoby, *Employing Bureaucracy: Managers, Unions, and the Transformation of Work in American Industry, 1900–1945*, New York, Columbia University Press, 1985, pp. 102–4.
14. *Ibid.*, p. 103.
15. Araki, *op. cit.*, p. 2.
16. *Ibid.*, pp. 4–5.
17. *Ibid.*, pp. 7–8.
18. *Ibid.*, pp. 8–11.
19. *Ibid.*, p. 28.
20. *Ibid.*, pp. 23–33.
21. Personal communication from Faith (Araki) Barcus.
22. Personal communication from Faith Barcus.
23. Araki, *op. cit.*, p. 63 for dance hall episode. Personal communication from Faith Barcus regarding opium den visit.
24. Araki, *op. cit.*, pp. 122–27. Personal communication from Faith Barcus.
25. Araki, *op. cit.*, pp. 129–34. Interview with Asanoma Seishirō.

26. Araki, *op. cit.*, pp. 50–51.
27. *Ibid.*, pp. 80–92.
28. *Ibid.*, pp. 11, 80–81.
29. In a number of cases he dealt with multiple problems, while in several other cases the memoir does not make clear what he did. The total of known problems tackled just happens to equal the number of clients.
30. Aoki Kōji, *Nihon rōdō undō shi nenpyō* (Chronological history of the Japanese labor union movement), 1968, p. 732.
31. Araki, *op. cit.*, pp. 15–17. Andrew Gordon, *The Evolution of Labor Relations in Japan*, Cambridge, Council on East Asian Studies, 1985, pp. 165–67, 173–74. When I wrote this book I did not know that Araki had been responsible for the NKK system. The description of the NKK rationalization drive in my book, derived from documentary records and interviews with retired company personnel managers, matches Araki's account of the NKK reforms.
32. Gordon, *op. cit.*, p. 174.
33. Araki, *op. cit.*, p. 17.
34. *Kanagawa rōdō undō shi* (History of the labor union movement in Kanagawa prefecture), Vol. 1, 1966, pp. 377–78, 460, 623 for details on these strikes.
35. Araki, *op. cit.*, p. 18.
36. *Ibid.*, p. 55.
37. *Ibid.*, p. 100.
38. Gordon, *op. cit.*, p. 279, on wartime impact of Yokohama Dock model.
39. For a more detailed account of this strike, *ibid.*, pp. 184–88.
40. *Ibid.*, p. 186.
41. Araki, *op. cit.*, p. 36.
42. Interview with Sugino (Araki) Eisen.
43. It is not clear whether he was an additional member or one of the nine management representatives.
44. For the average Dock Company worker, a 34-year old with 5 years' tenure, this portion would be ¥1.4, 65% of the ¥2.1 average day wage. This would vary by ¥0.1 per year of age and year of seniority above or below the average, so that a 40-year-old worker with 11 years on the job would receive ¥1.42 as the age-base portion of the day wage. Gordon, *op. cit.*, p. 187.
45. *Ibid.*, pp. 186–88.
46. Araki, *op. cit.*, pp. 41–42.

47. Minami Manshū Tetsudō, ed., *Naichi ni okeru kōjō chingin seido no kenkyū* (A study of the wage system in Japanese factories), 1930. The other three were Mitsubishi Electric and Japanese National Railways, which had both implemented "American-style" rationalization in the 1920s, and Yahata Steel.

48. Mori Kiichi, *Jūkōgyō no chingin to seikatsu* (Wages and livelihood in heavy industry), Minzoku Kagakusha, 1944, pp. 139, 141–42, 146.

49. Araki, *op. cit.*, pp. 34–43. The account of his work for the Manchurian Railway is a bit longer, but it covers a number of separate Mantetsu ventures.

50. *Ibid.*, p. 43.

51. *Ibid.*, p. 95.

52. *Ibid.*, pp. 112–15.

53. *Ibid.*, pp. 156–57, 183–85 for examples.

Comment

Kenji Okuda
Sophia University

Many of the conventional studies on Japanese labor management in the past might be described as having fallen into oversimplification in line with stereotyped perceptions. Typical as a case in point is the "triad divine symbolic concept" of lifelong employment, seniority-based wage system, and the in-house union structure. Moreover, traditional paternalism in Japanese management is stressed as one basic factor for the appearance of this sort of phenomenon. It has been thought by many people that workers may settle down and the lifelong employment system may take root by "warmly treating workers" in line with the principles of paternalism.

Nevertheless, it is evident that approach of this sort is an over-simplification and therefore is misleading when it comes to elaborate studies on the business history of Japan. Professor Gordon's paper is primarily designed to pursue trends in the labor management o Japan's prewar heavy industries, particularly casting light on the actual state of conditions in which brisk attempts were made for an improvement in work efficiency. Gordon's paper must be highly rated in the sense that he asserts labor management in prewar Japan was full of diversity.

1. Methodology. The methodology Gordon used in his book *The Evolution of Labor Relations in Japan* is also employed for his latest paper. First, he is not trapped by the erroneous practice of ascribing the features of labor management to Japan's traditions and regarding those features as something fixational. Like that of many other countries, Japan's business history has also dynamically changed in line with trends in the economic, social, and technological conditions.

After efforts of industrialization for 40 years following the Meiji Restoration, the managerial echelon began to make a conscious review of the way in which corporate management ought to be. Particularly in order to survive an intensifying international competition following World War I, Japanese industry was forced to raise its managerial efficiency. Also buffeted by international criticisms through the International Labor Organization (ILO) and further by a rising labor movement within the country stimulated by the Russian Revolution, Japanese corporate managers in those years were compelled to consciously strive for a streamlining of their management practices. In such efforts, many corporate managers went in for paternalism, but it does not follow that all of them praised paternalism in a stereotyped manner. In his paper, Gordon probes into the activity of one of the efficiency engineers in those years, thus casting light on the diversity of Japanese labor management.

Second, when it comes to a historical analysis of labor management, it is indispensable to pay due consideration to the position of workers and, in particular, to the influence of labor unions which work for their benefit. Essentially, the policy and substantive measures of the management on labor management are formed as a response of the management to the posture of workers as well as to criticisms from the labor union. In other words, it has been dynamically formed in the process where the conflict of interests between management and labor is regulated. In attempts to explain their position to their advantage, the management deliberately came out with rhetorics which attune to managerial paternalism.

In making a historical analysis, therefore, we would be inadvertently trapped by the illusion that paternalism was dominant in the past if too much stress was put on management rhetorics. The viewpoints contained in Gordon's paper are excellent in the sense that he has cast legitimate light on the assertions and responses of workers in the process of the shaping of Japanese labor management.

2. Diversity of Japanese Efficiency Movement. In Japan, efficiency movement was just as diversified as labor management. With this in mind, therefore, it is necessary that we should consider Araki Tōichirō was none other than one of those who played a part in the efficiency movement.

In incorporating Taylor's perception of scientific management, there was a debate between scholars and corporate managers. This debate is well discernible from Table 1.

TABLE 1   Views on the Introduction of Scientific Management in the 1920s.

(1) Views Against Introduction of Scientific Management from the Standpoint of Paternalism
     Suzuki Tsunesaburō, *Rōdō mondai to onjōshugi* (Labor problems and paternalism), Yōryokusha, 1915
     Uno Riemon, *Shokkō yūgū ron* (On favorable treatment of workers), Kōgyō Kyōikusha, 1915

(2) Views Against Introduction of Scientific Management from the Standpoint of Social Policy
     Kitazawa Shinjirō, "Kagakuteki kanrihō to rōdōsha" (Scientific labor management and the worker), *Kaihō* (March 1922)
     Horie Kiichi, "Kagakuteki keieihō to rōdōkumiai" (Scientific labor management and labor unions), *Mita gakkai zasshi* (Aug. 1920)
     Morito Tatsuo, "Kagakuteki kanrihō no shakaiseisakuteki kachi" (Scientific labor management practice and the importance of social policy), (I), (II), *Kokka gakkai zasshi*, Vol. 30, Nos. 11, 12
     Nakatsumi Tomokata, "Kagakuteki kanrihō ni taisuru gensei hihan" (A critique of scientific labor management), *Kokka gakkai zasshi*, Vol. 36, No. 2

(3) Criticism Concluding Scientific Management Not Scientific from the Standpoint of Labor Science
     Teruoka Yoshito, "On labor science," *Rōdō kagaku*, Vol. 1, No. 1

(4) Views for Introduction of Scientific Management
     Muramoto Fukumatsu, "Horie Hakase oyobi Teruoka Gakushi no kagakuteki keieihō ni kansuru hihan o yomite" (A comment on the critique on the scientific labor management practice of Horie and Teruoka), *Shōgyō oyobi keizai kenkyū*, No. 20
     Noda Nobuo, "Kagakuteki kanrihō to rōdōsha no fukuri" (Scientific labor management and the welfare of workers), *Shakai seisaku jihō*, No. 41 (Feb. 1924)

(5) Views on Japanese Amendment of Scientific Management
     Wakabayashi Yonekichi, "Kagakuteki kanrihō hihan" (A critique of scientific labor management), *Shakai seisaku jihō*, No. 20
     Kanda Kōichi, *Rōdō nōritsu kenkyū* (Studies in labor efficiency), Tōjō Shoten, 1922

For the argument of each author, refer to Okuda Kenji, *Hito to keiei, Nippon keiei kanrishi kenkyū* (Man and management), Managementsha, 1985.

Efficiency engineers such as Ueno Yoichi and Araki Tōichirō might be regarded as belonging to the fourth category.

Araki underestimated the activity of the Production Management Committee of the Ministry of Commerce and Industry in the 1930s, but this underestimation is nothing but a reflection of the position in which he considered his position absolute. In attempts to overcome a depression, Araki thought it necessary to step up a planned economy on the basis of the state's centralizing power. He was dissatisfied with the devotion of the Production Management Committee to an enlightenment movement for a streamlining of the management system.

The Production Management Committee made propositions on 33 themes on improvements in management, discussed each theme with experts on a national level, and evolved an enlightenment movement to streamline management. From 1932 to 1941, national forums were held on 20 themes.

In order to carry out the propositions made by the committee, the Japan Industrial Association was established in 1931. A three-month training course was established by the association to train industrial engineers, and about 300 persons took this course from 1937 to Japan's defeat in the Pacific War. From those trainees, there emerged leading industrial engineers for the postwar industry. The Japan Industrial Association turned itself into the Japan Management Association, which is playing an increasingly great role.

The Production Management Committee published a proposal under the title of Work Study in 1938 (one of the aforementioned 33 propositions). The position in which this suggestion was made is identical with that of Wakabayashi and Kanda in Table 1.

Unlike the view of workers in Taylor's scientific management, workers were accepted as coresearchers in a work study. In the selection of survey subjects, it was considered necessary not to choose "first-class men," but to choose not only persons capable of realizing the genuine purpose of the work study, but those who would be readily acceptable by coworkers. This is, it was argued, because there was a need to see to it that the results of the work study would be acceptable to a broad segment of workers. Such rectification of the view of workers in the scientific management system might be described as being grounded on Committee Chairperson Yamashita Okiie's assertion that "it is necessary to develop concepts and methods of the kind which is in line with the reality of Japanese industry."

There seems to be a need to take note of the fact that the efficiency movement in Japan's prewar industry, as was the case with that of many other countries, was diversified.

3. Danger of Dichotomy. I wish to comment more or less on the danger of dichotomy in which paternalism in Japanese industry is utterly heterogeneous to scientific management in American industry.

Naturally, there is much difference between the two. The former is an irrational approach in which emphasis is put on an appeal to human affection, whereas the latter puts stress on a quantitative approach and therefore is a rational way of perception. But it is to be noted that there exist similarities between the two against the background of such differences.

In paternalism, management is likened to a family. The workers who are likened to members of the family are placed in an instrumental position to contribute to the family's prosperity. Also in scientific management, workers are called for to devote themselves to the accomplishment of jobs assigned by the management for more efficient corporate management. In paternalism, the autocratic power of the entrepreneur is sugar coated, but it is essentially designed to strengthen an extremely centralized system. On the other hand, scientific management was also an attempt to completely eliminate the position of skilled workers as subcontractors and try to establish a centralized rule by the entrepreneur.

On this score, the two systems were common. This parallelism enabled some of the Japanese corporations to carry out labor management based on paternalism in parallel with scientific management. But this phenomenon was also observed in the United States in the 1920s. The dichotomy in which both are simply considered heterogeneous makes it impossible to cast light on the reality of industry.

Response

Andrew Gordon

Professor Okuda's comments are extremely helpful. They clarify the broader context of enthusiasm, doubt, and debate over scientific management ideas in interwar Japan. The bibliography in Table 1 will help me and other researchers who pursue this topic further.

I would simply add the comment that the lines between the five types of response to scientific management are blurry when we look at individual cases. Okuda suggests that Araki might be placed in the fourth category, that of unambiguous supporters of scientific management. As I argue in the paper, I see him moving over time from this position to the fifth group, those advocating some amendment of scientific management to serve the practical goals of motivating labor and securing loyalty to the goals of the enterprise. This, of course, is not a shift particular to Japan; American industrial psychologists also made significant "amendments" to the early scientific management ideas.

From this perspective, I agree wholeheartedly with Okuda's comment on the danger of positing a sharp dichotomy between Japanese paternalism and American scientific management. This is a point I tried to make in the paper, perhaps not clearly enough. In the United States as well as in Japan, pragmatic managers freely combined approaches we might consider "paternalistic" with those seeming to derive from scientific management ideas. This was the case at General Electric in the 1920s, and it was the case with Araki, who mixed his obsession with efficiency with appeals to workers to consider the good of the enterprise and the nation to be their own good. But in Araki's case, he persistently sought to reinforce loyalty to the enterprise community less with expressions of affection and more with palpable benefits such as profit sharing and premium wages conceived as a "sharing" of gains in productivity.

The Development of Machine Industries and the Evolution of Production and Labor Management

Minoru Sawai
Hokusei Gakuen University

I. Introduction

The primary purpose of this paper is to survey the development of the machine industries, in particular, the rolling stock, spinning and weaving machine, machine tool, and electric machinery industries. Its second purpose is to examine the conditions which gave rise to technological innovations and independence. Finally, this paper will study the structure of workshop organizations and the corresponding evolution of production and labor management.

As is well known, machine industries consist of many distinctive industries. This was also the case in the prewar period when they were divided into groups according to their relative degree of dependence upon orders from the public sector (including military demand from the army and the navy). There were also two types of production: mass production of small items mainly based on projected demand, and order production of large items in small amounts. In addition, production systems even in the same industry varied according to the size of the firm. Thus, the existence of the so-called dual structure problem has been discussed from various viewpoints.

The variety in production systems by industry and firm-scale, as indicated above, does not permit hasty generalizations in regard to the machine industries sector. The next section will therefore trace the characteristic development process of four machine industries and consider the conditions which brought about their technological

development. The third section will examine the structure of workshop organizations and the evolution of production and labor management between the wars.

II. The Characteristic Development of Four Machine Industries

1. Rolling Stock

The establishment of the "designated factory" system in 1912
was a key factor in the development of the rolling stock industry.[1]
In 1909, Japanese National Railways (JNR) resolved to acquire
new rolling stock from within Japan and thus end dependence on
foreign rolling stock, especially steam locomotives. In 1912, JNR
launched the new purchasing method. It would buy new rolling
stock from only four designated companies: Kisha Seizō, Nippon
Sharyō Seizō, Kawasaki Shipyard, and Amano Factory. In this
way, the establishment of the designated factory system gave rise
to an oligopoly within the rolling stock industry. The position of
the first three companies remained strong, but Amano Factory was
absorbed by Nippon Sharyō Seizō in 1920. The predominant position of the three original companies was based on their close connections with JNR as the largest user in Japan,[2] sales to which were
generally more profitable than to other private railway companies
or for export.[3] Many other companies, such as Hitachi Engineering
Works, Niigata Iron Works, Tanaka Sharyō, Umebachi Iron Works,
Mitsubishi Kobe Shipyard, Fujinagata Shipyard, Osaka Iron Works,
and so forth, became designated factories during the twenties.

High profitability and large, continuous demand from JNR were
business conditions that the rolling stock industry, earlier than
many other machine industries, used to gain technological independence from advanced countries such as the U.S.A., the U.K.,
and Germany. The role of JNR in the development of the rolling
stock industry, however, was not limited to the orders it placed.
Since the designated manufacturers had not yet reached the level
of technology that JNR required, JNR, which employed the largest
number of engineers in Japan at that time,[4] gave systematic technological support to the manufacturers in order to bridge that
technological gap. JNR made drawings for steam locomotives and
issued them to the manufacturers with the necessary materials,

essentially directing the duplication of imported locomotives. In addition, JNR tried to upgrade rolling stock and reduce repair time by means of establishing various kinds of standards for rolling stock parts. JNR dispatched its engineers to the designated factories where they stayed on as inspectors to guide the production process. Engineers were also sent to foreign countries to learn advanced technology. JNR consolidated the research and development departments that could not have been run on a paying basis in the case of private companies and during World War I led the designated companies by building special and new types of cars. In the 1920s JNR actively promoted cooperative design with the designated companies and sponsored the "conference on rolling stock."

The conference on rolling stock was set up in 1922 as an annual meeting, changing to a bi-annual format after 1925. The majority of the members were JNR engineers, with the remainder composed of engineers from companies such as South Manchurian Railways, Korean and Formosan Government Railways, local railways, and street railways, as well as material and parts makers and members from the designated companies. Topics for the meetings were announced in advance so that members could carry out related research in their own workshops beforehand. The results of the research, some of which would be promptly put into practice by JNR, were discussed at the meetings. JNR endeavored to standardize models by establishing common goals for the design of electric locomotives, motors, air brakes, and so forth in cooperation with the designated companies as equal partners.[5]

It should be noted that technical support from JNR had changed along with the technological upgrading within the designated companies over the years. In the production of steam locomotives from the end of the Meiji era to World War I, the leadership of JNR over the private companies was absolute. However, the designated companies acquired a relatively independent technological base after World War I, which became increasingly evident during the rapid expansion of electric railways during the twenties. As a result, there was very little one-way technology transfer from the public to the private sector at the conferences on rolling stock and cooperative design. Rather, a kind of cooperative R&D activity between equal

partners developed, though JNR maintained the function of or-
ganizer. Through these processes, the rolling stock industry gained
the ability to build most types of cars, including their parts, by the
end of the 1920s.[6]

2. Spinning and Weaving Machines

The development of weaving machines, especially those for cotton, seems to have advanced in distinct stages.[7] Power looms were
produced, replacing hand looms after the middle of the Meiji era.
At first, power looms were narrow and made of wood, or wood and
iron. Later, wide power looms made of iron, of which the H-type
made by Toyoda's Loom Co., Ltd., was the first example, became
dominant after the 1910s. By the late 1920s, Japanese weaving machine technology had caught up to the level of the advanced countries, and the industry even began producing automatic looms as an
epoch-making technological innovation.

The role of narrow power looms made of wood and iron in the
development of weaving machines is noteworthy. In the Meiji era,
large-scale spinning companies with their own weaving departments, whose products were mainly exported, imported wide power
looms made of iron. On the other hand, what the small weaving
sheds demanded in the way of narrow cloth for Japanese kimonos
was the low-priced power looms made by the Japanese manufacturers. In short, the domestic market for power looms was not
homogeneous but divided into two fields. At the outset, Japanese
manufacturers did not advance to the market level where there was
severe competition with foreign builders, but accumulated their
technological base through mass production of narrow power looms
made of wood and iron, gradually advancing to the wide power
loom and finally to the automatic loom markets. The market's
dual structure functioned as a non-tariff barrier securing sufficient
time for the infant machine manufacturers to learn the imported
technology. The fact that the supply of Japanese power looms had
already surpassed imports before World War I was made possible
only under these circumstances.[8]

Compared with early import substitution in power looms, the
domestic production value in spinning machines had barely sur-

passed imports even by the late 1920s.[9] This difference was based mainly on a homogeneous market structure composed exclusively of the spinning companies, and an extreme gap in productivity between modern, imported technology and indigenous hand spinning. There existed therefore no market that was virtually free from foreign competition such as was the case with power looms. The spinning machine manufacturers, who were not able to supply entire plants, ought to have advanced in successive stages, from parts repair, through the production of partially finished machines, and finally to the technologically most difficult stage, namely the outfitting of whole plants. In fact, between the wars, the spinning machine industry was in a state of transition from manufacturers of partially finished machines to builders of whole plants.

The top producers in the spinning and weaving machine industries around the 1930s, when import substitution became pronounced, were Toyoda's Loom Co. and Toyoda Automatic Loom Company. These were not only loom makers but manufacturers of entire plants of spinning machines, and they were followed, in decreasing order of firm scale, by loom or partially finished spinning machine manufacturers, and then by parts makers who produced spindles, rings, and rollers for spinning machines, or reeds, healds, shuttles, and so forth for looms. In addition, there were a number of small subcontracting factories related to the three abovementioned groups.[10] Therefore the relatively high proportion of medium-sized firms in the spinning and weaving machine industries resulted from the large number of makers of finished machines and parts.

The technology necessary for mass production had already begun consolidating after the 1920s, and by the mid-1930s, the representative companies in the spinning and weaving machine industries had established such systems.[11] This development was supported by various conditions, such as the introduction of jigs, limit gauge systems,[12] and special machine tools for the manufacture of spinning and weaving machines,[13] as well as the establishment of these companies' own foundries for producing founding products.

3. Machine Tools

Although machine tools were already being built in the early

Meiji era, it was not until the Sino- and Russo-Japanese wars that
the machine tool industries, as such, became established.[14] During
World War I, the machine tool industry became firmly established
in Japan's industrial structure.[15] The number of builders increased,
and although there were certainly limitations on the types of machines which could be produced, the manufacturers came to supply
many types of machines for a complex market, which ranged from
army and naval arsenals to small machine shops. The machine tool
manufacturers during the war could be divided into two groups:
the large and medium-sized factories which could supply machines
to the military and the small makers whose markets were mainly
limited to the private sector.[16]

In the 1920s, when a long stagnation period beset the industry,
this multi-tiered characteristic in the supply and demand structure
of machine tools became more pronounced.[17] The markets were
divided into the following three fields: (1) the monopolistic market
of high-quality and high-priced foreign machines, (2) the competitive market among foreign and Japanese manufacturers, and (3)
the monopolistic market of low-quality and low-priced Japanese
machines. The third market was further surrounded by a market
for the exchange of second-hand machines, which were in abun-
dance during the depression.

On the other hand, the manufacturers also came to be divided
into three groups: the five big manufacturers, Ikegai, Ōkuma,
Karatsu, Niigata Iron Works, and Tokyo Gas and Electric Co., who
were the only makers capable of consolidating the technological
conditions required to meet military demand, followed by medium-
sized, and finally small-sized makers. This multi-tiered structure in
the supply of machine tools appeared to be divided not only in
quality but also in price. This heterogeneous structure in both the
supply and demand sides of machine tools, similar to the case of the
narrow wood and iron power looms, functioned as a non-tariff barrier, preventing imported machines from an overall invasion of the
domestic market. Also, there was a relatively high proportion of
small- and medium-sized users in the domestic markets. For example, in 1929 the percentage of lathes and milling machines
possessed by firms with less than 200 employees in the eight sectors

of the machine-producing industry reached 70.5% and 59.4%, respectively.[18] The existence of a large number of small- and medium-sized users who did not want or feel the need to equip their machine shops with high-quality imported machines was the major factor in the large proportion of small- and medium-sized builders in the machine tool industry.

After the Manchurian Incident, the market for machine tools expanded much more than it had during World War I. In response to demand, the five big manufacturers, as well as some medium-sized ones, gradually upgraded the quality of their products.[19] However, in spite of these technological improvements, the dependence upon imports for some types of machines continued. As a result, the rate of dependence on imports grew to around 40 to 50% in terms of value during the first half of the 1930s, though it barely exceeded 10% in terms of number of machines.[20] This was due to the price gap between Japanese and foreign machines. The military, which had prepared a plan for total mobilization, had strong misgivings concerning this deep dependence on imports.[21] Dependence on imports continued, in spite of the upgrading of quality and the expanded variety of products, because of the development of demand for machine tools. In the 1930s, demand grew as a result of the rapid expansion of the "new industries," such as automobiles and aircraft construction, in parallel with the army arsenals, the naval yards, large-scale electric machinery companies, and so forth. Thus, while the representative makers were trying to catch up to the technological level of imported machines and begin competing with them, they also faced the problems of a demand structure which was constantly changing to reflect new stages in the growth of technology.

4. Electric Machinery

Before World War I, the Japanese electric machinery industry had been overwhelmed by imports in its main product area of heavy electric machinery. In comparison with foreign manufacturers, the Japanese industry produced low-capacity machinery and consequently advanced mainly into the field of small-sized machinery, depending on imports for large-capacity and high-voltage machinery. Shibaura Engineering Works was predominant among the domestic manufacturers, and Hitachi Engineering Works was just beginning to sell its products to outside customers after 1911.

This situation changed drastically during World War I in heavy electric machinery and other machine-producing industries. Domestic builders responded to the expansion in demand brought about by the decrease or stagnation of imports by advancing into the field of high-capacity and high-voltage machinery, at the same time expanding their ability to produce a variety of items.[22] After World War I, imports increased again and the rapid development of the electric power industry required high-capacity, heavy electric machinery. Consequently, the rate of dependence on imports reached around 30 to 40% between 1922 and 1926.[23] This demonstrated that technological development during World War I had not yet reached the level where competition with foreign machinery was feasible.

In the second half of the 1920s, especially after the tariff reform of 1926, the Japanese makers gradually secured the domestic market. This tendency was evident even in generators, in particular water turbine generators, whose production had been delayed in Japan. The production of high-capacity steam turbine generators also became possible by the end of the 1920s.[24]

The development of domestic production in the 1920s, in particular the latter half of the decade, was accompanied by severe competition among manufacturers as shown by the rapid decrease in the prices of their products.[25] Shibaura, Hitachi, Mitsubishi Electric, and Fuji Electric had grown through cut-throat competition and formed the so-called Big Four in the heavy electric machinery industry. During the Great Depression, several famous companies disappeared, including Okumura Electric, which had been established in the middle of the Meiji era, and Kawakita Electric Engineering.[26] Thus the development of the electric machinery industry in the 1930s was led by the Big Four, followed by specialty companies such as Yasukawa Electric, which changed from the overall production of heavy electric machinery to the mass production of motors and controllers, Meidensha Electric, which was deeply dependent on the production of motors, and Osaka Transformer Co., Limited.[27]

5. Conditions for Technological Independence

The four abovementioned industries developed through the introduction and diffusion of new technology, each forming its own unique industrial organization. Next, we will examine the conditions for technological development and independence, beginning with the role of the government.

Among these four industries, the rolling stock industry was the one most influenced by the activities of the government. Fundamental conditions for the technological development of the rolling stock industry included not only high profitability and steady and large demand from JNR, but also the transfer of engineers from JNR to the designated companies. In 1912, for example, a JNR engineer by the name of Nogami Yaeharu transferred to Nippon Sharyō Seizō, where he reformed workshop practices, promoting stricter materials management and attention to the appointed date of delivery. He observed that "workers look upon workshops not as the company's, but as their own. Therefore, they do not mind coming 5 or 10 minutes late, nor do they care about the appointed date of delivery for orders."[28] In Kisha Seizō, the limit gauge system had been adopted since 1914. This was one of the earliest private machine shops to do so, and the system could only be executed on abundant orders of standardized rolling stock for JNR. Thus, the orders and transfer of engineers from JNR greatly influenced the modernization of labor, production management, and cost control for the designated manufacturers.

The Big Five as well as some medium-sized manufacturers in the machine tool industry were closely related to parts of the government sector, such as the army arsenals, the naval yard, and JNR. The first linkage was the transfer of engineers in the army arsenals and the naval yard to the main machine-tool builders. For example, during World War I, some engineers in Sonoike Engineering Works were former Kure naval yard engineers. The factory superintendent of machine tools in Kubota Iron Works was a former naval yard engineer, and Niigata Iron Works also carried out technological upgrading by recruiting engineers from naval yards.[29]

Another link between the government sector and the private machine industry was the loan of imported machines from the army arsenals and naval yards to the manufacturers for the purpose of duplication. The development of new types of machines was also promoted by distributing drawings of imported machines.[30] In this regard, JNR established greater systematic cooperation with machine tool makers than the military had, organizing cooperative design and design testing with the manufacturers.[31]

Tariff policies were another important part of the government's role. The tariff reform of 1911 increased the former 5% ad valorem tariff to 20% for locomotives and to 30% for passenger and freight cars. This enabled manufacturers to secure a competitive position with foreign makers regarding locomotives, except for small locomotives mainly used in light railways.[32] The machine tool industry, being relatively undeveloped, received no tariff increase in the 1911 reform,[33] but in the 1926 reform it received from 1.7- to 3.1-fold increases, thus decreasing the import of certain types of machines.[34] The 1926 tariff reform, which included an average increase in tariffs of 75%, also had a considerable impact on electric machinery. As a result, domestic manufacturers of electric machines were able to make great advances in securing the domestic market.[35]

Although the role of the government, as outlined above, was important, the main factor for technological independence was the continuous effort on the part of the private companies to develop technology by themselves. The usual procedure among the four industries was first to produce "dead copies" (structurally identical but qualitatively inferior copies) of the imported machines. In the production of "dead copies," the knowledge possessed by engineers was the key difference between understanding the mechanism of modeled machines (as well as being able to judge the quality of materials) and "just duplicating the model by relying on only workers' skill."[36] There was a gap in the ability to copy the imported machines between large-scale manufacturers and medium- and small-sized manufacturers, who could not afford to employ the university and technical college graduates.

In addition to the informal methods for learning foreign technology, for example, the production of "dead copies," there were many systematic and formal measures, such as tie-ups with foreign firms, which were of particular significance for electric machinery manufacturers. Among the Big Four, Shibaura tied up with General Electric in 1909, Mitsubishi with Westinghouse Corporation in 1923, and, as is well known, Furukawa Electric with Siemens to establish Fuji as their joint concern. These three companies were greatly influenced by their foreign partners, not only in design and production technology, but in various management techniques as well. Between 1923 and 1940, for example, Mitsubishi Electric sent 55 engineers and 5 staff members to Westinghouse in order to study products, design, production technology, and management, and to enter the apprentice course.[37] In the major companies of these four industries, it was not rare for managers and engineers to go abroad to absorb new technology unrelated to technical tie-ups,[38] occasionally to purchase foreign technical magazines as well.[39]

III. Workshop Organizations and the Evolution of Production and Labor Management between the Wars

1. Engineers, Foremen, and Workers

In this section, we will examine the workshop organizations, focusing on their engineers, foremen, and workers. Table 1[40] shows the educational background of the engineers, assistant engineers, and foremen employed in the factories of the main machine companies. The greatest percentage of engineers were graduates of colleges, followed in order by those of universities, vocational schools (which were mainly for manufacturing), and continuation schools. Most assistant engineers were graduates of vocational schools, followed by those of continuation schools and finally of colleges. On the other hand, foremen were overwhelmingly persons who had only finished elementary school. More than 90% of university and college graduates were promoted to the post of engineer or assistant engineer, but the ratio decreased to 37.3% among those who had only finished vocational school, 15.2% in the case of continuation schools, and 1.1% in the case of elementary schools.

Table 2 shows the ratio of technical college and vocational school graduates by position and years after graduation in 1933. This is not time-series data; therefore, we cannot directly confirm the promotion routes by school careers. Roughly speaking, however, it can be said that university and technical college graduates entered

M. Sawai

TABLE 1 Male Employees in Machine Industries by School Career and Position, June 1930.

	University graduates	Technical colleges and other colleges	Higher schools & preparatory courses for universities	Vocational schools (manufacturing and other)	Middle schools	Continuation schools	Elementary (primary and higher)	Total
Department heads and above (Buchō)	(8.8) [46.5] 47	(4.7) [35.6] 36	(7.1) [1.0] 1	(0.7) [7.9] 8	(1.0) [6.9] 7	(0.3) [2.0] 2		(1.8) [100.0] 101
Section chiefs (Kachō)	(10.1) [30.9] 54	(10.0) [44.0] 77		(1.5) [9.7] 17	(1.5) [6.3] 11	(1.0) [3.4] 6	(0.5) [5.7] 10	(3.1) [100.0] 175
Chiefs (Shunin)	(11.6) [19.9] 62	(14.3) [35.3] 110	(7.1) [0.3] 1	(4.0) [15.1] 47	(6.1) [14.1] 44	(3.9) [7.7] 24	(1.5) [7.7] 24	(5.5) [100.0] 312
Staffs (Shain)	(65.2) [11.3] 348	(62.0) [15.5] 477	(85.7) [0.4] 12	(64.0) [24.4] 753	(64.4) [15.1] 465	(57.5) [11.6] 359	(35.7) [21.8] 672	(53.9) [100.0] 3,086
Others	(4.3) [1.1] 23	(9.1) [3.4] 70		(29.9) [17.1] 351	(27.0) [9.5] 195	(37.3) [11.4] 233	(62.5) [57.5] 1,178	(35.8) [100.0] 2,050
Total of office	(100.0) [9.3] 534	(100.0) [13.5] 770	(100.0) [0.2] 14	(100.0) [20.6] 1,176	(100.0) [12.6] 722	(100.0) [10.9] 624	(100.0) [32.9] 1,884	(100.0) [100.0] 5,724

Engineers and above (*Gishi*)	538 (50.9) [25.0]	703 (46.9) [32.7]	3 (15.8) [0.1]	484 (8.4) [22.5]	48 (7.3) [2.2]	214 (3.6) [10.0]	161 (0.3) [7.5]	2,151 (2.8) [100.0]
Assistant engineers (*Gite* or *Gishu*)	474 (44.8) [11.5]	660 (44.0) [16.0]	7 (36.8) [0.2]	1,664 (28.9) [40.4]	106 (16.0) [2.6]	684 (11.6) [16.6]	528 (0.8) [12.8]	4,123 (5.3) [100.0]
Foremen (*Shokuchō*)	13 (1.2) [0.4]	21 (1.4) [0.6]		254 (4.4) [7.3]	37 (5.6) [1.1]	607 (10.3) [17.5]	2,533 (4.0) [73.1]	3,465 (4.4) [100.0]
Workers (*Shokkō*)	31 (2.9) [0.1]	90 (6.0) [0.1]	9 (47.4) [—]	3,288 (57.1) [4.8]	459 (69.3) [0.7]	4,356 (73.7) [6.4]	59,835 (94.7) [87.9]	68,068 (87.1) [100.0]
Others	2 (0.2) [0.6]	26 (1.7) [7.9]		73 (1.3) [22.3]	12 (1.8) [3.7]	52 (0.9) [15.9]	163 (0.3) [49.7]	328 (0.4) [100.0]
Total of workshops	1,058 (100.0) [1.4]	1,500 (100.0) [1.9]	19 (100.0) [—]	5,763 (100.0) [7.4]	662 (100.0) [0.9]	5,913 (100.0) [7.6]	63,220 (100.0) [80.9]	78,135 (100.0) [100.0]
Total	1,592 [1.9]	2,270 [2.7]	33 [8.3]	6,939 [8.3]	1,384 [1.7]	6,537 [7.8]	65,104 [77.6]	83,859 [100.0]

Notes:
1. Percentage by position is shown in parentheses and by school career in brackets.
2. This table is the total of 59 main factories in machine industries including the major companies in rolling stocks, spinning and weaving machines, machine tools, and electric machineries industries.

Source: Ministry of Education, ed., *Kaisha kōjō jūgyōin gakureki chōsa hōkoku* (Reports on school careers of employees in companies and factories), investigated in June 1930, n.d.

TABLE 2 Graduates of Technical College and Vocational Manufacturing School by Position and Years after Graduation, 1 March 1933 (percentage).

	Within 5 years after graduation	10 years	15 years	20 years	25 years	30 years	35 years	Total
Engineers and above	6	12	27	66	85	66	87	(3,257)
Assistant engineers	59	78	68	27	11	32	0	(9,550)
Foremen	7	2	0	0	0	0	0	(661)
Workers	9	1	0	2	0	0	0	(658)
Others	19	7	5	6	4	2	13	(1,784)
Total of technical college graduates	100	100	100	100	100	100	100	(15,910)
Engineers and above	0	1	4	12	30	43	32	(1,541)
Assistant engineers	7	27	53	59	53	42	35	(9,731)
Foremen	6	10	7	9	3	3	5	(2,698)
Workers	55	32	15	4	2	2	2	(12,967)
Others	32	30	21	16	12	9	26	(10,154)
Total of A-type vocational schools for manufacturing	100	100	100	100	100	100	100	(37,091)

Engineers and above	0	1	2	1	2	22	28	(78)
Assistant engineers	3	7	26	27	33	51	48	(738)
Foremen	2	9	7	14	11	1	8	(357)
Workers	77	60	47	42	36	11	8	(4,122)
Others	18	23	18	16	18	15	8	(1,257)
Total of B-type vocational schools for manufacturing	100	100	100	100	100	100	100	(6,552)

Notes: 1. The actual numbers of persons are shown in parentheses.
       2. Percentages are round numbers taken from the graphs in the original data.
       3. Students entering A-type vocational schools entered after finishing higher courses in elementary schools; students entering B-type schools were not required to do so.

Source: Tanaka Yasuhei, "*Kōgyō kyōiku*" (Industrial education), in Kōgyō Chōsa Kyōkai, ed., *Saishin zusetsu Nippon kōgyō sōran* (The newest illustrations of manufacturing in Japan), 1937, pp. 43–44.

companies as assistant engineers and were promoted to engineers after gaining experience in production technology through contact with workers in workshops. On the other hand, the majority of vocational school graduates started their vocational life as workers and were promoted to assistant engineers with some being further promoted to engineers. Those who finished elementary school could be promoted to the post of foreman.[41] Of course, for vocational school graduates to start their careers not as workers but as assistant engineers was a striking illustration of the scarcity of engineers that existed at various times and in various sectors.

2. *The Evolution of Production and Labor Management*

Before we trace the evolution of production and labor management between the wars, we must examine the separation or independence of the design department from workshops. In the electric machinery industry, Shibaura, in an organization reform in 1915, expanded a design and drafting section into six design sections: alternating current machinery, direct current machinery, transformers, distributors, tool design, and drafting. These sections were supervised by a head of the works department.[42] Hitachi, on the other hand, enlarged a design section into a design department consisting of four sections organized according to machine type.[43] In this way, these two advanced companies responded to the diversification of items produced in World War I by reinforcing the autonomy of their design departments. The electric plant of Mitsubishi's Kobe Shipyard (the forerunner of Mitsubishi Electric) where "technology specialization had not proceeded, and where the interchange of personnel between design sections and workshops was common," carried out a reform in 1916 which separated design sections from workshops.[44] This reform emphasized the responsibilities of engineers with regard to production and design technology and was the beginning of the end of dependence upon workshops.

The organizational reform at Kisha Seizō around 1915 was very thorough. It abolished the post of foreman and gave engineers the responsibility of directly supervising workers in workshops. This indicated a change from the attitude that "designs are too precise and difficult to work with in workshops" to one maintaining that "designers should concentrate on design, and workers should do their utmost to produce accordingly."[45] At Ikegai Iron Works, during World War I, the core of a design section came to consist not of persons who had received practical training in workshops, but of university and technical college graduates, with up to 40 persons in a design section.[46] This development of the design departments and their independence from workshops could also be seen in the spinning and weaving machines industry. At Toyoda's Loom, for example, the design section that had had the function of research and development was enlarged, and at Toyoda Automatic Loom, the R&D department began to separate from the design department after the end of the 1920s.[47]

One of the important changes in the machine industries after World War I was the independence of design sections from workshops. During the highly competitive 1920s, workshops were being asked to produce for lower prices and by the appointed date of delivery. Meeting these demands, while at the same time achieving design objectives, required both changes in production and labor management that coordinated relationships between design sections and workshops as well as greater control over the actual production processes in the workshops. The electric machinery industry was probably the most advanced among the four machinery industries in regard to the evolution of management. For this reason, the above changes will be traced by discussing mainly the situation in that industry.

The production systems in the electric machinery industry were, roughly speaking, divided into order production and production for projected demand. In the case of order production, the biggest problem was strict observance of the appointed date of delivery. Process controls (the observation and control of variables which affected the production process) were the key to total production management.[48] From World War I to the early 1920s, Shibaura and Hitachi had attempted to introduce process controls by establishing a factory system, which in response to the diversification of products, was organized according to the type of machine produced.[49] The establishment of process sections was the next important step in achieving greater process control. Hitachi Engineering Works established a process section at its Hitachi plant in 1919, under which a wage team was set up in 1924.[50] Time study specialists were posted on the wage team, thereby permitting the determination of standard times for fundamental jobs. The process section was led by an engineer who was a technical college graduate, and the level of its investigation and control of production processes was very advanced.[51] Also, the responsibility for both deciding wage levels and allocating work in workshops was transferred from foremen to management. At Mitsubishi Electric's Kobe plant, the previous "controls without controls" (*nariyuki kanri*) were reformed, and chart controls modeled on practices at Shibaura and Hitachi were initiated in 1923.[52] A standard process chart and a works controls board were introduced in 1926. Furthermore, meetings on external process controls continued, and as a result, Mitsubishi Electric achieved total process control around the end of the 1920s.

Thus, in the area of order production by large-scale electric machinery manufacturers, process controls had developed greatly. As illustrated by changes such as those regarding wage decisions and the allocation of work in workshops, engineers played a greater role with increased control over the workshops, paralleling the diminishing authority of the foremen. The same trends could be seen in some advanced machine tool builders. At Ikegai, for example, staff replaced foremen for investigating the rate for piece work and recording work orders and designated piece rates, thereby measuring idle time in order to reduce manufacturing costs.[53] At Karatsu Iron Works, five persons, among whom were four employees whose seniority ranged from 12 to 20 years, were posted in a process section whose chief was a Tokyo Technical College graduate.[54]

The other production system to be examined is production for projected demand. Osaka Transformer, a specialty maker of small-sized transformers which commanded a large share of the market in the 1920s, adopted a flow system which was named "unit operation" by the company's division of labor.[55] This mass production method, later called "conveyor system without conveyors," enabled Osaka Transformer to produce at much lower prices than preceding makers. Yasukawa Electric, which stopped the production of generators and transformers to become a specialty maker of motors and controllers, also actively developed the mass production of small items after the end of the 1920s. Process simplification and product standardization advanced after the introduction of production for projected demand of small motors in 1928.[56] In addition to the process inspection system adopted in 1927, the limit gauge system was introduced despite initial resistance from the workshops. On the basis of these mass production methods, the regular flow system was introduced in factories of small- and medium-sized motors established in 1935 and 1937.[57]

Making the mass production system of small items for projected demand a reality required the consolidation of certain conditions, such as the subdivision and coordination of production processes, improvements in conveying equipment, individual motor-drives for machine tools and their allocation (rather than collective drives linked to pulleys), and the introduction of limit-gauge systems. The introduction of limit-gauge systems was also important as a means for engineers to control workshops through designation of parts tolerances. According to reports by the Ministry of Agriculture and Commerce around 1925, however, there were only 24 main companies and plants which had adopted the limit-gauge system. These included the Kure and Hiro naval yards and the army arsenals in the public sector and such firms as Kisha Seizō, Toyoda's Loom, Niigata, Ikegai, Karatsu, Tokyo Gas and Electric, Shibaura, Hitachi, and Fuji in the private sector.[58] This indicates that mass production or precision workings on limit-gauge systems were not necessarily widespread among machine manufacturing industries.

The introduction of the time study method in Mitsubishi Electric's Kobe plant illustrates the problem of wage management.[59] Engineers and staff at the electric fan shop in the Kobe plant introduced the time study method modeled strictly on the practices at Westinghouse, as a result of which it became possible to implement standard times after 1925. The time study method was adopted, after a literal translation, in its original form. On the other hand, there were two aspects to wage management at the Kobe plant. First, there was the characteristic of "the seniority wage on job evaluation." This meant that the evaluation of workers' skills was carried out on the basis of seniority, with the results set up as the standard wage rate in 13 stages. Secondly, there was the factor of "livelihood wages" for the purpose of attaining the average wage level in a given industry by adding premiums. These factors of seniority and livelihood wages became increasingly important in wage management. During the war, for example, when the idea of livelihood wages was widespread, Nippon Sharyō Seizō, while never actually institutionalizing these factors, stated that "although the piece wage rate system is adopted, adjustments are made in the allocation of work."[60]

After a successful introduction at the electric fan shop, the time study method and the new wage rate based on it gradually spread to most work at the other shops in the Kobe plant. The development of the time study method, by promoting the further evolution of process and cost controls, greatly contributed to innovations in overall management at Mitsubishi Electric. During World War I, Yasukawa Electric also tried to introduce a premium system based on standard time. However, this trial ended in failure because it was based on a rough estimate of standard time instead of accumulated operation studies.[61] As shown in the two cases above, the introduction of time studies depended greatly on the help of engineers and staff and on favorable market conditions.

As has been pointed out, seniority was a factor in wage management. Although some have asserted that this seniority wage was an important factor in the development of so-called Japanese management between the wars, certain reservations ought to be added. As indicated, regular wage increases were limited mainly to large-scale enterprises, even in the heavy industries. Also, wage increase curves were different for foremen and for the rank and file. A foreman could gain wages which, for the most part, increased according to his seniority, while in the case of workers, such wage increases ceased after a certain length of time, following which the disparity between them expanded. Finally, it should be noted that workers' wage increases were not necessarily across the board but, in some cases, selective.[62]

Figure 1 shows an example of seniority wages. Wage rate trends showed no increase during the depression between December 1929 and January 1933, although we can see increases once or twice a year before the war with China and a large increase during the war. There were no distinct increases in the total earnings and wages for regular and overtime work in spite of the increases in wage rates between the latter half of the 1920s and the first half of the 1930s. This was due to the stagnation of real working hours (regulated by market conditions), premiums, bonuses, and various allowances. In wartime, wages for regular and overtime work expanded because of the rapid increase in wage rates and real working hours and, especially during the Pacific War, because of a rapid increase in various allowances, bonuses, and premiums. As a result, total nominal earnings soared, though of course the real standard of living drastically decreased due to inflation and the severe lack of essential commodities.

This evolution in production and labor management greatly influenced the workshop organizations. Thus, the following discussion concerns the engineers and foremen who played leading roles in

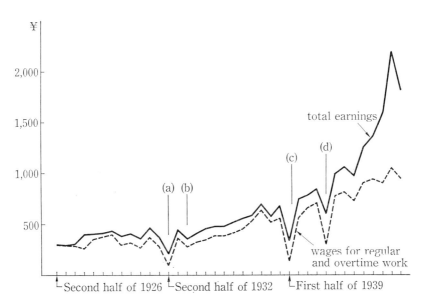

FIG. 1(a)   Total Earnings and Wages for Regular and Overtime Work: The Case of Mr. Y in Osaka Transformer Co., Ltd.

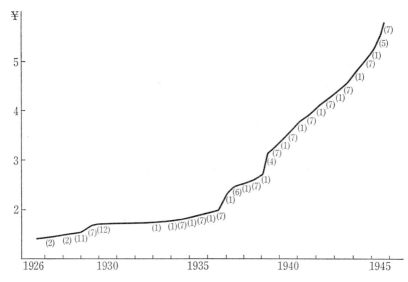

FIG. 1(b)   Daily Wage Rate for Mr. Y.

Notes: 1.   Personal history of Mr. Y: He was born in 1905 and in 1926 entered the
              transformer department as an iron-core cutter of Torishima Works,
              which changed its name to Torishima Transformer and was merged
              with Osaka Transformer Co. He had worked as an iron-core cutter until
              1942 and retired in 1961.
         2.   (a) absence of 113 days from July to November; (b) absence of 36 days
              in August and September; (c) absence of 116 days from February to
              June; (d) absence in March and April.
         3.   The numbers in parentheses show the month when the wage rate was
              increased.
         4.   The differences between total earnings and wages for regular and over-
              time work reflect premiums, bonuses, and various allowances.
         5.   Wages for regular work in 1942 and 1943 include premiums.
         6.   Data for August 1942 not available.
         7.   In 1939, 270 yen, not shown here, was paid in advance as part of the
              retirement allowance.
Source: Osaka Transformer Co., Ltd., ed., *Osaka hen'atsuki 50 nenshi* (A 50-year
          history of Osaka Transformer), 1972, pp. 596–615.

this developmental era. Table 3 shows data concerning engineers
employed in 1924. At least 55.2% of the 411 engineers employed in
1924 still remained with their respective companies in 1934, with
no large difference between those who graduated before or after
1914 (i.e., old and middle-aged, or younger engineers). Those who

transferred out accounted for 19.5% of the total number of engineers, and again there was no significant difference between older and younger engineers. The number of engineers who transferred to other machine building, railway, and electric power industries, so-called transfers within a sector, were 32 against a total of 80 transfers.

The percentage of engineers remaining within the same company differed widely from company to company. At Hitachi, for example, as can be seen from Table 3, 64.4% of the engineers remained for at least ten years. On the other hand, only 46.0% of the workers who graduated from Hitachi's Totei Yōseijo (apprentice school) in 1926, and only 33.3% who graduated in 1928, remained in 1936 and in 1938, respectively.[63] In 1933, the proportion of graduates of Kobe Mitsubishi Shokkō Gakkō (workers training school) remaining seven and ten years after graduation was 43 and 35% respectively.[64] However, in the case of engineers who supervised workers at Mitsubishi Electric, the figure was 69.2%, according to Table 3. Even though the number of samples is small, it can be said that the percentage of engineers remaining in the main machine enterprises was much higher than in the case of workers whose turnover ratio had decreased in the interwar period. This relatively high percentage of retention of engineers compared to workers, holds for both old and middle-aged as well as for the younger ones. Engineers who graduated from universities and technical colleges advanced not only into the design sections, which began to be separated from workshops, but also into the process and cost sections. In the advanced companies, the responsibilities of engineers, especially in production management, increased accordingly.[65]

This advancement of engineers into workshops was accompanied by diminishing responsibilities for foremen in the areas of production and operation management. As a result, according to the report from the Ministry of Commerce and Industry in 1928, it was factory managers, rather than foremen, who not only looked after production problems, quality improvement, and production cost, but also supervised plans for new factories, the distribution of wages, and the efficiency of machines.[66] The same situation existed in the area of production controls for most advanced companies,

TABLE 3 The Transfer of Engineers in the Main Machine Companies, 1924 to 1934.

	Total number of engineers, 1924	Of total engineers		Graduates prior to 1914			Graduates after 1914			Total		
		Graduates prior to 1914	Graduates after 1914	Remain	Transfer	Unknown	Remain	Transfer	Unknown	Remain	Transfer	Unknown
Shibaura Engineering Works	124	55	69	23	(8) 16	16	38	(7) 14	17	61	(15) 30	33
Hitachi Engineering Works	87	30	57	18	(2) 4	8	38	(3) 6	13	56	(5) 10	21
Mitsubishi Electric	39	12	27	8	3	1	19	(2) 4	4	27	(2) 7	5
Tokyo Gas and Electric	33	6	27	2	3	1	9	(5) 11	7	11	(5) 14	8
Kisha Seizō	26	13	13	9		4	10	2	1	19	2	5
Niigata Iron Works	21	9	12	8		1	7	1	4	15	2	4
Yasukawa Electric	16	5	11	5	(1) 1	4	6	2	3	6	(1) 3	7
Ikegai Iron Works	16	9	7	5	(1) 1	3	3	2	2	8	(1) 3	5
Nippon Sharyō Seizō	12	5	7	2	(2) 2	1	2		5	4	(2) 2	6
Fuji Electric	11	5	6	1	1	3	4	2		5	3	3

Toyoda's Loom	11	4	7	2	1	1	3	(1) 2	2	5	(1) 3	3
Karatsu Iron Works	7	7	6							6		1
Ōkuma Iron Works	3	2	1	1	1			1		1		2
Osaka Engineering Works	2	1	1	1						2	1	
Enshū Loom	1	1			1							
Osaka Kikō	1	1	1				1			1		1
Osaka Transformer	1		1	1				1				
Total	[100.0] 411	[100.0] 165	[100.0] 246	[52.7] 87	[20.6] (14) 34	[26.7] 44	[56.9] 140	[18.7] (18) 46	[24.4] 60	[55.2] 227	[19.5] (32) 80	[25.3] 104

Notes: 1. Remain = those who still remained in 1934.
   2. The numbers of transfers to other machine-building, railway, and electric power companies are shown in parentheses and are included in the numbers of transfers.
   3. The remain, transfer, and unknown percentages are shown in brackets.
   4. Engineers are university and technical college graduates.

Source: Kōgyō no Nippon Sha, ed., *Nippon kōgyō yōkan* (The directory of the Japanese manufacturings), 15th edition, 1924; Nikkan Kōgyō Shinbunsha, ed., *Nippon gijutsuka sōran* (The directory of engineers in Japan), 1934; Karatsu Iron Works, *Shain shirabe* (List of staff), 1936.

though to be sure, not in every industry or enterprise. Although even in wartime, engineers in the advanced companies of the machine tool industry, such as Ikegai and Karatsu, actively advanced into the workshops, problems such as the following were commonplace: "There is poor coordination between design sections and workshops in small companies as well as in large ones," and, "engineers in workshops don't have enough ability to control the operations of workers."[67] These problems were particularly evident in the production of large items in small amounts, such as in the machine tool industry, where product variety made it difficult to organize processes on the basis of production schedules. The disparity between engineers, who had the technical knowledge but insufficient workshop experience, and the foremen and workers, who had been trained in workshops but lacked the technical theory, were repeatedly pointed out. The evolution of production management was the attempt to control experience with knowledge. However, where there existed a great gap between domestic and foreign technology, even in knowledge itself, such as in the electric machinery industry before World War I and the machine tool industry between the wars, processes were forced to rely upon accumulated experience. Moreover, in areas where experience played an extremely important role, such as in the precision manufacturing of machines, it was much harder to overcome the abovementioned disparity.

Although the foreman's position in production management continued to decline, the above-quoted report from the Ministry of Commerce and Industry also pointed out that "it was common for foremen to hold real power over the personnel affairs of workers, such as their attendance, increases in wages, changes of posts, reward and punishment, premiums, and other pay in general." The report asserted that foremen still had powerful authority in labor management and workers' personnel affairs.[68] Thus, the foreman as the chief of a working group still played an important role in workshops.

3. *The Significance and Limitations of the Intra-Company Training System*
   It is well known that worker turnover in large enterprises in

heavy industry decreased in the 1920s. The evolution of production and labor management was able to take advantage of this situation. The loyalty of workers to the companies was supposed to promote firm-specific labor and technology. But this raises the question of to what extent the enterprises between the wars actively demanded firm-specific labor. Below, we will examine the development of the intra-company training systems as one of the most important measures for recruiting firm-specific labor.

There exist two opposing opinions regarding the development of intra-company training systems in the 1920s: one stresses the system's positive role, while the other asserts its retarding and retrocessive effect.[69] The following discussion is limited to the four machine industries. Table 4 shows the number of educational facilities in the four machine industries in 1930. Firstly, only Hitachi maintained a school within the company itself, while Shibaura, Mitsubishi Electric, Kawasaki Shipyard, Nippon Electric, Oki Electric, Tōyō Electric, and Tanaka Sharyō relied on outside schools. Among the enterprises not shown in Table 4, we can confirm intra-company training systems only at Karatsu, Okumura Electric, Nippon Sharyō Seizō, Kawakita Electric Engineering, Yasukawa, and Toyoda Automatic Loom. However, Okumura and Kawakita disappeared in the depression, and Yasukawa abolished its apprentice school in 1927, substituting short courses the next year.[70] Thus, it was the electric machinery industry which led the development of systematic skills training, including schooling inside and outside the company. Only in a small number of advanced companies in other industries could we confirm similar cases of such schooling. Karatsu and Hitachi were, therefore, representative of the companies which continually developed intra-company training within these four industries in the 1920s.[71]

Next, we shall examine the intra-company training system at Karatsu Iron Works in detail. Since its establishment, Karatsu had adopted the apprentice (*minarai*) system in such jobs as pattern makers, molders, machinists, finishers, electricians, and draftsmen. It employed apprentices who finished the higher courses at elementary schools and provided a training period of at least three years. Training expenses, which had been lent to apprentices, had to

TABLE 4   Educational Facilities in Four Machine Industries, June 1930.

	Company schools	Short courses and lecture meetings in companies	Schools outside of companies	Short courses and lecture meetings outside of companies
Factories with a thousand and over employees				
Shibaura Engineering Works		1	1	1
Shibaura, Tsurumi plant		1	1	
Tokyo Electric		1		
Aichi Watch and Electric		1		
Mitsubishi Electric, Nagasaki plant			1	1
Kawasaki Shipyard, Hyōgo plant			3	
Hitachi Engineering Works, Hitachi plant	2			
500–999				
Hitachi Engineering Works, Kameido plant		1		
Nippon Electric			1	
Oki Electric			1	3
Below 500				
Tōyō Electric			2	
Tanaka Sharyō			1	1
Total	2	5	11	6

Source: Ministry of Education, ed., *Kōjō jūgyōin kyōiku shisetsu chōsa hōkoku* (Reports on educational facilities in companies and factories), n.d.

be paid back between the end of training and when the apprentice turned 20 years of age.[72] Between World War I and the early 1920s, Karatsu had employed from approximately 100 to 250 apprentices, and the ratio to total employees reached around 30 to 40%.[73] As the depression deepened in the 1920s, however, Karatsu almost stopped acquiring apprentices in 1921, 1923, and 1924, and as a result, by the end of 1924, the number of apprentices had dropped to 54 (19.9% of employees), the lowest figure in the 1920s. Thereafter, the number of apprentices recovered, except in 1931 and 1932, reaching 193 (25.7% of employees) by the end of 1936. Thus, apprentices, whose employment was greatly regulated by market conditions, made up a relatively large proportion of total employees.

The intra-company training system in Karatsu, however, had to face several difficulties. Firstly, the turnover of apprentices during the training period continued and from 1918 to 1928 the rate of apprentice turnover ranged from 4.2 to 21.9%, except in 1922, the year of the labor dispute, and 1923.[74] Many apprentices were fired due to the labor dispute of 1922. Of 61 workers who completed training from 1918 to 1921, only 18 remained at the end of 1922, just after the labor dispute, and 6 of these left Karatsu by 1928. Of the 23 workers who finished in 1924, 17 remained in 1928, indicating at least an increase in labor stability for several years after the labor dispute.

In comparison, at Hitachi Engineering Works' Hitachi plant, the ratio of apprentices to the total number of employees ranged from 3.4 to 8.4% in the 1920s. After 1923, however, the rate of apprentice turnover decreased by several percentage points, and in the 1930s, since the social status of employees at Hitachi had greatly increased in the local area, around 40% of the graduates of the apprentice school remained.[75]

Though there was a great difference in turnover between Hitachi and Karatsu, the intra-company training system was an important means for securing future skilled workers for the two companies. "There was an era from around 1921 to the late 1920s, when many companies had their own apprentice schools. This situation, however, was gradually reversed due to various reasons: firstly, the powerful left-wing movement, secondly, the turnover of graduates of apprentice schools, and lastly, the depression. Thus, companies no longer train apprentices at their own schools."[76] As the above quote indicates, Karatsu and Hitachi's activities in the development of intra-company training systems were exceptional within the four machinery industries in the 1920s.

Furthermore, it is significant that even in Hitachi's case, around 60% of the apprentice school graduates ultimately transferred to other firms. This meant that the skills taught within the company, although necessary for the development of that company's production and labor management, might well end up being applied outside the company. In this sense, we must not overestimate the importance of firm-specific labor and technology between the wars. At the same time, the following observation is significant: "Where workers' skills required to suit job offers from the small factories are concerned—the case of turners, for example—small factories expect all-round workers who are used to operating every type of lathe possible. The skills of workers in Kawasaki (Shipyard) are extremely specialized, however. Turners are acquainted with only one type of lathe. As a result, the large proportion of ex-workers in Kawasaki were not matched with the job offers from small factories."[77] We should notice not only the firm-specific aspect of labor but also that specific to firm scale.

It was usual for turners to be able to operate drilling machines and shapers in addition to lathes, and in the small factories and workshops they were even acquainted with operating a forge. "The technology of the universal and general shop"[78] was available in these factories. There, the acquisition of skills was based on on-the-job training; in fact, apprentices "were discouraged from going to evening schools."[79] The skills formed under these circumstances would have been different from those at the advanced companies. These differences would have been an obstacle, although not an insurmountable one, to the transfer of workers as shown in the case of Kawasaki workers. Thus, the number and influence of advanced companies, which had developed production and labor management and which attempted to develop skilled labor suitable for the evolution of their management, was limited by sector and firm scale. Changes in this demarcation first became apparent during wartime.

IV. Conclusion

The active evolution of production and labor management between the wars occurred mainly within the large-scale companies and some medium-sized enterprises. Various trends developed simultaneously, such as the establishment of mass production for projected demand, the evolution of production management to strictly observe appointed dates for the delivery of orders, as well as labor management to support these activities. The engineers who graduated from universities and technical colleges led these developments through their advancement into the workshops and design sections. They accumulated ability as engineers by recognizing the gap between the knowledge taught at schools and the practical experiences available in the workshops and by trying to overcome this disparity through their assistant engineer post. Consequently, they were never separated from the workers.

Accompanying the advancement of engineers was the diminishing authority of foremen in production management. The foremen, however, still had powerful authority in labor management or over personnel as the heads of working groups. This ambivalent and transitional characteristic of foremen differed vastly by sector and firm scale. In the field of precision manufacturing by machines, the knowledge of engineers could not effectively supplant the experiences of the working groups headed by foremen. Or, in the case of medium and small factories which had an insufficient number of engineers, the foremen were still leaders even in production management. The powerful authority of foremen and their working groups in workshops resulted from the tradition of producing "dead copies" of imported machines, which was one of the most important and informal measures used to catch up with the technology of the advanced countries. Such production was first made possible by these working groups. Workshops and workshop operations were a kind of black box for engineers at the outset; however, as they slowly but steadily became understood, the autonomy of working groups and their foremen gradually diminished. We should notice, however, that working groups were neither actively nor passively controlled through orders from designers and engineers. Thus, they were not deprived of their autonomy and were able to plan and arrange their own work. Moreover, their production technology was acquired through the production of "dead copies" in workshops.

Notes

I am indebted to Professor William D. Wray and Dr. Herbert Brauer for their help on the English version of this paper.

1. On the development of the rolling stock industry from the middle of the Meiji era to the 1920s, see Sawai Minoru, "Senzenki Nippon tetsudō sharyō kōgyō no tenkaikatei" (The development of the Japanese rolling stock industry, 1890s–1920s), *Shakai kagaku kenkyū*, Vol. 37, No. 3, 1985.

2. For example, production of 12 designated factories for JNR in 1930 showed 91 locomotives, 296 passenger and electric cars, and 1,221 freight cars. Three companies, Kisha, Nippon Sharyō, and Kawasaki, produced 70 locomotives, 210 passenger and electric cars, and 1,064 freight cars. *Ibid.*, pp. 156–59.

3. For Nippon Sharyō, sales to JNR were more profitable than for other users, except for a period during World War I. *Ibid.*, pp. 66–67, 114–15, 182–83.

4. The academic background of engineers in JNR in 1910 was 271 university graduates and 243 technical college graduates. This was 1.49 times those in the military, which had naval yards and army arsenals. See Uchida Hoshimi, "Meiji kōki minkan kigyō no gijutsu-sha bunpu" (Employment of engineers in the Japanese industry, 1900–1910), *Keiei shigaku*, Vol. 14, No. 2, 1979, p. 7.

5. Sawai, *op. cit.*, pp. 167–71.

6. As a result, the ratio of imported rolling stock to the total domestic production values in the years between 1927 and 1930 was only 6.0%, and the ratio decreased to 0.6% in the years between 1930 and 1937. *Ibid.*, pp. 146, 189.

7. The following discussion is based primarily upon Ishii Tadashi, "Sen'i kikai gijutsu no hattenkatei: Shokki bōsekikikai seishiki no dōnyū fukyū kairyō sōzō" (The development process of textile machineries technology: The introduction, diffusion, improvement, and creation of weaving, spinning, and silk reeling machines), in Nakaoka Tetsurō, Ishii Tadashi, Uchida Hoshimi, *Kindai Nippon no gijutsu to gijutsu seisaku*, Tokyo, University of Tokyo Press, 1986; idem, "Rikishokki seizō gijutsu no tenkai" (The development of power loom manufacturing technology), in Minami Ryōshin, Kiyo-

kawa Yukihiko, eds., *Nippon no kōgyōka to gijutsu hatten*, Tokyo, Tōyō Keizai Shinpōsha, 1987.

8. Ishii, 1986, *op. cit.*, p. 131.
9. *Ibid.*, p. 142.
10. Itō Taikichi, "Kikai kōgyō no hattatsu: Tokuni menbōshoku kikai kōgyō no hattatsu o chūshin to shite" (The development of machine industries: Especially the development of cotton weaving and spinning machines industries), in Arisawa Hiromi et al., ed., *Chūshō kigyō kenkyū I: Chūshō kigyō no hattatsu*, Tokyo, Tōyō Keizai Shinpōsha, 1960, pp. 65–66, 80–91.
11. The annual production capacity of Toyoda's Loom Co. in 1936 was 15,000 looms and 700,000 spindles for cotton spinning machines. See Toyoda's Loom Co., Ltd., *Sōritsu 30 nen kinen shi* (A 30-year history of Toyoda's Loom Co.), 1936, p. 139.
12. Ishii, 1987, *op. cit.*, pp. 144–45.
13. Sawai Minoru, "Kōsaku kikai kōgyō no jūsōteki tenkai: 1920 nendai o megutte" (The multi-tiered development of the Japanese machine tool industry: The 1920s), in Minami and Kiyokawa, *op. cit.*, p. 191.
14. Chokki Toshiaki, *Nippon no kōsaku kikai kōgyō no hatten katei no bunseki* (Analysis of the process of development of the Japanese machine tool industry), Tokyo, published by the author, 1963, pp. 62–70.
15. On machine tool builders during World War I, see Sawai Minoru, "Dai ichiji taisen zengo ni okeru Nippon kōsaku kikai kōgyō no honkakuteki tenkai" (The development of the Japanese machine tool industry around the time of World War I), *Shakai keizai shigaku*, Vol. 47, No. 2, 1981.
16. Some of the medium-sized makers located in local industrial cities, like Nagaoka in Niigata prefecture, were not as linked to the military's demands as their counterparts in large cities, thus drastically decreasing their production during the stagnation of the 1920s. However, they formed one of the centers for the production of machine tools through the expansion of production after the Manchurian Incident. *Ibid.*, pp. 53–54; Sawai Minoru, "1930 nendai no Nippon kōsaku kikai kōgyō" (The Japanese machine tool industry, 1930–1937), *Tochi seido shigaku*, No. 97, 1982, pp. 47–48.
17. Sawai, 1987, *op. cit.*, pp. 177–85.
18. *Ibid.*, p. 180. The eight sectors in machine-producing sectors were prime movers, pumps, hydraulic and gaseous presses, machine tools, printing and book making machines, weaving and spinning machines, electric machineries, and locomotives.

19. Sawai, 1982, *op. cit.*, p. 43ff.

20. *Ibid.*, p. 35.

21. For the plans for the expansion of production of machine tools by the military, the Department of Commerce and Industry, and Bureau of Resources (Shigen Kyoku) just before the Sino-Japanese War, see Sawai Minoru, "Senji keizai tōsei no tenkai to Nippon kōsaku kikai kōgyō: Nitchū sensōki o chūshin to shite" (The intensification of wartime economic controls and the Japanese machine tool industry, 1937–41), *Shakai kagaku kenkyū*, Vol. 36, No. 1, 1984, pp. 151–55.

22. Ōshio Takeshi, "Nippon ni okeru denki kikai kōgyō shihon no chikuseki yōshiki" (The capital finance of the electric machinery industry), *Shakai keizai shigaku*, Vol. 39, No. 3, 1973, pp. 42–43.

23. Hasegawa Shin, "1920 nendai no denki kikai shijō" (The Japanese electrical equipment market in the 1920s), *Shakai keizai shigaku*, Vol. 45, No. 4, 1979, p. 40.

24. *Ibid.*, pp. 57–60.

25. The following discussion is based on Hasegawa Shin, "1920 nendai no denki kikai kōgyō: Hatten yōin to sono tokushitsu" (The electrical equipment industry in the 1920s: A study of its growth factors and characteristics), *Rekishigaku kenkyū*, No. 486, 1980, pp. 19–20.

26. *Ibid.*, p. 20, and Yamada Ryōzō, Takenaka Kazuo, and Miwa Yoshirō, "Denki kikai kōgyō no tenkai to gendankai" (The development and the present stage of the electric machineries industry), in Arisawa Hiromi, ed., *Gendai Nippon sangyō kōza VI, Kikai kōgyō 2*, Tokyo, Iwanami Shoten, 1960, p. 41.

27. Hasegawa Shin, "Senkanki no jūdenki kōgyō ni okeru senmon mēkā no hatten: Yasukawa Denki Seisakusho o chūshin ni" (The specialization of the Japanese electrical equipment manufacturers in the interwar period), *Shizuoka daigaku kyōiku gakubu kenkyū hōkoku*, No. 33, 1982, pp. 28–32, 38–39.

28. Sawai, 1985, *op. cit.*, pp. 65–66.

29. Sawai, 1981, *op. cit.*, p. 48.

30. *Ibid.*, pp. 48–49.

31. Sawai, 1987, *op. cit.*, pp. 187–88.

32. Sawai, 1985, *op. cit.*, pp. 60–62.

33. Department of Agriculture and Commerce, Bureau of Commerce and Industry, ed., *Shuyō kōgyō gairan* (The survey of the major industries), 1914, p. 283.

34. Sawai, 1987, *op. cit.*, pp. 176–77.

35. Hasegawa, 1979, *op. cit.*, pp. 43–44.

36. Kōsaku Kikai Tenrankai Kyōsankai, ed., *Kōsaku kikai tenrankai hōkoku furoku* (Report on the machine tool exhibition: Appendix), 1922, p. 173.

37. Mitsubishi Electric Co., Ltd., *Kengyō kaiko* (A company history of Mitsubishi Electric Co.), 1951, pp. 69–71.

38. For example, Ikegai Kishirō of Ikegai Iron Works visited more than 80 companies within his stay of three months in the United States. See Hayasaka Tsutomu, ed., *Ikegai Kishirō tsuisō roku* (Memoirs of Ikegai Kishirō), Tokyo, Kikai Seisaku Shiryō Sha, 1943, p. 234.

39. Karatsu Iron Works continually subscribed to such periodicals as *American Machinist, The Engineers, The Foundry, Foundry Trade Journal, General Electric Review,* and *Machinery* (published in the United States) from 1916 to 1928, and furthermore, *Drop Forger, Engineering, Industrial Management, System* and *Machinery* (published in the United Kingdom) for some duration. See Karatsu Iron Works Co., Ltd., *Kessan chōsho* (Reports on settlement of accounts), each term.

40. On p. 69 in Fukuda Kōichirō, "Nippon ni okeru dokusen shihon shugi dankai no rōdōsha tōkutsu kikō: Shokuchō seido to kōgyō kyōiku" (Labor control in Japan during the period of monopolist capitalism), *Nihonshi kenkyū*, No. 131, 1973, Table 8, which is based on Tanaka Yasuhei, "Kōgyō kyōiku" (Industrial education), in Kōgyō Chōsa Kyōkai, ed., *Saishin zusetsu Nippon kōgyō sōran*, 1937. As is shown, however, we made Table 1, which is based on the original data that would have been used in Tanaka's work in order to clarify the classification by industry.

41. According to the investigation by Kyōchōkai at the end of the 1920s, the composition by age of foremen in machineries and equipment building factories were: 3.5% for those under 30, 44.0% aged 30–39, 44.2% aged 40–49, and 8.2% for those over 50. See Kyōchōkai, ed., *Honpō kōjō kōzan shokuchō seido gaiyō* (Survey of the foreman system in factories and mines in Japan), 1929, p. 16. The workers who finished the higher courses at elementary schools, therefore, would have needed a career of over 15 years in order to become foremen. For example, according to the report of Yahata Ironworks in 1932, workers needed, on the average, a tenure of around 10, 16, and 21 years for acceptance to become *gochō, kumichō,* and *kōchō,* respectively (names for foremen). See Rōdō Undō Shiryō Iinkai, ed., *Nippon rōdō undō shiryō* (Documents on the labor movements in Japan), Vol. 7, Tokyo, University of Tokyo Press, 1964, p. 86.

42. Shibaura Engineering Works, ed., *Shibaura Seisakujo 65 nenshi* (A 65-year history of the Shibaura Engineering Works), 1940, pp. 139–40.

43. Yoshida Masaki, "Hitachi Seisakusho seiritsu ni kansuru ichi kōsatsu" (The early history of Hitachi Electric Company: A study of the genesis of Hitachi group), *Mita shōgaku kenkyū*, Vol. 17, No. 4, 1974, p. 23.

44. Mitsubishi Electric Co., *op. cit.*, pp. 37–38.

45. Dewa Seisuke, "Kikansha no seisaku ni tsuite" (On the manufacture of locomotives), *Kikai gakkaishi*, Vol. 18, No. 40, 1915, p. 80. In Kisha Seizō, almost at the same time, group contract work conducted by foremen was changed to the system of time work. See Kisha Seizō Co., Ltd., ed., *K S K nenpyō chū*, (Notes of the chronological tables of Kisha Seizō), n.d., p. 1,133.

46. Hayasaka Tsutomu Zenshū Kankō Iinkai, ed., *Hayasaka Tsutomu zenshū; Kōsaku kikai to bunmei* (Collected works of T. Hayasaka: Machine tools and civilization), Tokyo, Komine Kōgyō Gijutsu, 1964, p. 466.

47. Taniguchi Yutaka, "Senkanki ni okeru Nippon bōshoku kikai kōgyō no tenkai: Menbōshoku kikai kōgyō no kenkyū kaihatsu" (The development of the Japanese spinning and weaving machinery industry during the interwar period: Research and development in the cotton spinning and weaving machinery industry), *Sangyō keizai kenkyū*, Vol. 26, No. 1, 1985, pp. 60–63.

48. Yoshida Masaki, "Seisan kanri no keieishi: Senzen no jūdenki seisan o chūshin ni" (The history of production management in the electric manufacturing industries), *Keiei shigaku*, Vol. 5, No. 1, 1970, p. 41.

49. Yoshida, 1974, *op. cit.*, p. 23; Shibaura Engineering Works Co., Ltd., *op. cit.*, pp. 270–81.

50. The following discussion is based upon Hasegawa, 1980, *op. cit.*, p. 29.

51. Hitachi Engineering Works, Hitachi Plant, ed., *Hitachi kōjō 50 nenshi* (A 50-year history of Hitachi Plant), 1961, p. 21; Kōgyō no Nippon Sha, ed., *Nippon kōgyō yōkan* (The directory of Japanese manufacturing), 15th edition, 1924, p. 171.

52. The following description is based on Hasegawa, 1980, *op. cit.*, pp. 29–30 and Yoshida, 1970, *op. cit.*, pp. 63–64.

53. Sawai, 1987, *op. cit.*, p. 186.

54. Karatsu Iron Works Co., Ltd., *Shoin shirabe* (The list of staff), 1932;

Nikkan Kōgyō Shinbunsha, ed., *Nippon gijutsuka sōran* (The directory of engineers in Japan), 1934, p. 434.

55. Osaka Transformer Co., Ltd., *Osaka Hen'atsuki 50 nenshi* (A 50-year history of Osaka Transformer Co.), 1972, pp. 71–72, 83.

56. The following discussion is based on Hasegawa, 1982, *op. cit.*, pp. 32–33; Yasukawa Electric Co., Ltd., *Yasukawa Denki 40 nenshi* (A 40-year history of Yasukawa Electric Co.), 1956, p. 321.

57. It was an engineer who had learned operation, motion, and time studies at Osaka Prefectural Institute of Industrial Efficiency who led the introduction of the flow system. See Yasukawa Daigorō Den Kankōkai, ed., *Yasukawa Daigorō den* (Biography of Yasukawa Daigorō), 1977, p. 142; idem, *Yasukawa Daigorō Den: Bessatsu* (Separate volume), 1977, p. 512.

58. Nagata Eisuke, "Kikairui no kōsaku ni mochiuru rimitto gēji ni tsuite" (On limit gauges used in the manufacturing of machineries), *Kōgyō chōsa ihō*, Vol. 3, No. 3, 1926, pp. 211–12.

59. The following description of Mitsubishi Electric Co. is based upon Sasaki Satoshi, "Mitsubishi Denki ni miru kagakuteki kanrihō no dōnyū katei: Jikan kenkyūhō no dōnyū o chūshin ni" (The introduction of the time study method into Mitsubishi Electric Co. at the Kobe works), *Keiei shigaku*, Vol. 21, No. 4, 1987, pp. 37–50.

60. Nippon Kōgyō Kyōkai, ed., *Chingin seido* (The wage system), Tokyo, Kyōritsusha, 1940, p. 22.

61. Yasukawa Electric Co., Ltd., *op. cit.*, p. 53.

62. This discussion is based on Shimada Haruo, "Nenkō sei no shiteki keisei ni tsuite: Senzen Yahata Seitetsusho no jirei kenkyū" (On the historical formation of the seniority system: A case study of prewar Yahata Ironworks), *Mita gakkai zasshi*, Vol. 61, No. 4, 1968, p. 63. and Hyōdō Tsutomu, *Nippon ni okeru rōshi kankei no tenkai* (The evolution of labor relations in Japan), Tokyo, University of Tokyo Press, 1971, pp. 442–46, 454–56.

63. Sugayama Shinji, "1920 nendai no kigyōnai yōseikō seido: Hitachi Seisakusho no jirei bunseki" (The corporation apprenticeship of the 1920s), *Tochi seido shigaku*, No. 108, 1985, p. 47.

64. Fukuda, *op. cit.*, p. 65.

65. In Oki Electric, the "joint-piecework system" was adopted until the latter half of the 1920s but was abolished in a new factory established in 1927 in the course of the modernization of production management led by the engineers, who were the graduates of universities or technical colleges and who were regularly employed after World

War I. See Chokki Toshiaki, "Senzen Nippon no denki kikai seisaku kigyō ni okeru gijutsu to rōdō no chikuseki" (Accumulation of technology and work force in Japanese electric machinery manufacturing companies before World War II), *Keiei shirin*, Vol. 23, No. 3, 1986, p. 15.

66. Okamoto Hideaki, *Kōgyōka to genba kantokusha* (Industrialization and foremen), Tokyo, Nippon Rōdō Kyōkai, 1966, pp. 114–15.

67. "Kōsaku kikai gijutsu kōjō zadankai" (A symposium on the advancement of machine tools technology), *Mashinarī*, Vol. 3, July 1940, pp. 81, 89.

68. Okamoto, *op. cit.*, pp. 116–17.

69. Sugayama, *op. cit.*, 34–35.

70. Sumiya Mikio, ed., *Nippon shokugyō kunren hattatsu shi* (The history of development of industrial training), Vol. 2, Tokyo, Nippon Rōdō Kyōkai, 1971, Tables 1–11, and 2–22; Toyoda Automatic Loom Works, Ltd., ed., *40 nenshi* (A 40-year history), 1967, pp. 178–79; Yasukawa Electric Co., Ltd., *op. cit.*, p. 391.

71. The details of the intra-company training system in Nippon Sharyō Seizō are unknown.

72. This discussion is based on Chūō Shokugyō Shōkai Jimukyoku, ed., *Kakushu kōjō totei ni kansuru chōsa* (Report on various kinds of factory apprentices), 1926, pp. 155–59.

73. The following description is based upon Karatsu Iron Works Co., Ltd., *Eigyō hōkokusho* (Annual reports) and *Kessan chōsho*, each term.

74. Computed on the basis of Karatsu Iron Works, *Kessan chōsho*.

75. Sugayama, *op. cit.*, pp. 38, 42–49.

76. "Jukurenkō yōsei mondai zadankai" (A symposium on the problem of training skilled workers), *Kyōiku*, Vol. 5, No. 7, 1937, p. 67.

77. Kobe Shi Shakai Ka, ed., *Kaiko kara kisū made* (Discharge and its consequences), 1928, pp. 72–73.

78. Kiuchi Takaji, "Nippon ni okeru gijutsu suijun to gijutsu kyōiku-ginōsha yōsei (3)" (The technological level and technical education for the training of skilled workers in Japan), *Kyōiku*, Vol. 8, No. 5, 1940, pp. 19–20. On the conditions of small and petty machine factories in the first half of the 1930s, see idem, "Kikai kōgyō ni okeru shōkibo kōjō no jissō" (The real state of small factories in machine industries), *Shakai seisaku jihō*, No. 188, 1936.

79. Chūō Shokugyō Shōkai Jimukyoku, ed., *Shokugyō betsu rōdō jijō (3): Kikai kōgyō* (Labor conditions by industry [3]: Machine industries), 1927, p. 51.

Comment

Eisuke Daitō
University of Tokyo

As is summarized skillfully by Professor Sawai, the four industries varied widely in their process of development as well as in their structures and the firms resulting from it. It goes without saying, therefore, that we must be careful not to jump to hasty conclusions. Sawai tells us in the second section of the paper that the development of the four industries was one based on import substitution. According to Sawai, firms in these industries could attain "technological independence" owing to the support by the government on the one hand and the continuous efforts on the part of private companies on the other.

In my opinion, however, the strategy of import substitution is not always successful. As is widely known, after World War II, many policy makers in developing countries thought their economies could be industrialized through the strategy of import substitution. In other words, they tried to establish domestic industries, whose products had been imported in quantity, behind the tariff wall and other protective measures. It was hoped that imports would be replaced by domestic products and that internal growth would be stimulated. Regrettably for many developing countries, experiences with this strategy have been disappointing. They are suffering from trade deficits, which means that their dependence on imports from advanced countries has not been reduced yet. These facts lead me to a series of questions: Why was the development by import substitution successful in Japan? Did the strategy not have any adverse side effects? Who bore their cost? Was the development of user industries not discouraged as they might have to purchase inputs at cost above world market levels from domestic firms operating under the protection? My first request is to elucidate a little more analytically the condition of "technological independence."

The third section of the paper deals with many important topics concerning production control and labor management. I believe that almost everyone agrees that success or failure of a manufacturer depends as much on its products as on any other factor. I think it very important, as is pointed out by Sawai, that after World War I, designing sections were established in the machinery industry. But the problem is how powerful they were and to whom the task was assigned. Theoretically, it is advisable that a new product is developed through the joint effort of a design engineer, a production control man, a process or method engineer, a purchasing agent, a market analyst, and others. In reality, however, it is sometimes difficult to put this theory into practice. Although Sawai points out the importance of the coordination between design sections and workshops, it seems to me that in the subsequent pages he does not explain how this coordination was conducted. Take the introduction of limit-gauge systems, for instance. It is certainly an innovation. But it is very important for us to know how tolerance limits were determined. If tolerance is too tight, it entails much unnecessary work and increases manufacturing costs. Many unsatisfactory parts and products may result from loose tolerance specifications. I wonder how tolerance limits, in which both design sections and workshops have large interests, were determined.

Concerning the wage administration, I think that the hyper-inflation of the late 1910s exerted more serious influence on the wage administration of a firm than any other factor. Between 1918 and 1920, wage rates of many trades were more than doubled. Many firms introduced a series of fringe benefits, such as family allowance, temporary allowance, children's allowance, and housing benefit. The management considered these allowances as an alternative to wage increases. In addition, the inflation made the management take the cost of living into consideration when they designed payment systems. Although after World War I some of the benefits were abolished, these developments were a clear departure from the past practices, which had relied heavily on the piece-rate system.

Although I agree with Sawai in his argument on the so-called *nenkō* wage, more attention should be paid to the abovementioned developments.

Sawai believes that there is a popular view that trainees in the in-house training schools acquired a firm's specific skills which could not be transferred to other employers. In my opinion, that is not always the case. At well-organized training schools for future straw bosses and foremen, trainees acquired not only manual skills of various kinds but also theoretical knowledge, which were not firm-specific but were a sound base for versatile skills. Firm-specific skills were acquired through more informal on-the-job training, especially in large factories where many firm-specific jobs existed because of the minute division of labor. According to Seike Tadashi, the most effective method with which an employer could retain talented workers is to assign a set of tasks and jobs which were specific to his factory. In addition, during the training period, employers could screen and select trainees. It can be argued, therefore, that on-the-job training sometimes could be utilized more effectively as a method of labor management in many ways than well-organized training schools.

As is pointed out by Sawai, many training schools could not survive the depressions in the 1920s. Some of them were, however, essentially very small and could accomplish their purpose in a short period of time. For example, the case of Nikkō Works of the Furukawa Electric Co.: Suzuki Kōzaburō, the factory manager famous for his labor management policies, inaugurated a *totei gakkō* (apprentice school) in 1913. The school was closed in 1918 because all the posts for foremen could be filled by 87 apprentices who had graduated during the period. In 1928, a training school started to accept trainees again but closed in 1934. During the period, 94 persons graduated. Again, this number was large enough to fill all the vacancies for the first-line supervisors in the near future. Since the factory was the biggest employer around the city of Nikkō and the purpose of the school was so attractive, every year many talented boys took the entrance examination. As a result, the school could scoop the cream of the community. In short, in order to draw a definite conclusion on in-house training systems in the 1920s, we must pay careful attention to their purposes.

Response

Minoru Sawai

Firstly, as Professor Daitō points out, the strategy of import substitution is not always a sufficient condition for industrialization in many developing countries. The multi-tiered structure in the market as a non-tariff barrier, however, gave infant machine tools and spinning and weaving machines builders time to absorb imported technology. The domestic makers could enlarge markets by using low prices as a weapon, and through this process upgrade the quality of their products as well. For the rolling stock and electric machineries industries, in which the markets were relatively homogeneous, the support by the governmental sectors and the technical tie-up with foreign makers were respectively decisive.

Secondly, the coordination between design sections and workshops varied widely by firm. In Ikegai, for example, when management staff estimated the rate for a certain piecework and the foremen wanted a different rate applied, they compromised on the rate established. But, in the introduction of limit-gauge systems in Kisha Seizō, tolerance limits were supposedly determined not by the cooperation with workshops but by the design sections, because JNR standards already existed, and Kisha could not deliver their products unless they reached the designated levels.

Thirdly, the acceleration of inflation in the 1910s, as Daitō stresses, was the driving force for the evolution of wage administration. At the same time, we cannot neglect the impact of the frequent turnover of workers on management at that time. The high turnover rate under inflation was one of the main factors which forced management not only to evolve the new wage administration but to introduce intra-company training systems. These systems were composed of schooling and on-the-job training at the workshops. As Daitō states, the skills taught in the systems were not necessarily firm-specific, as long as we take schooling into consideration. There was presumably, however, a decisive difference in the devotion of workers to their companies in the cases where skills were acquired through on-the-job training and schooling, in which engineers were teachers, and in the cases where workers aquired skills as they transferred from factory to factory. The intra-company training systems, therefore, were effective for the training of workers who could respond well to the evolution of production and labor management.

Factory Legislation and Employer Resistance: The Abolition of Night Work in the Cotton Spinning Industry

Janet Hunter
London School of Economics and Political Science

One of the most contentious issues raised by the movement for factory legislation in pre-1945 Japan was the abolition of night work for women. The cotton industry was highly dependent on night work by women, and the movement for prohibition developed within a context of international pressure for labor legislation and acute competition in overseas markets. A ban eventually came into effect on July 1, 1929, after over three decades of controversy.

This paper is not directly concerned with the economic rationale of employers' use of night work. It seeks instead to use the abolition debate as a case study to elucidate the perceptions of women which governed women's position in the labor market and informed attitudes to protective legislation as a whole. As such it has an important bearing on the economic arguments.

I. The International Context

The first legislation restricting night work by women was passed in England in 1844.[1] During the latter half of the 19th century, France, Germany, Russia, and other industrializing nations also introduced legislation restricting night work by women, but night shifts for male and female labor remained widespread in many countries, stimulating an international movement for prohibition. The Sixth International Congress on Hygiene and Population held in Vienna in 1887 proclaimed that prohibition was necessary for hygienic and moral reasons, and in 1890 the International Congress on Workers' Protection in Berlin resolved to suppress night work for women.[2] An International Association for Labour Legislation was set up to promote research activities and act as a pressure group on individual governments.[3] Early campaigners were concerned with the detrimental effects of night work on both men and women workers. Accident rates were higher at night and workers less efficient. Night shifts led to chronic overwork, lack of family life, and premature aging.[4] However, the implementation and enforcement of general international regulations seemed unrealistic at this time, and partial prohibition was likely to be complex and ineffective. In this context the movement concentrated on special protection for women. Women, it was said, were more prone to morbid germs than men; they tended to be ill more frequently and for longer. Experience showed a ban on night work reduced female and infant mortality.[5]

The arguments for a ban on night work for women were initially those of health and efficiency, but the issue of gender roles soon became all-pervasive. Cultural perceptions of the social role of women, in particular the ideology of domesticity, became the single most important factor behind the arguments of all protagonists in the debate. Implicit in the arguments was a recognition that a woman had duties to her family beyond a greater daily participation in family life. Etienne Bauer of the International Association for Labour Legislation claimed in 1903 that the longer night's rest a woman received and the earlier she finished work on Saturdays,

> the more can the woman basically occupy herself with her household. Children will no longer grow abandoned to the care of mercenaries without being exposed to the salutary influence of their parents. The maintenance of the house in the desired state of cleanliness, the careful preparation of food have only been possible once night work has been banned. All these advantages are for working families ample compensation for the pecuniary losses consequent upon the suppression of night work.[6]

The IALL campaigned for the setting up of a congress to discuss an international convention banning night work, and a memorial in support of the case was handed to various governments. This memorial was explicit in its aim of protecting "the mothers of the young working generation, these guardians of the workman's home," from abuse in their employment.[7] It outlined the improvements in health, education, and family life which would result from a ban, and stressed: "The greater resistance and improved health verified among women ... have allowed of housewives attending better to their home duties; preparing meals, education and training of children, tidying the linen and the home etc."[8] The IALL opposed a ban on night work for married women only, on the grounds that it would discourage marriage. It further argued that an international convention was the only means of overcoming employers' financial scruples borne of intense competitive pressure in international markets. Not surprisingly, the concept of a convention was supported most fully by those countries which had already implemented restrictions on night work by females.

In 1906, the Berne Diplomatic Conference drafted a convention on abolition which was signed by 14 European states, 12 of which had ratified the convention by 1914. In 1919, the inaugural conference of the International Labour Organization in Washington drafted a convention regarding women's night employment, which had a significantly broader scope of application. Night work was thereafter increasingly considered within the context of pressure for shorter working hours and the movement for the eight-hour day. By 1931, 20 states had ratified the 1919 convention. Japan was not among them.[9]

II. The Japanese Context

> In our country we can say that social policy has still not been realized. For example, even though we have moved toward establishing factory laws, the goal of these laws is not the reverence of the workers' personality, or the increase of the class profit of the working class. As much as possible we consider [the workers] to be the tools of national industry. The improvement of these tools is necessary for the healthy advancement of the nation's industry. (Kawakami Hajime)[10]

Night work for women in factories was first adopted in 1882 at the Kuwanohara Cotton Spinning Mill.[11] The practice spread rapidly to Shibusawa Eiichi's Osaka Spinning Company and a number of other large mills. Unlike the female industrial labor force in some other countries, the labor force in Japan's cotton industry consisted largely of young, unmarried women. These women, who were mostly under 20, worked for a few years at most before returning to their villages to marry or moving elsewhere. At work they lived in dormitories attached to the mill, making it easier for management to employ workers on two 12-hour shifts, enabling 24-hour operation. The continuous running of the machinery was adopted to minimize production costs, and pay off heavy capital investment necessitated by construction costs and importing of expensive equipment. By the 1890s, 24-hour running was the norm in almost all modern cotton mills, and in 1904 the IALL estimated that around 250,000 Japanese workwomen were doing night shifts.[12] In the 1920s, around 65% of women spinners were working alternating stints of seven to ten days on day and night shifts.[13] A survey in 1926 estimated that 180,400 women and minors were still engaged in night work in Japan, of whom 99% (178,800) were in spinning and other textiles.[14] Outside the cotton spinning industry women's night work was not common. The other large industrial employer of women, the silk reeling industry, was seasonal in nature. In peak periods it utilized extended daytime shifts of up to 17 hours, but not night shifts as such, although it was inevitably affected by the general movement for shorter working hours. The cotton spinning industry thus became the major target of the abolition movement and its employers the most vocal exponents of the anti-abolition point of view.

The possibility of a ban on night work for women was first seriously mooted in the *Shokkō jōrei* (Regulations for workers) of 1887 as an integral part of a protective legislation package.[15] Economic expansion, especially after the Sino-Japanese War, brought with it social problems and an emerging labor and social movement. Elements of the bureaucracy and intellectuals showed themselves for various reasons concerned over conditions in factories, and there was widespread discussion. Prefectural governors were sounded out upon the desirability of protective legislation for workers, and in October 1896 the first session of the authoritative Nōshōkō Kōtō Kaigi (Higher Council on Agriculture, Commerce, and Industry) was convened. Calls for protective legislation met with strong resistance from the industrial side, and the issue was deferred. The third session of the Council convened in October 1898 discussed a draft Factory Act. Industry's representatives still raised objections to the concept of legislation, but the growing importance of a new generation of entrepreneurs less implacably hostile to a change in the existing *modus vivendi* led to a subcommittee of the Council's being requested to produce an amended draft. This draft was duly adopted by the Council but failed to reach the Diet because of political difficulties.[16]

In the autumn of 1902 a new draft Act was put forward by the government. Article 5 provided for a ban on night work by women between the hours of 10 P.M. and 4 A.M., but permitted its indefinite continuation in rotating alternating shifts, i.e., as it already functioned in the cotton spinning industry. The Russo-Japanese War halted discussions, and new proposals in November 1909 contained the same exemption clause.[17]

By contrast, the draft Factory Act submitted to the Diet in January 1910 proposed to ban all night work by women ten years after the legislation came into force. A storm of employer-led protest caused its withdrawal, but a committee headed by entrepreneur Shibusawa Eiichi produced a revised draft, which eventually passed the Diet in March 1911. The new Factory Act provided for a ban on night work by women under the age of 20 between 10 P.M. and 4 A.M. Special exemptions allowed for work until 11 P.M., and the ban was to be implemented 15 years after the Act came into effect. In fact, the exemption clause was widely exploited, and since the Act did not come into effect until September 1916, night work for women would become illegal only in September 1931.[18] Night work for women over 20 was permitted by the Act, but since the cotton spinning labor force was predominantly young, the ban on under-20s meant almost total restraint on night operations by cotton employers.[19]

As domestic economic and social pressures increasingly intertwined with international ones after the founding of the ILO in 1919, demands grew for a ban on night work before 1931. A revised draft Factory Act was submitted to the Diet late in 1922. After extensive discussions over the length of the transition period needed by employers, the revised Act was passed March 1923. It provided for a ban on night work for all women three years after the law came into effect. Despite bitter criticism, promulgation of the law was delayed by employer protest and the disastrous Kantō earthquake of 1923, but an imperial decree of June 1926 prohibited night work by women from July 1, 1929.[20] From this date, as scheduled, factory work by women was prohibited between the hours of 10 P.M. and 5 A.M., although "general special permission" allowed for work until 11 P.M.—a device derided by a Western economist two years later as "a typical Japanese expedient for appearing well in foreign eyes and yet carrying on as nearly as possible in the same way as before."[21]

A closer look at the main strands of the argument will demonstrate how far the various parties focused their arguments on the women who were the objects of discussion. The main advocates of a ban on night shifts and other protective legislation included members of the intelligentsia, the state, the ILO, and other international organizations, Japan's industrial competitors, organized labor, and, occasionally, women themselves. The employers and their organizations constituted the major opponents of a ban on night work. The argument evolved over time as each side was forced to respond to the claims of the other.[22]

III. Journalists and Intellectuals

An awareness of industrial realities was spread in the 1890s by journalists who inspected modern mills and saw firsthand the appalling conditions under which many workers spent their working hours. In his famous *Nihon no kasō shakai* (Lower social strata of Japan), published in 1898, Yokoyama Gennosuke attempted to comment dispassionately on the arguments of those who believed that the lives and health of workers should not be an impediment to the advance of industry, and those who believed it was humanly unacceptable to make people work at night so that the public might sleep easy in their beds.[23] Put in such terms it seemed a stark choice. Ushiyama Saijirō's reports on factory visits were published in the *Jiji shinpō* newspaper October-November 1897. Ushiyama tried to present objectively employers' arguments in favor of night work, but his description of some mills suggested that night shifts were harmful to workers and inefficient in terms of production:

> From 1 A.M. to around 3 A.M. the bodies of the girl workers are like those of "boiled octupuses"; some are in a dream, some fall asleep at the machines, some are lying down in corners, but even so the supervisors themselves are overtaken by drowsiness and cannot keep effective watch, and the soulless machines turn endlessly. If the all-important worker does not use them, the progress of production is sluggish and has to go along crudely by itself, so isn't the working of the machines during this time almost useless?[24]

Intellectuals opposed to both laissez-faire and socialism saw protective legislation as integral to reform within the status quo which would help to still the more vocal forms of worker unrest and the appeal of socialism in the wake of the economic difficulties of the post Sino-Japanese War years. Members of the influential Shakai Seisaku Gakkai (Social Policy Study Group), many of them teachers at state institutions of higher education, supported the concept of factory legislation as part of a program to improve social conditions from above. Influential on their thinking was the work of individuals such as Kuwada Kumazō, whose study of industrial health led him to become a vocal exponent of the ban when the draft Act eventually reached the Diet. Kuwada argued that traditional employer-employee relations could not be maintained in large companies operating in a highly competitive economic situation, that product quality would not improve while workers' hours remained long, and that conditions reduced the number of healthy recruits for the army.[25] The Shakai Seisaku Gakkai embraced intellectuals of a wide range of views, but many so-called liberals adhered to a German-influenced organic view of the state, which held it was fallacious to distinguish between the interests of the state and the individuals who comprised it. Their statements created the impression that the benefits of the individual must be sought for the purposes of the state.

In this context, too, gender roles were of importance. Writing in his *Nihon no shakai* (Japanese society) in 1911, Toda Umiichi argued that the employment of women and minors impeded technological advance, which was essential to Japan's future competitiveness.

However, given the necessity of such employment, the abolition of night work was imperative, since it was a major factor in the high labor turnover which hindered technological advance. Toda added: "If we subject our fragile womenfolk to the extremes of harsh employment we cannot have healthy mothers. Moreover, once they are mothers they will be unable to govern the household and bring up children. . . ."[26] Kanai En, professor at Tokyo Imperial University, commented that if married women sought work outside the home at all it implied that their husbands were unable to protect them, and unmarried women were, in the final analysis, "the weaklings of society."[27] The "statism" of the arguments of many intellectuals was not dissimilar to that favored by leading bureaucrats.

IV. The State

In Japan the state was the main agent in the implementation of factory legislation. Bureaucrats were not united in their support for protection for women workers. The French legal adviser, Boissonade, found some backing when he stated in 1892 that only minors and pregnant women required legal protection; married women were protected by their husbands and adult women could look after themselves.[28] For the most part, though, the authorities argued that protective legislation would stem the advance of socialism, curb the social evils which accompanied the industrialization process and achieve cooperation between labor and capital for the benefit of Japan's future.[29] Economic conditions and social unrest combined to produce a movement for state compulsion which was an extension of the *fukoku kyōhei* (rich country, strong army) slogan of the early Meiji period. The state not only needed a generation of young men who would provide healthy and reliable conscripts for the armed forces, but a healthy and efficient labor force in the nation's productive industries. A report by the Agricultural Affairs Bureau in 1900 confirmed that night work gave rise to physical attrition, high labor turnover, low efficiency, and hence lack of technical progress.[30] Sitting on an official committee, Kanai En claimed that the government was "not just moved by feelings of benevolence, but the health of the working classes is crucial for the prosperous existence of the nation as a whole."[31] Kaneko Kentarō, Minister of Agriculture and Commerce in 1898, argued in support of a Factory Act that greater labor productivity and a more able and willing work force would increase the efficiency, competitiveness, and profitability of industry: "This Japan of ours is an industrial nation, and anyone who is unwilling for industry to become the basis of the state is gambling with the future of Japan. . . . We wish Japan to become competitive not only in Asia, but in the world as a whole."[32]

Officials expressed concern about the health and welfare of all workers:

> The young workers in our factories must become mothers and fathers in the future, and should the development of their bodies be inadequate, this will not only be a tremendous disadvantage to industrialists, but from the point of view of the country as well, when we get a succession of people of this kind [i.e., unhealthy] it will be a deplorable thing for a nation which today has a system whereby all men enlist in the army.[33]

The state took the view that it had a particular duty towards women. When the Factory Act reached the Diet in 1911 Oka Minoru, Head of the Industrial Affairs Bureau, claimed that it was needed to protect women "who are future mothers of the nation."[34] Oka expanded on this view that the health of future mothers was essential for industrial development and defense in his *Kōjōhō Ron* (On the Factory Act) of 1917.[35] Yamaguchi Yoshinori, head of the Labor Section of the Social Affairs Bureau when the ban came into effect in 1929, said that women and children required special protection because "their resistance is weak." He added that night work made young women suffer a gradual loss of body weight; they returned to their villages unaware of frequent chest complaints and infected others with the tuberculosis bacillus, thereby becoming "a huge threat to the health of our villages . . . which were so pure."[36] Some argued that night work by women was morally inappropriate, as it made women less able to fulfill their "normal" functions within the family. More seriously, Ushiyama's suggestions that night work could make women prey to unscrupulous foremen and male fellow workers in the obscurity of the more dimly lit parts of the mills had serious implications for the family-oriented morality propounded by the state.[37] Nevertheless, the abolition of night work would make available greater leisure time in which girls could, if not strictly supervised, indulge in *warui asobi* (lit. bad play).[38] Girls must be occupied by new pastimes and activities, preferably those which would better fit them to become wives and mothers in the future.

The bureaucracy rarely viewed the conditions of factory workers from a perspective of genuine altruism. While it frequently found itself in opposition to the business community on the question of protective legislation, the success of employers in resisting legislation up to 1911, and in postponing its implementation thereafter, showed that the state was never inclined, or able, to force through a Factory Act. Yamaguchi Yoshinori's statement in 1929 that "the attitude of businessmen in our country toward their workers is for the most part progressive and in accordance with the paternalism (*onjōshugi*) which they have long professed" was more than bureaucratic rhetoric.[39]

The state in Japan could not argue that female workers should cease working at night in order that they might better fulfill their role as wives and mothers. Even as late as 1955 only 20% of all female employees were married.[40] It nevertheless maintained the importance of gender roles by arguing for protection on the grounds that workers would be wives and mothers in the future. The protection of women workers was seen as vital to the integrity and success of the state *per se*.

V. International Organizations and Competitors

The IALL, ILO, and other international bodies pressing the case for reform were primarily concerned with the health of future generations and the degree to which women were able to fulfill their dual role as housewives and employees. An ILO report in the 1930s stated that the abolition of night work was desirable for both sexes, but particularly for women and young persons, in order to minimize fatigue and enable workers to enjoy a normal family life.[41] The assumption that women should still do housework and childcare even if they were employed full time outside the home was less significant in Japan, where few married women were employed in the textile factories, so the Japanese branches of these organizations considered workers as future wives and mothers. In October 1926 the Commission on General Problems of the Japanese Association for International Labour Legislation called for the immediate prohibition of night work, which "is injuriously affecting not only the health of the women workers themselves, the majority of whom are not fully matured, but also, through them, the health of future generations."[42]

However, statements by Japanese representatives of these organizations also showed intense concern for the interests and pride of the nation. Prohibition would lead to better health among operatives, reduce turnover and absenteeism, increase efficiency and productivity during working hours and thereby give a new lease of life to the textile industry.[43] The Japanese branch of the IALL, meeting in October 1925 in Osaka, mentioned that the government had claimed exemption from the 1919 Washington Convention, but had undertaken in return to enforce the provisions of the convention, including a ban on night work. This had not been done, and "the honor of our country has thus suffered in no small measure."[44] A year later the same organization, at a meeting chaired by Abe Isoo, censured the government for postponing implementation of a ban, which meant that Japan "not only stands in the way of the development of human civilization, but is also unfairly competing with the textile industries of British India and other countries where the Draft Convention has been ratified and enforced."[45]

This "unfair competition" on the part of Japan became a particular grievance during the 1920s, when competition in Asian markets became acute. Night work continued to be legal in China throughout the interwar period, and this fact was frequently used as an argument to retain night work in Japan. Once an end to night shifts in Japan was certain, Japanese entrepreneurs sought to establish mills in China to avail themselves of, among other things, the lower levels of worker protection. The fiercest criticism of "unfair competition" came from Japan's other major competitors, India and Britain. Some of this criticism was disguised as altruism. Margaret Bondfield, British trade unionist and later minister of labor, speaking at the ILO in Geneva in 1926, said that night work by girls in Japan's spinning industry was "a blot on human civilization."[46] The Indian representative at the 8th ILO Conference in 1926 accused Japan of perfidy over the postponement of the ban on night work, which seemed to make a nonsense of the 1919 Washington Convention.[47]

VI. Organized Labor and the Male Work Force

Organized labor in early 20th-century Japan was largely the voice of the male work force, and labor's support for protective legislation for women was not totally unambiguous. The early labor movement actively supported a ban on night work, and it was part of the platform of the 1901 Shakai Minshutō (Social Democratic Party). The Rōdō Kumiai Kiseikai (League for Founding Labor Unions) argued that welfare legislation would increase the efficiency of labor and promote Japan's rapid industrialization:

> We can only raise the quality of workers if we improve their work places, namely, the factories, if we take care of workers' health, if we allow them time to educate themselves by shortening their working hours, if we raise their living standards through genuine increases in wages and improve their technical abilities through serious efforts at worker training. To achieve this a Factory Act, or a Workers' Act, is essential.[48]

Katayama Sen was more direct:

> We know that female cotton spinners work overly long hours in unhealthy factories, and this is injurious to the state itself. Everyone knows this. . . . It is an outrageous crime to know of this and yet not to do anything about it. He who loves his people and his state should rise up and demand that the present deplorable state of affairs should be brought to an end.[49]

Support for the prohibition of women's night work was, however, conditioned by the conciliatory attitude of some labor organizers toward both government and employers. An article in the *Yūai fujin* of 1916, for example, while concluding that night work was undesirable, urged female workers to keep up their good efforts for the sake of the country and remarked on the improvements wrought by benevolent management in the character and behavior of country girls.[50]

In the upsurge of labor activity after 1917, male unionists began to take more cognizance of the presence of female co-workers, and women's sections were founded by some organizations, but union leaders remained relatively reluctant to organize women workers, regarding them as short-term workers, uncommitted to the labor force, and passive and indifferent to organization. In fact, the lack of female unionization effectively reduced the labor movement's power to regulate female workers. Legislation seemed to offer some control over female access to the work force without the expense of organization.

Women's night work had a direct bearing on men's own employment and position in the work place. While a genuine element of concern doubtless existed, male support for a ban was premised on a belief that women could not be equal competitors in the work place. Kato Kanjū, for example, spoke of the cruel and long hours worked by "weak" women and minors, and among the less radical, elaborate flattery about the "uniqueness" of Japanese women was the norm.[51] However, female workers, like minors, offered cheap competition in the labor market, and in the circumstances of the 1920s were also seen as a threat. The industries where night work by women was carried on on any scale, notably cotton, employed relatively few men.[52] In the male-dominated heavy industries, night work, though not the norm, was often undertaken for technical and not purely economic reasons. By supporting a ban on night work for women, male workers were ensuring their own continuing dominance of these industries. Protective legislation could exclude women from many male-dominated sectors, thus partly laying to rest the specter of women's encroachment on the work place. Yet differing interests between male and female workers could provoke opposition to protective legislation. In 1910, Katayama Sen argued that while shorter working hours and the ban on night work would undoubtedly benefit female workers, the maximum working day permitted under the new Act was in excess of hours already being worked by many male workers and was in danger of leading to an *increase* in working hours for such workers.[53] The feeling that male workers should not sacrifice their own gains for the sake of female co-workers seems to have been broadly shared.

On the occasion of abolition in 1929, the Japanese press reported that piece work rates in most mills were to remain the same, as were daily wages, but in many mills, day wage earners were to get up to two days extra wages per month:

> Generally speaking the operatives paid by days are men, and they are the dangerous element in the spinning mills because of the fact that it is always these men operatives paid by days who initiate and organize strikes. On the other hand, most of the operatives paid in accordance with the amount of work done are girls, and these job work operatives seldom start labour disputes.
>
> With this in view the management carries [sic] favour with the 'dangerous' day-wage men operatives by paying two days extra wages a month, thus taking over the loss resulting from the shortening of working hours entirely on the part of the management, and unconditionally at that. On the other hand the management requests the job operatives to improve their efficiency in order that they may be able to maintain their monthly income at the same level after the practice of the new system.[54]

Tanino Setsu, the first female factory inspector, who carried out an extensive survey on the effects of the abolition of night work, reported that its abolition had had only a marginally negative effect on wages, but female workers' wages had fallen more than men's.[55]

The effect on relative wages was conditioned by the degree, or absence, of overlap of the male and female labor markets. In a female-dominated industry many tasks were specified as women's work, and market logic suggested that women workers would bear the brunt of the pecuniary loss occasioned by shorter working hours. Nevertheless, employers afraid that male worker discontent could be exploited by "extremist" groups outside the factories made sure that the burden was not spread to male workers, and this strategy provoked few objections from male workers fully aware of their greater industrial muscle. A lack of male-female solidarity at the work place increased the possibility of such discrimination.

Outside the work place, male workers, in Japan as elsewhere, had an interest in preserving the traditional role allocation within the household and were likely to support any measures which enabled their own domestic needs to be better catered for. In Russia, for example, male workers took partisan positions for and against night work according to abolition's perceived effects on their own wage superiority and the family's income, as well as more immediate domestic considerations: "The men, especially the weavers, announced that they are parted from their wives and must sleep separately from them, and that for them the law [prohibiting night work] is not advantageous, since each member of the family must keep house for himself."[56]

VII. Women's Interests

In the international movement for the abolition of night work, women's pressure groups were of considerable importance. The majority of women's groups campaigned for protective legislation on the grounds that it would ease the load on women who already bore a double burden, but support for a ban on night work for women was not unanimous. The Russian feminist M. I. Pokrovskaia, for example, argued in 1906 that a prohibition on night work diminished women's ability to find employment, deprived them of higher wages, and often drove them into prostitution.[57] Some feminists in the United Kingdom saw protective legislation as a male trade union strategy to restrict the number of jobs open to women, thereby compelling them to take up unskilled, low-paid jobs. They complained that women were to be protected because of their reproductive capacity at the expense of their right to work.[58] The inherent conflict between support for sexual equality and support for protective legislation for women was never resolved.

In Japan, women's feelings and organized protest were scarcely significant in the implementation of early protective legislation, although the strikes and protests of the 1880s and the acute competition for labor in the 1890s reinforced management's desire to have a more docile and easily controlled work force. Even after the emergence of a small women's movement in the years following the founding of the Seitōsha, women's organizations did not constitute a powerful pressure group. The majority of women's leaders supported a ban on night work. Like many of their counterparts overseas, they were anxious to alleviate the conditions of individual working women and regarded the role of women as present or future wives and mothers of prime importance. They shared the assumption widespread in Japanese society (and elsewhere) that it was undesirable for women to work at all outside the home, but should they be forced to do so, the hours should be made as short, and the burden as light, as possible.[59] There were few feminists to argue that this amounted to a fundamental denial of equal rights.

It is far more difficult to judge what women workers themselves felt about night work. Ushiyama reported in 1897 that workers in general preferred to work the day shift, although a few outside workers preferred to work at night to avoid the excessive cold in winter.[60] Other outside workers preferred night work for domestic reasons, as it maybe enabled them to look after their children during the day.[61] The abolition of night work frequently appeared in demands on the occasion of strikes, but vocal opposition does not appear to have been widespread. A survey conducted by the labor organization Nihon Rōdō Sōdōmei in 1928 reported that only 168 out of 1,177 mill girls regarded it as the most painful experience of their factory lives.[62] This apparent passivity—or fear of alienating employers—was one reason why others felt it incumbent upon them to campaign on these workers' behalf.

VIII. Employers

Opposition to a ban on night work was spearheaded by employers in the cotton spinning industry, who were well organized, particularly through the Dainihon Bōseki Rengōkai (Greater Japan Cotton Spinners' Federation). In the early years, cotton employers could count on the support of employers in the silk industry, who felt themselves to be equally threatened by a move to impose shorter working hours. As heavy industrial employers became more influential in business circles, all semblance of a united front in opposition to legislation disappeared.[63]

Employers had a variety of reasons for opposing the introduction of a ban on night work, but their early arguments in the 1890s seemed more instinctive than realistic.[64] They initially tried to deny that night work had any harmful effects at all. They protested that workers preferred night work to day work because factories were cooler at nights in summer; poor workers unable to keep warm at night in winter were better off at work, and workers earned more. Employers claimed that workers in their own homes worked around the clock anyway, and that the hours were no longer than those of workers in other "lower social strata." In any case, the need for Japan to compete with the West entailed sacrifices on the part of all Japanese.[65] Some employers, such as Kashima Manpei and Dan Takuma, even argued that the provision of work was essentially a social service, keeping formerly idle women off the streets. If the price of this service was night work, then so be it.[66] *Shokkō jijō* reported others as saying that the abolition of night work and shorter working hours would corrupt morals further.[67]

As research substantiated the detrimental effects of night work on the health of all workers, it became more difficult for employers to defend the practice. They now claimed to be in principle in favor of an end to night work, but resisted its abolition on two grounds in particular. The first set of reasons was largely economic. The second revolved around the statement that it was foolish to imitate Western countries in an unthinking fashion.

At the core of the economic reasoning was the claim by mill owners that they had to run their machinery continuously in order to defray the extensive capital outlay involved in setting up production, i.e., Japan was a late starter and could not afford to pander to the welfare of workers at such an early stage in development. The abolition of night work would cause a dramatic fall in working hours and hence in production. Japan would be unable to compete effectively in foreign markets, or fulfill existing market demand, and once these markets were lost, Japan would be unable to regain a foothold. Countries such as China, where night work by women was still allowed, would be put at an advantage. The Spinners' Federation argued:

> If night work is actually abolished in ten years' time, that can lead to two possible results: there will either be a falling off in exports of cotton yarn and cotton cloth, or a severe shortage of supplies within Japan itself. The former will be a great setback, while the latter will put the spinning industry into disarray. In short, the draft Factory Act put forward by the administration endangers not only the development of our spinning industry, but . . . the basis of our whole cotton industry.[68]

As early as 1897, Ushiyama Saijirō reported the management at the Nagoya Spinning Mill as saying that an abolition of night work could cause a 40% drop in profits, since business was more constrained by going on the gold standard and the slackness of the China trade.[69] At Hirano Spinning the management claimed that abolition would cause problems in the economical use of coal and care of running machinery, a fall in production, and a greater fall in profits. If the dividend to investors were to fall below 10% per annum, investment would dry up, and in a risky business like cotton there would be imminent danger of bankruptcy.[70] At Kanakin Seishoku the chief engineer said that if a ban were introduced, many companies would go bankrupt and thousands of workers would end up jobless, and therefore worse off.[71] The Spinners' Federation claimed that Japan's ability to compete in external markets "must be seen as a result of the savings in costs resulting from day and night operation"[72] and in January 1910 petitioned both houses of the Diet, arguing that the proposed ban on women's night work would remove Japan's ability to compete effectively with China and India.[73] The same year Hibiya Heizaemon, director of Kanegafuchi Spinning, stated: "If there were any absolute prohibition of night work or enforcement of limitations on hours [of work], the volume of production would decrease [from ¥120 million] to ¥60 million, exports would cease, and we would have to import."[74]

In the forefront of opposition on economic grounds was the cotton center of Osaka, where companies felt they stood to lose more by a ban than spinning firms in areas such as Kantō. Significantly, entrepreneurs in the two regions later disagreed on the length of transition time required before a ban came into operation. In the late 1890s, Osaka entrepreneurs maintained that the city had suffered particularly badly from the price rises of the post–Sino-Japanese War period, hence from demands for higher wages, as well as an acute shortage of labor and the threat of Chinese competition.[75] Twenty years later, employers were using the same Chinese threat in their arguments for a lengthy transition period:

> It seems as if [the ILO] has totally forgotten the question of limitation of working hours in China, which is very important for our country. . . . If things remain as they are and industry in China is not limited in its work hours, there will be a danger of our in-

dustry . . . losing competitiveness in China. Then the export industry of our country will be hindered from developing further. This is primarily regrettable for our workers; capital can easily be switched to China, but not workers.[76]

How far these arguments were valid is a matter of some debate.[77] Employer resistance certainly gave managers a lengthy period in which to make a smooth transition to a day-oriented system. After the early twenties employers were less concerned by the idea of a ban "because the postwar slump had calmed down, and exports of cotton thread and cloth were showing a tendency to advance even more than in the war period."[78] The introduction of shorter working hours was ultimately delayed until declining demand and overcapacity in the late 1920s necessitated a cutback in production which made shorter working hours even welcome.

The second main thread running through employers' arguments was that of Japan's uniqueness and difference from the West and the reflection of this difference in the emergent pattern of labor-capital relations. Employers were from the start averse to the idea of state interference in their business affairs. An attempt to do so was taken as a reflection upon their ability to cope with their labor forces, and they reacted indignantly to what seemed almost a personal insult.[79] Response to the "threat" posed by state intervention could not be made on economic grounds. Instead, employers sought to emphasize Japan's difference from the West, which made Western-style protective legislation totally inappropriate. A Spinners' Federation report of 1898 opposed imitation of the West on the grounds that Japanese workers lacked factory discipline. They told jokes and fooled around at work; therefore, Western legislation geared to an industrial sector where workers worked diligently for a stipulated length of time was erroneous.[80] In discussions with the Shakai Seisaku Gakkai in 1908, Shibusawa Eiichi warned that while a Factory Act was no longer premature, it was important not to take other countries' models too literally.[81]

This desire to draw a line between Japan and the West, which was not restricted to employers, led logically to a strong emphasis on Japanese "tradition." Employers claimed that the old relationship between employer and employee was a "beautiful" one, with mutual respect and affection on both sides. From the 1890s onward, employers argued forcefully that Japan had unique moral qualities; the model of the family, the existence of labor-capital harmony, and the implicit effectiveness of informal social controls rendered state intervention superfluous and even harmful.[82] Speaking in the Diet in 1909, Tanabe Kumaichi, industrialist and Lower House member, claimed that Japan was quite different from other countries: "The Japanese people are truly of a mind to serve their master and are faithful workers in their employment. Moreover, the entrepreneurs are imbued with a profound benevolence, affection, and compassion. Japan is thus quite different from the West in manners and customs."[83]

Japanese employers had long claimed to act *in loco parentis* for the young women they employed. They continued throughout the period of the debate to emphasize their pursuit of a truly paternalist (*onjōshugiteki*) or familistic (*kazokuteki*) management policy based on a harmonious relationship between employer and employee. This claim was, ironically, used to oppose calls for a ban on night work for women. After 1890 the majority of cotton employers fought a sustained rearguard action against the prohibition of women's night work, regardless of whether or not the paternalist rhetoric was translated into practice. Mutō Sanji, famed as a paternalist employer, was among the most vocal supporters of the use of night shifts. Companies such as the Gunze Spinning Mill, whose management criticized night operation as undertaken for greed rather than profit, were not representative.[84] When employers did have to come to terms with a ban, it was against a background of rationalization, of advances in scientific management and technology which offered labor-saving gains in productivity, thereby facilitating a compromise, and of advances in labor activism which suggested that it was worth employers' while to use such legislation as a palliative for male workers and a means of keeping women out of unions.[85]

Unlike the other participants in the debate, employers rarely referred to the sex of their employees. Hibiya Heizaemon of Kanegafuchi did oppose a night work ban on the grounds that eight or nine out of every ten workers were temporary, most of them working only to obtain dowries; thus the harmful physical effects of a year or two's work were negligible, but the use of gender issues to support the employers' case was unusual.[86] Employers were not less conditioned by the perception of women as present or future wives and mothers. Management policies adopted toward women workers tended to reinforce gender roles. After the ban was implemented in 1929, employers sought to fill their employees' greater leisure time with instruction geared to their future as wives and mothers, and were proud of doing so.[87] Here, though, any mention of the "weakness," special role, and status of women in society, and their role as wives and mothers, threatened to undermine employers' arguments. The prime considerations of employers were economic, and employers did not perceive this particular aspect of paternalism and differential treatment for women to be in their economic interest. When it came to male-female wage differentials, for example, greater docility of labor, or stricter control over the work force, employers were only too ready to exploit the fact of gender.

That this should have been the case is not particularly surprising. What is conspicuous is the degree of cynicism with which employers approached their female workers in an era when the state, and they themselves, were propounding the sanctity of Japanese womanhood. Employers were relatively in touch with the aspirations and expectations of most women workers, but at a basic level female labor was a factor of production lacking even the dignity accorded to elements of its male counterpart. It took employers several decades to be persuaded that paternalist practices—as opposed merely to paternalist rhetoric—were not necessarily detrimental to their economic interests.

In using the post-1929 fate of the cotton industry as the yardstick for assessing the validity of employers' arguments against a ban on night work, it is too easy to confuse sequence with consequence, to argue *post hoc ergo propter hoc*. It is certainly a mistake to see abolition as defeat for employers and victory for workers. The 1930s was not marked by a disastrous decline in the cotton industry in Japan, and many cotton entrepreneurs sought to capitalize on the continuing possibility of night work in China by investing in new plants there. Employers were accused of skillfully using the abolition of night work to gloss over the rationalization of industry.[88] Abolition was broadly assumed to have certain non-economic advantages for women workers, but even this was called into question. Girls complained that the effective shortening of rest times and eating periods meant they had to eat "like express trains" and that their monthly wages were only maintained at the same level by fewer holidays and rest periods, since the daily wage was lower than previously.[89]

IX. Women and Protective Legislation

Some feminists believed that the abolition of night work for women alone would serve to undermine women's equal employment prospects. The experience of other countries suggested even at the time that where an industry had a predominantly female labor force, protection for women became protection for all workers, but where the number of women workers was relatively few, legislation acted to exclude women.[90] The Japanese cotton industry was clearly in the former category. No attempt was made to maintain night work by restructuring the work force. After 1929, despite an absolute decline in the number of workers, women continued to form around 80% of the labor force,[91] and the age structure of the female work force changed only slightly.[92] Employers' response to the prospect of a ban was to increase productivity and capital investment, a process which was assisted by technological advances. If, as has been suggested, the financial burden from shorter working hours was borne disproportionately by women workers, this is likely to have enhanced the desire of some employers to continue employing them.

The decision to press for protection for women workers as a group was based on certain presuppositions about women as a class. Yet women workers were not a homogeneous group, but experienced huge variations in status and conditions depending on the nature of their employment. The disparity of interest between the *dekasegi* majority and other, longer-term women workers was particularly great. The categorization of women as a separate group within the work force was based not on occupational or economic circumstances, but simply on sex. Ascribed gender roles and greater physical weakness caused women in most countries to be regarded as a distinct group within the work force and undermined their ability to protect themselves in dealings with employers. This vulnerability was rendered more acute in prewar Japan by the legal position of women—most women, like minors, were legal incompetents—and the youthfulness and temporary nature of the work force. This character of the labor force was constantly reinforced by prevailing social mores and the expectations of women workers and their families. The extreme ideology of domesticity in Japan which presupposed, for example, that women were working temporarily only to secure dowries (a statement used to argue both for and against protection) perpetuated the existence of a work force in special need of protection.

The problem of how far women needed to be protected cannot, therefore, be separated from the conviction that women's employment was not merely supplementary, but peripheral. It was widely assumed that ideally women, particularly if married, should not be in paid employment, and this assumption was reinforced by the rhetoric of "good wife, wise mother." Employment for single women became an education and a service, a temporary financial bonus rather than a necessity. This assumption was clearly incompatible with economic realities, as men were not paid according to the logic of the concept that women's work was supplementary. Toda Umiichi in 1911 concluded that the widespread use of women employees lowered male wages and that women should therefore be removed from the work force,[93] but in general the problems of the family wage were little discussed.

The widely shared assumption manifest in the night-work debate, that women needed to be protected for the sake of their families, was rarely extended to men, despite the fact that male health was a proven significant factor in the health of families and the pivotal role of men in families was widely accepted. Moreover, there was a widespread belief that it was possible to separate the underpayment, poor health, and bad working conditions of women from those of men, whereas conditions in the two labor markets were inextricably intertwined. The rural sector's high degree of dependence on female *dekasegi* workers was only one aspect of this. The degree of interdependence between male and female employment conditions was disregarded by many, and the view that a ban on night work for women would lead to general improvement does not appear to have been widespread in Japan.

The debate demonstrates that Japan shared with many other countries an ideology of domesticity which raised fundamental questions concerning the nature of women's employment. The issue of prohibition of night work highlighted the prevailing idea of dependency and productive function. Some saw it as a means of controlling women's job opportunities to reinforce this role. The rejection of general welfare led to a heightened emphasis on women as child-bearers, rearers, and husband carers. The argument that a ban on night work was necessary on physical and moral grounds reinforced the idea of women's different physical status and of women's possession of unique mental and moral attributes, a concept fully in line with official dogma on women. Where the Japanese case stands out is in the application of these arguments to a non-married work force free of the dual burden imposed by domestic responsibilities.

Japanese employers were caught in a dilemma. Until the 1920s, most perceived the proclaimed virtues of paternalism and the ideal of the Japanese woman to be incompatible with their need to make profits and exploit female workers to the full as a factor of production. They therefore turned, unlike the advocates of a ban, to economic and other arguments which did not constantly refer to gender roles. Yet they, too, regarded women workers as a distinct class of labor, with specific attributes and greater physical and mental weakness than their male counterparts. In a society where the determination to impose gender roles was stronger than many others and was reflected in the nature of the female work force, protective legislation served further to reinforce a division among workers on gender lines and by implication to emphasize that in Japanese society women had little right to work for a living wage.

Notes

Sugihara Kaoru and Jay Kleinberg read an earlier draft of this paper. I am most grateful to them for their valuable comments. Professor Takamura Naosuke noted two errors in the conference paper which have since been corrected. I would also like to thank Professor Takamura for his constructive comments. The discussions at the conference exposed the relative lack of consideration paid to gender issues in the history of Japanese management. I am grateful to all the participants for confirming my view that this is a fruitful area for future study.

1. For the course of international legislation restricting night work by women, see International Labour Office, *Women's Work Under Labour Law* [Studies and Reports Series I (Employment of Women and Children) No. 2], Geneva, 1932, pp. 104–10.

2. *Ibid.*, p. 107; E. Bauer (L'Association internationale pour la protection légale des travailleurs), *Le Travail de Nuit des Femmes dans l'Industrie*, Jena, 1903, p. ix.

3. ILO, *op. cit.*, p. 107.

4. Bauer, *op. cit.*, p. xxxix.

5. *Ibid.*, p. xxxvii.

6. *Ibid.*, pp. xxxviii–xxxix.

7. International Association for Labour Legislation, *Memorial Explanatory of the Reasons for an International Prohibition of Night Work for Women*, 1904.

8. *Ibid.*, p. 9.

9. ILO, *op. cit.*, pp. 108–10.

10. Quoted in G. L. Bernstein, *Japanese Marxist: A Portrait of Kawakami Hajime*, Cambridge, Mass., 1976, p. 67.

11. Utsumi Y., *Rōdō jikan no rekishi* (History of working hours), Tokyo, 1959, p. 195.

12. IALL, *op. cit.*, p. 5.

13. P. Fuchs, "Das Problem der Frauennachtarbeit in Japan und die Argumentation der japanischen Unternehmer," *Nachrichten der Geschichte für Natur- und Völkerkunde Ostasiens* 107/108, Hamburg, 1970, p. 77. This is the only detailed treatment of night work in Japan in a Western language. It concentrates on the validity of employers' economic arguments, in particular those of Mutō Sanji.

14. Yamaguchi Y., "Kōjō ni okeru joshi oyobi shōnensha no shin'yagyō haishi ni tsuite" (On the abolition of night work by women and minors in factories), *Sangyō fukuri* 4, No. 8 (Aug. 1929), p. 2.

15. Utsumi, *op. cit.*, p. 213.

16. K. Taira, "Factory Legislation and Management Modernization during Japan's Industrialization 1886–1916," *Business History Review*, Vol. 44, No. 1 (Spring 1970), pp. 90–95.

17. Fuchs, *op. cit.*, p. 92.

18. Oka Minoru of the Industrial Affairs Bureau remarked subsequently that if they had been able to predict that it would take 6 years before the law came into effect, the 15-year postponement period would have operated from the time of promulgation, i.e., 1911 [Morita, Y. "Kōjōhō seiteiji no gikai to undō" (The Diet and lobbying at the time of the enactment of the Factory Act], *Shakai seisaku jihō* 100/101 (Jan.–Feb. 1929), repr. in R. Akamatsu, ed., *Nihon fujin mondai shiryō shūsei* (Collected materials on the woman problem in Japan), Vol. 3, *Rōdō* (Labor), Tokyo, 1977, p. 315.

19. As late as 1927, 61.5% of the 181,000 women in spinning were 19 years of age or younger (T. Izumi, "Transformation and Development of Technology in the Japanese Cotton Industry," Working Paper of Project on Technology Transfer, Transformation and Development: The Japanese Experience, United Nations University, 1980, p. 29).

20. Fuchs, *op. cit.*, pp. 97–98.

21. F. Utley, *Lancashire and the Far East*, London, 1931, p. 159.

22. R. P. Dore, "The Modernizer as Special Case: Japanese Factory Legislation 1882–1922" (*Comparative Studies in Society and History* Vol. 11, No. 4 [Oct. 1969]) looks at the arguments in the context of Japan's perceptions of how far it was inevitable or desirable that Japan should follow the Western pattern.

23. Yokoyama G., *Nihon no kasō shakai* (The lower social strata of Japan), 1898, repr. Tokyo, 1976, p. 162.

24. Ushiyama S., "Kōjō junshi ki" (Record of a tour of inspection of factories), *Jiji shinpō* 5035, 12 Oct. 1897. The whole series of Ushiyama's articles appear in *Meiji bunka zenshū* (Collected works on Meiji culture), Vol. 16, Tokyo, 1959.

25. Morita, *op. cit.*, pp. 312–14. Kuwada sat in the Upper House as a representative of highest taxpayers in Tottori.

26. Toda U., *Nihon no shakai* (Japanese society), Tokyo, 1911, p. 450.

27. Utsumi, *op. cit.*, p. 207.

28. *Ibid.*, pp. 205–6.

29. The emergence of state attitudes to protective legislation and the response of business are discussed in B. K. Marshall, *Capitalism and Nationalism in Prewar Japan: The Ideology of the Business Elite 1868–1941*, Stanford, 1967, pp. 53–75.

30. Nōshōmushō Nōmukyoku, *Nihon menshi bōseki ki* (Account of cotton spinning in Japan), 1900, section 2, ch. 7, repr. in *Nihon fujin mondai shiryō shūsei*, Vol. 3, p. 154.

31. Quoted in Nakamura M., *Rōdōsha to nōmin* (Workers and peasants), *Nihon no rekishi* (History of Japan), Vol. 29, Tokyo, 1976, p. 185.

32. Quoted in Fuchs, *op. cit.*, p. 89.

33. Quoted in Kobayashi T., *Kōjōhō to rōdō undō* (The Factory Act and the labor movement), Tokyo, 1965, p. 247.

34. Quoted in Mori K., *Nihon rōdōsha kaikyū jōtai shi (senzen)* (History of the circumstances of the working class in Japan [prewar]), Tokyo, 1961, p. 195. Dore mentions that the 1896 draft Factory Act affirmed that the state had a duty to protect women and minors since they could not protect themselves (*op. cit.*, p. 447).

35. Oka M., *Kōjōhōron* (On the Factory Act) (Sept. 1917) section 1, ch. 7, repr. in *Nihon fujin mondai shiryō shūsei*, Vol. 3, p. 329.

36. Yamaguchi, *op. cit.*, pp. 2–3.

37. Ushiyama S. in *Jiji shinpō* 5041, 19 Oct. 1897.

38. Mori, *op. cit.*, p. 195.

39. Yamaguchi, *op. cit.*, p. 5.

40. D. Robins-Mowry, *The Hidden Sun: Women of Modern Japan*, Boulder, Colo., 1983, p. 177.

41. ILO, *The World Textile Industry, Economic and Social Problem*, Studies and Reports Series B (Social and Economic Conditions), No. 27, 2 vols., Geneva, 1937, pp. 275–76.

42. ILO, *International Labour Information*, Vol. 21, No. 1 (3 Jan. 1927).

43. E.g., *ibid.*, Vol. 22, No. 6 (9 May 1927).

44. *Ibid.*, Vol. 16, No. 9 (30 Nov. 1925).

45. *Ibid.*, Vol. 21, No. 1 (3 Jan. 1927).

46. Quoted in Makise K., *Hitamuki no onnatachi* (Single-minded women), Tokyo, 1976, p. 48.

47. Utsumi, *op. cit.*, p. 245; R. Kumar, "Family and Factory: Women in the Bombay Cotton Textile Industry 1919–1939," *Indian Economic and Social History Review*, Vol. 20, No. 1 (Jan.–March 1983) pp. 102–3.

48. Quoted in Fuchs, *op. cit.*, p. 83.

49. *Ibid.*

50. Hirazawa K., "Jokōsan no seikatsu" (Life of factory girls), *Yūai Fujin*, Vol. 2 (Sept. 1916), repr. in *Nihon fujin mondai shiryō shūsei*, Vol. 3, pp. 232–35.

51. *Ibid.*, p. 232; Katō K., "Shin'yagyō kinshi ni saishite" (On the occasion of the abolition of night work), *Kaizō*, Vol. 11, No. 8 (Aug. 1929), p. 49.

52. In 1925, 81.4% of nearly one million workers in textiles were women,

whereas in the machine and tool industries, women accounted for little over 6% of the labor force of nearly 287,000 (I. F. Ayusawa, "The Employment of Women in Japanese Industry," pt. 1, *International Labour Review* [Feb. 1929] p. 201).

53. Katayama S., "Kōjōhōan o hyōsu" (Comments on the draft Factory Act), *Tōyō keizai shinpō*, Vol. 540 (5 Nov. 1910), repr. in *Nihon fujin mondai shiryō shūsei*, Vol. 3, pp. 326–27.

54. Quoted in A. S. Pearse, *The Cotton Industry of Japan and China*, Manchester, 1929, pp. 106–7. Kurashiki Bōseki Kabushikigaisha Shashi Hensan Iin, *Kaiko 65 nen* (Looking back over 65 years), Osaka, 1953, p. 385, supports this statement.

55. Tanino S., "Shin'yagyō kinshi no eikyō chōsa" (Survey on the effects of the abolition of night work) in Kitakawa, ed., *Fujin kōjō kantokukan no kiroku* (Reports of a woman factory inspector), 2 vols., Tokyo, 1985, p. 385.

56. R. L. Glickman, *Russian Factory Women: Workplace and Society 1880–1914*, Berkeley, Calif., 1984, p. 159.

57. *Ibid.*, p. 251.

58. J. Lewis, "Dealing with Dependency: State Practices and Social Realities 1870–1945" in J. Lewis, ed., *Women's Welfare, Women's Rights*, Beckenham, Kent, 1983, p. 31.

59. *Industrial and Labour Information*, Vol. 21, No. 1 (3 Jan. 1927); Fuchs, *op. cit.*, p. 98. F. Kaneko's claims ('Fujin rōdōsha no shin'yagyō—konjaku' [The abolition of night work for women workers—now and then], *Nihonshi kenkyū*, Vol. 113 [July 1970]) that women were a potent force pressing for legislation do not seem to be substantiated.

60. Ushiyama S. in *Jiji shinpō* 5062 (12 Nov. 1897).

61. Fuchs, *op. cit.*, p. 82. E. Honig (*Sisters and Strangers: Women in the Shanghai Cotton Mills 1919–1949*, Stanford, 1986, pp. 153–55) comments that Chinese workers had mixed attitudes toward night work, some preferring it because discipline was laxer at night.

62. "Bōseki kōjō ni okeru chōsa" (Survey at a spinning factory), *Rōdō fujin*, Vol., 4 (March 1928), repr. in *Nihon fujin mondai shiryō shūsei*, Vol. 3, p. 237. Responses may have been affected by the imminent ending of night work the following year.

63. Mori, *op. cit.*, (*senzen*), p. 190; Dore, *op. cit.*, p. 449.

64. Taira (*op. cit.*, p. 91) calls the level of debate at the first session of the *Nōshōkō kōtō kaigi* in 1896 "astoundingly low," with eminent entrepreneurs such as Ōkura Kihachirō barely able to put forward coherent views.

65. Marshall, *Capitalism and Nationalism in Prewar Japan*, p. 55; Dainihon Bōseki Dōgyō Rengōkai, *Bōseki shokkō jijō chōsa gaiyōsho* (Outline of survey on conditions of workers in spinning), 1898, repr. in *Nihon fujin mondai shiryō shūsei*, Vol. 3, p. 155. In opposing employers' claims that workers preferred to work at night, it was argued that it was employers' obligation to ensure that workers earned enough to ensure their economic welfare without sacrificing their health (M. Matsuzaki, "Le Travail de Nuit des Femmes dans le Développement de l'Industrie Moderne au Japon," in Bauer, *op. cit.*, pp. 293–94.

66. Both cited in Fuchs, "Das Problem der Frauennachtarbeit," pp. 102–3.

67. Quoted in Utsumi, *op. cit.*, p. 212.

68. Quoted in Fuchs, *op. cit.*, p. 109.

69. Ushiyama S. in *Jiji shinpō* 5029, 5 Oct. 1897.

70. *Ibid.*, 5038, 15 Oct. 1897.

71. *Ibid.*, 5039, 16 Oct. 1897.

72. Quoted in Mori, *op. cit.*, p. 193.

73. Petition in Morita, *op. cit.*, p. 317ff.

74. Quoted in Mori, *op. cit.*, p. 192.

75. Ushiyama S. in *Jiji shinpō* 5055, 4 Nov. 1897. In 1925, the Kinki area accounted for 32% of women doing night work, Tōkai (i.e., Nagoya) for 27% (Naikaku Tōkeikyoku, *Rōdō tōkei yōran* [Summary of labor statistics], Tokyo, 1930, p. 70).

76. Quoted in Fuchs, *op. cit.*, p. 114.

77. E.g., *ibid.*, pp. 116–36.

78. Kurashiki Bōseki, *op. cit.*, p. 381.

79. Taira, *op. cit.*, p. 89.

80. Dainihon Bōseki Dōgyō Rengōkai, *Bōseki shokkō jijō chōsa gaiyōsho*, 1898, p. 155.

81. Shibusawa E., "Kōjōhō ni taisuru iken" (Opinion on a Factory Act), April 1908, repr. in *Nihon fujin mondai shiryō shūsei*, Vol. 3, p. 324.

82. *Tōkyō keizai zasshi*, quoted in Taira, *op. cit.*, p. 89.

83. Quoted in Morita, *op. cit.*, p. 316. This is a rather different perspective on workers to that put forward by the Spinners' Federation in 1898 (see note 80).

84. Ushiyama S. in *Jiji shinpō* 5041 (19 Oct. 1897).

85. Kurashiki Bōseki, *op. cit.*, p. 381; K. Seki, *The Cotton Industry of Japan*, Tokyo, 1956, p. 311.

86. Quoted in Mori, *op. cit.*, p. 192.

87. Tanino, *op. cit.*, pp. 127–36.
88. Orimoto S., "Jokō o kataru" (Talking about factory girls), *Chūō kōron*, Vol. 44, No. 12 (Dec. 1929), repr. in *Nihon fujin mondai shiryō shūsei*, Vol. 3, p. 313.
89. *Ibid.*, pp. 240–42; Tanino, *op. cit.*, p. 127.
90. E. Lüders, "The Effects of German Labour Legislation on Employment Possibilities for Women," *International Labour Review*, Vol. 20, No. 3 (Sept. 1929).
91. Hirozaki S., *Nihon joshi rōmu kanri shi* (History of the management of women workers in Japan), Tokyo, 1967, p. 62.
92. In 1949, 60% of workers in the cotton industry were still under the age of 20 (Seki, *op. cit.*, p. 360).
93. Toda, *op. cit.*, p. 467.

Comment

Naosuke Takamura
University of Tokyo

Professor Janet Hunter examined debates over the abolition of night work in the Japanese cotton spinning industry as a case study which elucidated the perceptions of women. She made free use of many records and documents written in Japanese, and the facts described in her paper are quite accurate.

The thesis of the paper is as follows. Debates on the abolition of night work in Japan were held on the assumption of the ideology of domesticity, as they were in other industrially advanced nations. In Japan, the major aim in abolishing night work was to protect unmarried female workers as future wives and mothers, and the protective legislation served further to reinforce a division among workers on gender lines. I have no intention to raise any objection to this point. My role as a commentator is probably to connect Hunter's thesis to our common topic, "Japanese management in historical perspective," but it is more than I could do. So, I would like to present different approaches to the abolition of night work for discussion.

My question is how employers met the abolition of night work. The answer is that they fulfilled business growth, taking two measures: one is an attempt to increase labor productivity by strict labor management, and the other is an attempt for the so-called familistic management.

1. Increase in labor productivity by strict labor management. Before night work was abolished, working hours were usually ten, not including recesses, but they were reduced to eight and a half in July 1929. If employers intended to avoid the rise in wage costs on the assumption that day wages were invariable, they would be

required to fulfill as much production in eight and a half hours of work as in ten hours of work. The production of Japanese standard count cotton yarn (No. 20) per female spinning hand (including the production of male spinning hands converted into that of female hands, according to the ratio of wages) was 11.25 kg a day in 1928; it rose to 11.74 kg in 1929, 12.38 kg in 1930, and 14.40 kg in 1931, showing a 28% increase in the three years between 1928 and 1931, even though the working hours were reduced. Production per hour even increased by 50.6% in this period.[1] Moreover, the operation originally conducted by male hands was partially replaced by that of female hands, and the ratio of female workers among the whole workers increased from 76.4% to 80.6%.

What caused such a growth in labor productivity in spite of a decrease in working hours? Many scholars indicate the cause as the introduction of new machines such as small-sized motors, high-draft frames, and simplex frames. According to my research, however, it was only after 1932 that these new machines came into wide use.[2] Even in the Tōyo Spinning Company which was quite keen on the introduction of new machines, the progress in machine technology about the time of the abolition of night work was limited to partial improvement, such as the direct connection of the mixing machine with scutching machine and the improvement in carding machines.

In my opinion, the rise in operation efficiency which resulted from strict labor management increased labor productivity in the period up to 1931. By this period, 80% of female spinning hands had educational backgrounds, elementary or higher school graduation; employers gave aptitude tests at the time of employment and offered special training for newly hired female workers.[3] These employers had learned scientific labor management of Western nations since the end of World War I. Repeating motion studies of various operations, they set up the "standardized motion" for every particular operation which would most serve for rise in efficiency, and had female spinning hands fully understand this motion. It was in 1927 that the Dainippon Spinning Company adopted standardized motion, being the last of the big three spinning companies to introduce this new method. These companies tried to increase the number of spindles per female hand or to rev up spindles by enforcing thorough training for the standardized motion.

Moreover, the Great Depression which influenced the Japanese economy shortly after the abolition of night work gave an opportunity for cutting wages. Wages sharply dropped between 1930 and 1931. In 1931, the average wage of a female spinning hand fell to 75.5% of the wage level of 1928. In other words, not only day wages but also time wages dropped in 1931 to a level lower than that prior to the abolition of night work. Thus, employers successfully reduced wage costs by increasing labor productivity and cutting wages.

2. Establishment of the so-called familistic (*kazokuteki*) management. As Hunter observes, employers opposed the Factory Act, advocating paternalism (*onjōshugi*) and familisticism (*kazokushugi*) in their arguments against factory legislation. However, the actual situation differed from what the employers advocated. Though there were a few exceptions, most employers worked female workers hard and treated them like "speaking machines" or disposable swabs. It was after World War I that employers began to provide welfare facilities under the pressure of deteriorating supply-and-demand relations and with the necessity of improvement in quality of manufactured goods. However, the actual conditions of fringe benefits were generally poor, and female workers had no time to use welfare facilities under the conditions of longer working hours.

As leisure hours increased with the abolition of night work, employers offered fringe benefits so that female workers could physically and psychologically bear up under the harsh labor conditions. Fringe benefits were considered necessary for eliminating the popular image of female workers represented by the "miserable history of mill girls" and recruiting good female workers. According to the survey conducted by the government in late 1930 in the midst of the Great Depression, among 436 facilities for recreation in the cotton spinning industry, 103 were founded after the abolition of night work.[4] Among expenditures related to labor in the spinning industry, the share of wage expenses declined from 80.5% in 1926 to 75.2% in 1931; the share of expenditure on facilities increased from 19.0% to 21.5% in the same period.[5]

It is questionable whether the employers' eagerness for fringe benefits removed the difference between their propaganda of "familisticism" and reality, but there is no doubt that the difference was reduced. The form of wages which transformed after World War I from simple piece wages to piece wages plus seniority did not change with the abolition of night work and the Depression. Therefore, when employers attempted to cut wages, they did not choose to restore piece wages but to respect the seniority order linking it with "familisticism" as their fundamental policy for labor management.

NOTES

1. Takamura Naosuke, "Shihon chikuseki: keikōgyō" (Accumulation of capital: light industry), in Ōishi Kaichirō, ed., *Nippon teikokushugi-shi* (History of Japanese imperialism), Tokyo, University of Tokyo Press, 1987.
2. *Ibid.*
3. Hazama Hiroshi, *Nippon rōmukanri-shi kenkyū* (History of labor management in Japan), Tokyo, Ochanomizu-shobō, 1978, Section 3, Ch. 3.
4. Naimushō, Shakaikyoku, Rōdōbu (Department of Labor, Social Bureau, Ministry of Home Affairs), *Shin'ya eigyō kinshi no eikyō chōsa* (Survey on effects of the abolition of night work), 1931.
5. 1920-nendai-shi Kenkyūkai (Association for the Study of the 1920s), ed., *1920-nendai no Nippon shihonshugi* (Japanese capitalism in the 1920s), Tokyo, University of Tokyo Press, 1983, p. 201.

Summary of the Concluding Discussion: Human Resources and Organizations

Keiichiro Nakagawa
Aoyama Gakuin University

The final general discussion, chaired by K. Nakagawa, centered on two themes: first, the general trend and crucial stages of the development of managers, engineers, and workers in modern industries, and, second, the causal relationship between the development of such human resources and organizations characteristic of business enterprises.

T. Yui discussed that at the time of the enactment of the Company Law in 1893 businessmen were still not convinced of the future development of joint-stock enterprises. However, by the beginning of this century, they were fully confident of the success of joint-stock companies because many of the educated professional managers and engineers had already been promoted as members of the board of directors and the practice of companies issuing stocks and bonds had also been settled on the right track. Further, during and after World War I, product diversification was promoted in many industrial firms and sophisticated company management organizations were established, although the size of central offices remained generally small.

H. Uchida summarized the increase in engineers in three stages. In the formative years, between 1860 to 1885, most educated engineers were employed by government offices and enterprises. In the next stage, between 1885 to 1910, however, private industrial firms were able to employ an increasing number of graduates from the engineering department of the Imperial University and from the Tokyo Technical College, who were trained to implement newly introduced Western machines and equipment. In the third stage, between 1910 to 1935, further institutional development of technological education at three levels—high school, college, and university—made it possible to supply an adequate number of engineers and machinists to such newly rising industries as electric manufacturing, chemical, and electrolysis and also to afford qualified engineers for scientific management and factory rationalization.

A. Gordon argued that around 1900 Japanese labor relations turned from indirect employment based on the *oyakata* system to a direct employment system, partly as a response to the impending Factory Law, which was finally approved by the Diet in 1911. After World War I, to stimulate the workers' will to work, factory managers improved working conditions with *onjōshugi* as their motto, but such paternalism contradicted their resistance to the public demand for immediate abolition of night work. Gordon considers the government a major driving force for modernizing Japanese labor relations.

M. Fruin pointed out the insufficiency in dealing with each of the three human resources independently and suggested the concept of "organizational learning." This concept might be interpreted in the following way. The three individual resources—managers, engineers, and workers—which are expected to work together toward a common goal of an industrial firm usually try to build, through their mutual interaction, a new informal organization, which in turn leads them to work in a particular way to achieve their common goals. Fruin maintained that such organizational learning, based on the dichotomy of individuality and solidarity, has been a particularly important feature of Japanese business enterprises.

Following the above four presentations, the general discussion continued, first, to identify causal relations between the development of the three categories of human resources and the formation of Japanese management organization and, second, to identify the crucial periods and driving forces in the development of the management structure. As these topics generally concern not formal but informal organization, the discussion did not proceed in a straightforward manner, and the following is no more than a summary of the diverse themes and interpretations by the participants.

At the beginning of Japan's industrialization, learning through books and at school was the only way to learn about the Western industrial revolution. Usually, an additional year of apprenticeship at a British factory, for example, was a sine qua non for an educated engineer to become a chief engineer or manager of a pioneering mill, because the experience of such an apprenticeship was a unique opportunity for Japanese engineers to understand a modern industrial enterprise in its entirety and learn how to manage modern mills. As the merchant capitalists and aristocratic capitalists like Hachisuka, described by A. Fraser, knew nothing about and were indifferent to mill management, many of the educated engineers who had had opportunities to undergo apprenticeship extended their authority to management and, by 1900, dominated the top management of industrial firms.

In addition, higher education in technology spread with the establishment of engineering departments at the new imperial universities of Kyoto, Tōhoku and Kyushu and the establishment of about ten new technical colleges in Osaka, Nagoya, Kumamoto, Sendai, and other cities. As a result, the number of educated engineers employed in the private sector rapidly increased from 182 in 1880 to 10,368 in 1920, among whom university graduates increased from 131 to 3230 and college graduates from 34 to 7137. The supply of educated engineers for leading industrial firms was now adequate, and Tōyō Cotton Mills at the end of 1913, for example, employed 75 engineers: 11 university graduates and 64 college graduates, whereas the company employed only 16 university and college graduates for clerical work.[1]

Now, where were these growing number of educated engineers assigned? In the case of Tōyō Cotton Mills, its central office in Osaka employed only 1.3% of total employees, and it seems that most of the engineers were located not in the central office but at its 15 factories widely dispersed throughout the country. In fact, the heads of 12 out of 15 factories were educated engineers who had already served from 9 to more than 20 years as factory engineers. The earliest cotton mills built or acquired new mills at different sites and tended to merge with each other after the turn of the century. They thus had nationwide networks of factories, and, consequently, by the eve of World War I, most of the engineers were located in local factories, thus *genbashugi*, i.e., "shopfloor-centered management," had already become a dominant feature in leading industrial firms.

Genbashugi, which allocated human resources for management and engineering not to the central office but to the shopfloors, was closely related to the nature of the tasks required of engineers in the early stages of industrialization. Up until 1919 or 1920, their primary task was not to develop new products or technologies but to implement the technologies introduced from the Western industrial countries. This could be realized only on shopfloors through close cooperation with the workers. It should not be overlooked that the supply of skilled workers who could serve as foremen and supervise the workshops was very limited in the new Western-style industrial firms, simply because of the sharp discontinuity of technologies between the traditional craft industries and modern machine industries. Even the engineers themselves had to train the unskilled workers at workshops and teach the newly recruited primary school graduates in the company apprentice schools. It is no wonder that relations between engineers and workers became close and cooperative and that a sense of workshop community was created.

The development of such a shopfloor community was, needless to say, neither an easy nor effortless achievement. In many industries like mining and certain fields of engineering, skilled workers had established their control over workshops on the basis of their authority as *oyakata* or subcontractors, and, therefore, young college graduate engineers were not easily allowed to even enter such workshops. Nevertheless, working alongside workers in workshops had been virtually established as a norm or discipline, and only through their ability to do so successfully could young engineers be accepted by workers, senior engineers, and managers.

Above all, it was the aggressive introduction of new technologies and new industries that constantly undermined the domain of the *oyakata*, who gradually lost their control over workshops. In the meantime, the graduates of the company apprentice schools and government technical high schools increased considerably in number, and, during World War I, with the introduction of scientific management and the accompanying adoption of special purpose machine tools, these new lower-level engineers encroached on and took over the prerogatives of *oyakata*. At any rate, the indirect employment, or internal contract system, under the *oyakata*'s control, which began in the 1880s, was already being replaced in the 1900s. In other words, this indirect employment system was much shorter lived in Japan than in the U.K., the U.S.A., or other Western countries.

The growing number of engineers with various levels of education started, around the 1900s, to occupy all the ranks of the management hierarchy. They were interested in and involved in workshop operation, although workshops under the control by *oyakata* were, at the outset, most forbidding. For example, when a new plan for scientific management was drawn up by an engineer and proposed to a workshop, it was usually refused, and a revised plan had to be drawn up in close consultation with the workers. Such conflict and consultation usually resulted in a sudden burst of workshop solidarity between engineers and workers.

This close cooperation between engineers and workers, especially at the workshop level, seems to have been a prime source of energy for the incremental improvement of production process technology that has supported the modern economic growth of Japan. The

TABLE 1   Educated White-Collar Employees, 1930.

Engineering Industry (59 factories)			
	university graduates	college graduates	high school graduates
Clerical	535 (9.0)	772 (18.2)	1,192 (20.2)
Technical	1,592 (18.0)	2,272 (25.2)	6,966 (118.0)
Textile Industry (53 factories, each with over 1,000 employees)			
	university graduates	college graduates	high school graduates
Clerical	180 (3.4)	277 (5.2)	400 (8.3)
Technical	222 (4.2)	770 (14.5)	1,348 (25.4)

Note: Figures in parentheses designate number of workers per mill.
Source: Mombushō Jitsugyō Gakumukyoku (Ministry of Education, Industrial Education Department), "Kaisha kōjō jūgyōin gakureki chōsahōkoku" (Report on the education of employees in business companies and factories), 1930, in *Nihon rōmukanri shi shiryōshū*, ed. by Hazama Hiroshi, Vol. 9, 1988.

statistics in Table 1 on educated engineers in 1930 suggest the degree of domination of engineers at all levels of management hierarchy.

The growth ratio of educated engineers between 1880 and 1920 was higher in Japan than in the U.S.A., the U.K., Germany, and France, although the total number of engineers had not yet reached the level of that in France in 1920.[2] This rapid increase in educated engineers reflects the efforts by businesses and the government to fill the serious shortage of skilled workers. Some of these engineers had climbed the ladder of management hierarchy to become members of the board of directors; others cultivated, in workshops, cooperative relations between the workers and themselves. The sense of workshop community expanded into that of the entire company community. Needless to say, this sense of company community was the basis on which the lifetime employment system could develop.

Most of the participants of the meeting agreed that the 1900s were the crucial years for the development of the management structure discussed above. Promotion of educated engineers and managers to the board members was already prevalent at that time, and the labor employment system switched from an indirect one to direct in the same period. Another driving force for such managerial development was seen in the impact caused by three wars: the Sino-Japanese War (1894–95), Russo-Japanese War (1904–5) and World War I. Undoubtedly, during the wars the shortage of skilled workers was serious, and to prevent the workers from moving to other mills the industrial firms had not only to improve working conditions but also to strengthen the workshop community.

More noteworthy, however, is the fact that Japan had to introduce from the Western countries the newest technologies along with advanced business systems, such as corporate and managerial organizations, throughout the period of the three wars. S. Ericson stated, pointing out the importance of the 1900s, that the transportation revolution, managerial revolution, and educational revolution had to proceed during the early stages of the industrial revolution, and this multiple revolution led to the growing roles of professional managers and engineers in workshops as well as in central offices.

However, the central offices seem to have been relatively small for a long time because manufacturing firms could or had to rely on outside general merchants, *sōgōshōsha*, and the established traditional distribution system for selling their products and buying raw materials.

To conclude, in the case of Japanese industrial firms, educated engineers had to play important roles as the earliest professional managers as well; the development and accumulation of industrial skills had to be achieved not by skilled workers but through the close cooperation of engineers with workers. Further, on account of rapid technological and industrial changes, even modern zaibatsu managerial firms could not, once their conservative bureaucracies were established, seize new entrepreneurial opportunities in new industries like electrolysis, and therefore, in the 1920s, a group of new "scientist entrepreneurs" like Noguchi, elaborated on by B. Molony, had entered the new stage of heavy chemical industrial development.

NOTE

1. Uchida Hoshimi, "Gijutsusha no zōka bunpu to Nihon no kōgyōka" (Increase and distribution of engineers and Japan's industrialization), *Keizai kenkyū*, Vol. 39, No. 4 (1988). For Tōyō Cotton Mills, see *Tōyōbō 100 nenshi* (A century of Tōyōbō), 1986, Vol. 1, pp. 228–29.
2. Uchida, *ibid.*

MEMBERS OF THE ORGANIZING COMMITTEE

Chairman: Yonekawa Shin'ichi (Hitotsubashi University)
Fukuoh Takeshi (Tokyo Keizai University)
Kobayashi Kesaji (Ryukoku University)
Miyamoto Matao (Osaka University)
Ōkōchi Akio (University of Tokyo)
Yamazaki Hiroaki (University of Tokyo)
Yui Tsunehiko (Meiji University)
Secretariat: Abe Etsuo (Meiji University)
Yuzawa Takeshi (Gakushuin University)
Kasuya Makoto (University of Tokyo)
Kawano Aizaburō (Doshisha University)

Participants in the Fifth Meeting of the International Conference (Third Series) on Business History

Abo Tetsuo
(University of Tokyo)
Daitō Eisuke
(University of Tokyo)
Ericson, Steven
(Brown University)
Fraser, Andrew
(Australian National
University)
Fruin, Mark
(California State University)
Fujita Nobuhisa
(Ryukoku University)
Gordon, Andrew
(Duke University)
Hiroyama Kensuke
(Nagasaki University)
Hunter, Janet
(London School of Economics
and Political Science)
Itagaki Hiroshi
(Saitama University)
Iwauchi Ryōichi
(Meiji University)

Kudō Akira
(University of Tokyo)
Molony, Barbara
(Santa Clara University)
Nakagawa Keiichirō
(Aoyama Gakuin University)
Okayama Reiko
(Meiji University)
Okuda Kenji
(Sophia University)
Sawai Minoru
(Hokusei Gakuen University)
Takamura Naosuke
(University of Tokyo)
Uchida Hoshimi
(Tokyo Keizai University)
Yasuoka Shigeaki
(Doshisha University)
Yoshihara Hideki
(Kobe University)
Yui Tsunehiko
(Meiji University)

Index

285